JESUS OUR R.

Jesus Our Redeemer

A Christian Approach to Salvation

GERALD O'COLLINS, SJ

OXFORD

UNIVERSITY PRESS

OXFORD

UNIVERSITY PRESS

Great Clarendon Street, Oxford OX2 6DP

Oxford University Press is a department of the University of Oxford.
It furthers the University's objective of excellence in research, scholarship,
and education by publishing worldwide in

Oxford New York

Auckland Cape Town Dar es Salaam Hong Kong Karachi
Kuala Lumpur Madrid Melbourne Mexico City Nairobi
New Delhi Shanghai Taipei Toronto

With offices in

Argentina Austria Brazil Chile Czech Republic France Greece
Guatemala Hungary Italy Japan Poland Portugal Singapore
South Korea Switzerland Thailand Turkey Ukraine Vietnam

Oxford is a registered trade mark of Oxford University Press
in the UK and in certain other countries

Published in the United States
by Oxford University Press Inc., New York

British Library Cataloguing in Publication Data

Data available

Library of Congress Cataloging-in-Publication Data
O'Collins, Gerald.
Jesus our redeemer : a Christian approach to salvation / Gerald O'Collins.
p. cm.
ISBN–13: 978–0–19–920313–0 (alk. paper)
ISBN–10: 0–19–920313–X (alk. paper)
ISBN–13: 978–0–19–920312–3 (alk. paper)
ISBN–10: 0–19–920312–1 (alk. paper)
1. Jesus Christ—Person and offices. 2. Redemption. I. Title.
BT203.O26 2007
232'.3—dc22   2006030176

Typeset by
SPI Publisher Services, Pondicherry, India
Printed in Great Britain by
Biddles Ltd., King's Lynn, Norfolk

ISBN 978–0–19–920312–3 (Hbk)
ISBN 978–0–19–920313–0 (Pbk)

3 5 7 9 10 8 6 4 2

Preface

He [Jesus] became the cause of eternal salvation for all who
obey him.
Hebrews 5: 8.
For the world, I count it not an inn, but a hospital, and a place
not to live, but to die in.
Sir Thomas Browne, *Religio Medici.*

In the verse quoted above from the Letter to the Hebrews, we may
prefer to translate a key term in the original Greek as 'author' or
'source' rather than as 'cause'. But we are still left with the hard
question: how did the life, death, and resurrection of Jesus transform
humanity's relationship with God? Whether we call Jesus the 'cause',
'source', or 'author' of salvation, we still must ask ourselves: how can
someone who lived two thousand years ago effect our salvation
today? How has Christ made an essential difference for us, as individuals, as a human community, and as a whole created world? In
other words, in what ways does a past event of redemption or set of
such events work, both here and now and in the future, to save
human beings and their world? This is an issue that we may not
gloss or hedge.

In the past, many Western Christians associated the saving 'work'
of Jesus exclusively or almost exclusively with his suffering and death.
When 'making the Stations of the Cross' or devotedly following a
series of pictures or carvings that represent the last journey of Christ
from his condemnation by Pontius Pilate to his burial in the tomb,
Catholics and some other Christians would repeat the prayer that (in
a Latin form) dates back at least to the eleventh century: 'We adore
you, O Christ, and we bless you, because by your holy cross you have
redeemed the world.' Nowadays it is more usual and convincing to
acknowledge that the redemption of human beings and their world
was, is, and will be brought about through the entire Christ-story: by
his incarnation, life, suffering, death, and resurrection, the sending of
the Holy Spirit, and the transformation to come at the end of history.

But the key difficulty remains more or less the same, and one can phrase it in the light of the Letter to the Hebrews. The anonymous author of that treatise presents the sacrifice of Christ in a full sequence that stretches from Christ's coming into the world (10: 5–7), through his bloody death (9: 11–22), his entry into the 'sanctuary' of heaven (9: 24), the enthronement 'at the right hand of God' (10: 12), and his glorious 'second coming' to consummate the work of salvation (9: 28). Repeatedly the treatise insists that, while the self-offering of Christ took place only once and for all (9: 12, 25–6; 10: 11–12), it remains efficacious 'for all time' (10: 12) and for all people. How and why is it possible that some particular events in the ancient past can bring about such an effect two thousand years later and for the rest of human history? Thus my first hard question concerns Christ and the causality at work in what he achieved. How is Christ 'the cause of our salvation'?

A second such question concerns the supposed beneficiaries of his redeeming 'work'. Why do we need such redemption at all? Whatever our spiritual and other problems, surely we human beings can deal with them and solve them, provided we put our minds to it and make a real effort? Do we need Christ to make an essential difference to us? We must face this question, and will do so at length. We may not leave the issue of alleged self-sufficiency unexamined and unresolved. In the seventeenth century Sir Thomas Browne (1605–82) had no doubt that we do not finally control our lives but desperately require divine help to live and die as we ought in the 'hospital' of this world. But many people in the twenty-first century do not share that sense of need but live as if they were self-sufficient and truly autonomous.

The 'need' for redemption has been understood individually and collectively—another version of the classic issue of the 'one' and the 'many'. How should we interpret the relationship between individual and corporate salvation, both now and at the end? Getting the balance right between the individual and the collective is not easy, but St Paul's teaching about Christ as the last Adam and of salvation as entailing insertion 'in Christ' clearly indicates that human beings cannot live and be saved as isolated individuals. Add too the Apostle's hope for the redemption of the whole created order (Rom. 8: 18–25). If he is still allowed to set the standard, any approach to redemption that unilaterally emphasizes individual salvation does so at its own peril. The redemption of our bodily, social selves and of the present world, while not absent earlier, will emerge as a key issue in Chapter 12.

The third hard question bears on our image of God. Some images of God create special difficulties for those who elaborate a theology of redemption. Is God so removed from human history or so mysteriously beyond our ken, that it seems bizarre to talk about sinful human beings being personally reconciled with God through the saving actions of Jesus Christ? Or is God deeply involved with human behaviour, but as Someone who punishes wrongdoing, demands retribution, and even settles scores? The Scriptures, both the OT and the NT, speak of the 'anger' of God towards sinners and towards those who harm the chosen people. Some versions of redemption have pictured Jesus being punished in our place by an angry God, who begins to act mercifully once the strict demands of divine justice have been met through the terrible sufferings of the innocent Jesus. Such versions of redemption look incompatible with the image of God to be drawn from the parable of the prodigal son, better called the parable of the merciful father (Luke 15: 11–32). Beyond question, one's image of God will prove decisive for any understanding and interpretation of redemption.

Responses to these three questions will move in and out of what follows and give shape to this book. The permanent efficacy of Christ's saving activity, the human need for redemption (both individually and collectively), and the image of God implied by Christ's activity and human need will be the major themes of my study. I begin by critically assessing the terms that continue to be used for redemption (Chapter 1) and then move to the creation of the world as the 'ground' for redemption (Chapter 2). Chapters 3 and 4 will examine the human condition and its need for redemption. Chapter 5 moves to the coming of Christ and considers the salvific activity deployed in his full story, from the incarnation right through to his 'second' coming. The heart of the book takes up three pervasive approaches to redemption: as liberation from evil (Chapter 6), as cleansing from guilt (Chapters 7 and 8), and as the transforming power of love (Chapter 9). Chapter 10 considers the present mediation of salvation through the Holy Spirit to the Church, while Chapter 11 will reflect on the wider mediation of salvation to those who are not Christians. Finally, Chapter 12 will turn to bodily redemption and the transformation of the material world. At the end I add a bibliography and an index of names. As the themes for the chapters imply, the book moves from salvation as *past* 'fact' (Chapters 1–10), to salvation as *present* experience (Chapters 10–11), and on to salvation as *future* hope (Chapter 12).

Before plunging into the book, I should say something about the basis for the arguments which follow—right from the search for linguistic clarity in Chapter 1. Obviously the scriptures supply the primary norm for evaluating statements about redemption, as well as for evaluating symbolic actions (e.g. the celebration of the sacraments) and symbolic objects (e.g. paintings of the crucifixion). Yet it is by no means a straightforward operation to negotiate the passage from the biblical witness to theological positions. In *The Bible for Theology* (Mahwah, NJ: Paulist Press, 1997), Daniel Kendall and I proposed ten principles which can supply a method and criteria for using the scriptures in theology. In this present book I presuppose these principles: for instance, the third principle, which is concerned with interpreting and appropriating the scriptures within the living community of faith. From the start of Christianity, the biblical witness has been deployed in a living tradition, which has included liturgical celebrations, patterns of behaviour, art, music, and literature. At times the tradition has developed magnificently something which the Bible enunciates only briefly. Chapter 2 will provide an instance of such development: from St Paul's concise contrast between the First Adam and the Last Adam to the full elaboration of the two Adams in liturgy, icons, and literature. The ninth principle in *The Bible for Theology*, which concerns the necessary dialogue with philosophy, requires *coherent* positions that will rule out views of redemption which are in irreconcilable conflict with one's image of God. Those particularly interested in method and criteria can examine for themselves whether the principles set out in that earlier work are genuinely valid and whether *Jesus Our Redeemer* follows them.

In writing this book on 'soteriology' or Christ's saving work for human beings and the whole created world, I have to tell a story that is at least partly familiar and cannot promise to be constantly and startlingly original. I must engage in dialogue with my predecessors in the biblical period, the patristic era, and the subsequent history of church teaching and theology. Such a critical dialogue necessarily involves being selective. The material from the Bible, the Fathers, and later church history is complex and often controversial. Exegetes, patristic scholars, historians of doctrine, and philosophers will always want to hear more. But this present work introduces the biblical, historical, and philosophical contributions with the aim of constructing my own systematic soteriology which finds its primary interpretative key in the divine love, and not with the aim of writing a complete history of soteriology. One should not and cannot write a soteriology without paying attention to and drawing to some extent on what has gone before. Yet writing up the complete history of soteriological developments would be a quite different and much longer project.

Any dialogue with my contemporaries in soteriology also calls for selectivity. A full critical attention to all the major alternative positions would mean switching projects. My purpose is to write a systematic soteriology, not do something thoroughly worthwhile but quite different—namely, survey and appraise leading contributions to modern soteriology. In any case footnotes and the bibliography will establish one conclusion: that I am aware of alternative positions. Although the dialogue with my predecessors and contemporaries must be selective, on substantive issues this book will direct readers to some relevant works and/or major entries in dictionaries and encyclopedias. Through these references interested readers will easily find further bibliographical information. But, in general, an effort has been made to avoid the massive footnoting which brings some scholarly books almost to a standstill.

In his pioneering work William Wrede (1859–1906) wrote of 'the messianic secret of Jesus Christ'. I would talk rather to 'the messianic mystery' of Christ and his saving work. A secret can be revealed once and for all; a religious mystery invites a lifetime of reflection in which there can never be definitive statements and truly final conclusions. Both by themselves and in dialogue with others, workers in soteriology find themselves in the 'yes-but' situation. Every significant affirmation will always call for further qualifications, explorations, and additions. The messianic mystery of Christ's saving work, precisely as mystery, means that we can never expect to argue everything out in complete and final detail. At the same time, this 'yes-but' situation may never be an excuse for blatantly inadequate or simply inaccurate claims.

I am most grateful to many people for their help and encouragement in writing this book: Lloyd Baugh, Caroline Walker Bynum, Tom Casey, Charles Conroy, Stephen Davis, Mervyn Duffy, Francisco Egaña, Mario Farrugia, Paul Haffner, Michael Jones, Daniel Kendall, Lori King, George Lawless, Barry Meehan, Eamonn Mulcahy, John O'Donnell, Kevin O'Reilly, Jared Wicks, all the participants at the Redemption Summit held in New York at Easter 2003, those who attended a staff seminar at Georgetown University (October 2004), the members of other seminars and classes around the world, some anonymous advisers for Oxford University Press and at the Gregorian University, and Lucy Qureshi and her colleagues at Oxford University Press. With deep gratitude and affection I dedicate this book to all the students I have been privileged to teach at the Gregorian University since coming to live in Rome full time in 1974. May this book offer some help towards understanding that faith in the Redeemer which was at the heart of their existence and which led some of them to suffer like him a violent death.

Gerald O'Collins, SJ

Gregorian University, Rome
23 March 2006

Contents

Abbreviations

ABD	D. N. Freedman (ed.), *Anchor Bible Dictionary*, 6 vols. (New York: Doubleday, 1992)
DzH	H. Denzinger and P. Hünermann (eds.), *Enchiridion Symbolorum, definitionum et declarationum* (Freiburg im Breisgau: Herder, 37th edn., 1991)
LXX	Septuagint (the most important Greek version of the OT)
ND	J. Neuner and J. Dupuis (eds.), *The Christian Faith* (Bangalore: Theological Publications in India, 7th edn., 2001)
NT	New Testament
par. parr.	parallel passage(s) in the Synoptic Gospels
OT	Old Testament
Redemption	S. T. Davis, D. Kendall, and G. O'Collins (eds.), *The Redemption* (Oxford: Oxford University Press, 2004)
TRE	G. Krause and G. Müller (eds.), *Theologische Realenzyklopädie*, 36 vols. (Berlin: Walter de Gruyter, 1977–2004)

1

Terms and Images

Christ has died for us, but this is not to say that his death was a sacrifice.

Ingolf Dalferth, in S. W. Sykes (ed.), *Sacrifice and Redemption.*

It's not the thought; it's the words that count.

Anonymous.

Both the OT and the NT abound with salvific and redemptive terms and images. Either directly or indirectly, almost every page of the Bible has something to say about salvation and/or the human need for it. The same holds true of liturgical language, both in Western and Eastern Christianity. In praising God and imploring the divine help, the public worship of the Church draws on and 'performs' the redemptive language of the Bible. Anyone who reflects on the nature of redemption will find an astonishing amount of witness in scriptural and liturgical texts. Yet the very rich character of these sources may leave us puzzled about the correct lines to develop in terminology and theories. Let me explain.

Whereas controversies and official teaching (in the first seven general councils of the Church) about the person and natures of Christ helped to establish clear terminology for Christology or the doctrine of Christ 'in himself', such conciliar clarification has never taken place in soteriology or the doctrine of Christ's saving work 'for us'. Nevertheless, theological debates and official teaching on original sin, grace, the salvation of the non-baptized, justification, the Eucharist, and the other sacraments naturally raised questions about Christ's redemptive activity or at least about its appropriation by human beings. Yet no period of Christianity can claim to have produced a truly unified view of redemption. There has been a great variety of approaches in this sector, and sometimes a confusing, even careless use of words. At the very least, theology means 'watching one's language in the presence of God'. Perhaps in no area should we watch our language and images more closely than when we talk about redemption. Later chapters will have more to say about the terminology of salvation. Here let me begin with five key terms: redemption, salvation, atonement, reconciliation, and expiation. Where do these words come from, how have they been used, to what extent do they overlap, and what do they convey as images?

Before replying to the questions, we should recall two important points. First, these terms are not used alone but in biblical and liturgical texts, prayers, creedal statements, poems, novels, and literature of other genres. The scriptural language of redemption has been set to music in antiphons, canticles, and hymns of all kinds. Painting, sculpture, and architecture have portrayed 'materially' the nature and function of redemption. Such verbal, musical, and material expressions *show* God's redeeming actions rather than attempting to *explain* them. These primary expressions communicate meanings directly and appeal to the imagination and the heart. From the beginning of Christianity the fourth 'Servant Song' (Isa. 52: 13–53: 12), which pictures someone whose cruel suffering brings blessings to many, has functioned to show directly rather than explain intellectually what the death of Jesus meant. An early example of this usage comes from St Clement of Rome, who does not offer in his own words any explanation of the crucifixion but simply quotes the fourth 'Servant Song' from Isaiah (1 Clement 16). Nearly two thousand years later Franco Zeffirelli did the same in his film *Jesus of Nazareth*. Looking at Jesus hanging dead on the cross, Nicodemus (played by Sir Laurence Olivier) recites with moving gravity lines from Isaiah 53. Instead of expressing redemption directly through such verbal and visual images, our doctrinal, theological, and philosophical statements aim at explaining redemption in 'clear and distinct' ways. Much of this book will be doing just that. But any such second-level language of theological reflection and clarification, while it should bring precision, cannot take the place of the primary religious language and its 'showing'—a showing that links the present with the past and allows the saving events in the past to have their present impact.[1]

Second, let me also recall that frequent overlap in the lexical range of meanings of such words should not lead to any hasty conclusions about their being simply variant ways of saying the same thing. Words enjoy their specific denotations and meanings when used with other words in phrases, in entire sentences, or in whole paragraphs. I will not only summarize the general meanings of words for redemption but also add some specific expressions. In both cases we need to 'watch our language'. We also need to remember that such '-tion' terms as redemption, salvation, and reconciliation can be more verbs than nouns. They may point to the *process* of being redeemed, saved, and reconciled, to the *end-result* (the state of being redeemed, saved, and reconciled), or to both the process and the end-result. For that matter, various nuances in the use of related terms like atonement may highlight more the process or the end-result.

REDEMPTION

St Paul speaks of Christians being justified by the free grace of God 'through the redemption (apolutrôsis) that comes in Christ Jesus' (Rom. 3: 24). The Apostle even speaks of Christ himself becoming our 'redemption' (1 Cor. 1: 30). This image of 'buying back' has been connected with two practices in the Graeco-Roman world: the ransoming of prisoners of war out of captivity by a purchasing agent, and the sacral manumission of the slaves. In the latter case, a fictitious purchase by some divinity, owners would come with slaves to a temple, sell them to a god, and from the temple treasury

---

[1] The Eucharist offers a spectacular example of the primacy of 'showing' over theological 'telling'. It was only in the second millennium that St Anselm of Canterbury offered the first full-blown theological explanation of the redemptive significance of Christ's death: *Cur Deus Homo* (1098). But for a thousand years, by celebrating the Eucharist, Christians had already been expressing in a primary way the significance of Christ's death (and resurrection).

receive money which the slaves had previously deposited there out of their savings. Freed from their previous masters, the slaves became the 'property' of the god. At the temple of Apollo in Delphi, more than a thousand inscriptions record that 'Pythian Apollo purchased So-and-So for freedom'. This language could have provided a lively image in the thought world of such early Christian communities as that in Corinth. Paul was well aware of slavery and the emancipation of slaves (1 Cor. 7: 20–2). But the background to his usage of the image of 'redemption', as with almost all the Apostle's related terms and images, is to be found primarily in the terminology of the LXX. The verb 'apolutroô' is applied to the 'redeeming' of a slave (Exod. 21: 8); the simpler forms 'lutron' (ransom) and 'lutroô' (to redeem) turn up frequently (Exod. 6: 6; 15: 13–16; 21: 30; 30: 12). Associated with this usage is the image of God as 'go'el' (redeemer), the divine kinsman who fulfilled the duty of buying back an enslaved or captive relative (Isa. 41: 14; 43: 14; 44: 6; 47: 4). God was shown to be such a divine 'Redeemer' when he set Israel free from the slavery of Egypt (Ps. 111: 9) and 'acquired' a people as his own special possession (Exod. 15: 16; 19: 5). In the language of redemption there was a specifically Jewish reference to the divine rescue of the Israelites from the slave-market of Egypt. Later on God was again revealed as the 'Redeemer' who brought Israel home from the Babylonian captivity (Isa. 51: 11; 52: 3–9). In the final days God 'will come as a redeemer to Zion' (Isa. 59: 20), delivering Israel at the end of time (Hos. 13: 14). The psalmist celebrated this redemptive power of God to be deployed in the future: 'Let Israel hope in the Lord. For in the Lord there is steadfast love and great is his power to redeem. It is he who will redeem Israel from all their sins' (Ps. 130: 7–8).

The language of 'redemption', while having different linguistic roots in Hebrew, Greek, Latin, and English (which here, as elsewhere, draws many of these relevant terms from Latin), overlaps frequently with that of 'salvation', and with two less frequently used terms: 'liberation', and 'deliverance'. Whether it is a matter of rescue from physical dangers like disease and death or a matter of rescue from 'spiritual' threats like sin and judgement (or both), 'save (sôzô)' turns up frequently in the LXX and in the NT: for example, in the divine intention that 'the world might be saved' through Christ (John 3: 17). Along with the verb we have the corresponding nouns, 'salvation (sôtêria)' and 'saviour (sôtêr)': for instance, the 'Benedictus' speaks of 'salvation from our enemies and from the hand of all who hate us' (Luke 1: 71), and the 'Magnificat' of 'God my Saviour' (Luke 1: 47). In the OT, God is called the 'Saviour' (e.g. Isa. 45: 15, 21), who brings 'salvation' (e.g. Isa. 49: 6) and who raises up 'saviours' to deliver Israel (e.g. Judg. 3: 9, 15; 6: 36). The NT calls God (the Father) 'Saviour' eight times, and calls Christ 'Saviour' sixteen times, as in the angelic message to the shepherds: 'Today there has been born for you a Saviour who is Christ the Lord' (Luke 2: 11). While giving Christ the title of 'Saviour', the NT does not follow suit with the title of 'Redeemer (lutrôtês)'; that title occurs only once and is given to Moses (Acts 7: 35).

In his Gospel and Acts, the central message of Luke is that human beings are saved only through Christ. Luke's two-part work on Christian origins climaxes with the claim: 'There is no salvation through any else [than Jesus]; for there is no other name under heaven given among human beings by which we must be saved' (Acts 4: 12).[2] This claim from a speech by St Peter fits into a whole pattern of speeches in Acts and introduces recurrent themes: the universal significance of his message (for all 'human beings' 'under heaven') and the 'name' of Jesus. In Acts the apostles and others baptize 'in the name of Jesus', preach and teach in his name, and heal in his name; the 'name' is to be identified as Jesus himself. Ten times in his Gospel and Acts, Luke uses 'sôtêria', a term never found in Mark and Matthew and only once in John (4: 22). It is only here in Acts 4: 12 that Luke uses the definite article with 'salvation (hê sôtêria, the salvation)'. In short, this verse offers us Luke's primary message in miniature.[3]

---

[2] In his unpublished dissertation at the Gregorian University, Nazarene Soosai Fernando, ' "Salvation in No One Else": A Contemporary Theological Reading of Acts 4: 12' (Rome, 2002), drew from such standard authors on Luke–Acts as C. K. Barrett, J. A. Fitzmyer, E. Haenchen, J. Nolland, G. Schneider, M. L. Soards, C. H. Talbert, and J. A. Ziesler to establish that the central message of this two-part work on Christian origins is summarized in Acts 4: 12.

[3] Further lexical statistics suggest the key importance of what Luke writes in Acts 4: 12. 'Name' or 'the name' occurs 230 times in the whole NT, with well over a third of these occurrences coming from Luke (34 times in his Gospel and 60 times in Acts). Mark and Matthew each use the verb 'to save (sôzein)' 15 times, whereas Luke uses it 30 times in Luke–Acts. Luke calls Jesus 'Saviour (sôtêr)' (Luke 2: 11; Acts 5: 31; 13: 23); John does so once (John 4: 42), but Mark and Matthew never.

In the NT the language of 'liberate' or 'set free, liberate (eleutheroô)' and of 'freedom, liberation (eleutheria)' can overlap with that of 'redeem', as when Paul contrasts two 'laws': 'the law of the Spirit of life in Christ Jesus has set you free/liberated you from the law of sin and death' (Rom. 8: 2). The Apostle uses this language when he looks forward to the glorious consummation of all things: 'creation itself will be set free/liberated from the bondage of decay and will enter upon the glorious liberty of the children of God' (Rom. 8: 21). In John's Gospel, Jesus promises his audience that 'the truth will set you free/liberate you' (John 8: 32). This is to say, 'if the Son has set you free, you will be free indeed' (John 8: 36). In contemporary theology 'redemption' and 'liberation' can prove roughly equivalent, with the former suggesting an onerous (past) victory over evil and sin and the latter pointing more to a new situation of freedom that has been or will be brought about.

The version of the Lord's Prayer found in Matthew's Gospel introduces another relevant term, 'rescue, deliver (ruomai)': 'Deliver us from the evil one' (Matt. 6: 13). The word recurs in Matthew's passion story when the chief priests and others mock Jesus on the cross: 'He saved others; he cannot save himself... He trusted in God; let God now rescue him' (Matt. 27: 42–3). Here the Gospel-writer uses as equivalents, 'save (sôzô)' and 'rescue (ruomai)'. In the 'Benedictus' 'being rescued/delivered (rusthentas) from the hand of our enemies' obviously parallels 'salvation (sôtêrian) from our enemies' (Luke 1: 71, 74). A similar parallel turns up in Paul's letters: 'All Israel will be saved (sôthêsetai); as is written, "out of Sion will come the Deliverer (ruomenos)"' (Rom. 11: 26). The language of deliverance and that of salvation converge.

In this book I will pay more attention to the language of 'redemption' and 'salvation'. Yet we should remember that, both in the Bible and in the history of Christianity, some other word-groups overlap with these two terms. St Anselm of Canterbury, for instance, could use both the nouns 'redemption (redemptio)' and 'liberation (liberatio)' and the verbs 'redeem (redimere)' and 'liberate (liberare)' as equivalents (*Cur Deus Homo*, 1. 6). But we need to spend more time on sorting out the relationship between the language of 'redemption' and 'salvation'. Once again we find them functioning as synonyms in the writing of Anselm, as when he calls Christ

'Saviour (Salvator)' and 'Redeemer (Redemptor)' (*Oratio II ad Christum*, 42–7).

SALVATION AND REDEMPTION

In the original Hebrew from which it was translated into the Greek form in which we know it, the very name 'Jesus' meant 'God is salvation' or 'God saves'. Not surprisingly then the NT, as we saw above, sometimes calls Jesus 'Saviour'. In post-NT Christianity, the early third-century *Apostolic Tradition* combined 'Saviour' and 'Redeemer' and showed how they shared the same basic meaning: 'We thank you, God, through your beloved Son Jesus Christ, whom in these final times you have sent us as Saviour, Redeemer and Messenger of your will.'[4] Christian usage has often continued to employ 'Saviour' and 'Redeemer' or 'save' and 'redeem' as equivalents. The hymn 'Jesus Christ is risen today' from *Lyra Davidica* (1708), based partly on the fourteenth-century hymn 'Surrexit Christus hodie', tells of Christ who 'endured the cross and grave . . . sinners to *redeem* and *save*'. In the opening lines of 'The Table of Confession' William Dunbar (*c.*1460–*c.*1520) wrote: 'To thee, O merciful *saviour* mine, Jesus/my king, my lord, and my *redeemer* sweet.'[5] Since they continue to look interchangeable, 'redemption' and 'salvation' are often associated in the titles of books: for instance, *Jesus in the Drama of Salvation: Toward a Biblical Doctrine of Redemption*, and *Images of Redemption: Art, Literature and Salvation*.[6]

But sometimes the language of hymns supports the notion that 'redemption' points rather to the past activity of Christ, whereas

---

[4] This work is normally dated to the early third century and attributed to St Hippolytus of Rome (d. around 236).

[5] J. Kingsley (ed.), *The Poems of William Dunbar* (Oxford: Clarendon Press, 1979), 15.

[6] R. Schwager, *Jesus in the Drama of Salvation: Toward a Biblical Doctrine of Redemption* (New York: Crossroad, 1999); P. Sherry, *Images of Redemption: Art, Literature and Salvation* (London: T. & T. Clark, 2003).

'salvation' points to the present and future results of that activity.[7]
Thus the second verse of a traditional Sussex carol, 'On Christmas
night all Christians sing', associates redemption with the past: 'Then
why should men on earth be so sad,/ Since our *Redeemer* made us
glad,/ When from our sin he set us free,/ All for to gain our liberty?'
The first verse of an Easter hymn by the English composer Samuel
Sebastian Wesley (1810–76) likewise connects the redemption with
what Jesus did, once and for all, in his death and resurrection:
'Alleluia, sing to Jesus, his the sceptre, his the throne,/ Alleluia, his
the triumph, his the victory alone,/ Hark, the songs of holy Sion
thunder like a mighty flood:/ Jesus out of every nation hath *redeemed*
us by his blood.' A hymn by Matthew Bridges (1800–94), 'Crown him
with many crowns', concludes with the acclamation: 'All hail,
Redeemer, hail,/ For thou hast died for me.' Then one of the eucharistic acclamations contrasts the liberating or redeeming action of
Christ in the past with his present status as Saviour: 'Lord, by your
cross and resurrection you have set us free; you are the Saviour of the
world.'[8] A medieval prayer, ascribed (probably wrongly) to Pope
John XXII (d. 1334), recalls the blood and water which flowed out
when a soldier pierced the side of the dead Christ on the cross
(John 19: 32–7). But the prayer seeks blessings here and now from
'my Saviour'. In the words of an anonymous translation, 'Soul of
my Saviour, sanctify my breast;/ Body of Christ be thou my saving
guest;/ Blood of my Saviour, bathe me in thy tide,/ Wash me with
water flowing from thy side.'[9]

Christians have used the language of 'Saviour' and 'salvation' not
only of the present but also of the future. The Letter to Titus
describes Christian life as looking forward in hope to the time
when 'the glory of our great God and Saviour Jesus Christ will

[7] The title for a very good work by Paul Fiddes reflects such a frequent association
of salvation with the present: *Past Event and Present Salvation: The Christian Idea of
Atonement* (London: Darton, Longman & Todd, 1989).

[8] The reference to the present is made even clearer in the original Latin text of the
acclamation: 'Salvator mundi, salva nos, qui per crucem et resurrectionem tuam
liberasti nos.'

[9] 'Soul of my Saviour' is passionately concerned with the salvation of the
individual, but turns towards the salvation of others in the last two lines: 'when
I may praise thee/ with thy saints for aye'.

appear' (Titus 2: 13).[10] Here, as elsewhere (e.g. Acts 4: 12; Phil. 3: 20), the language of salvation gets linked not only to the present but also to the future. Paul strongly emphasizes the future aspect: 'our salvation is now closer than when we first believed' (Rom. 13: 11). He prays for the salvation of the Jewish people, and is convinced that 'all Israel will be saved' (Rom. 11: 26).

Nevertheless, a temporal difference does not always serve to distinguish the language of redemption and salvation, as if the former referred to the past and the latter to the present and future. Salvation is *also* used of Christ's past activity. The Letter to Titus declares that 'the grace of God has appeared bringing salvation to all human beings' (Titus 2: 11). In *Cur Deus Homo* St Anselm writes about 'salvation' as something brought about (in the past) by Christ's death (2. 19 twice). On Good Friday, in the 'showing' of the cross that precedes its veneration, the priest or deacon sings three times: 'Behold the wood of the cross on which hung the Saviour of the world.' Likewise the difficulty about linking 'redemption' primarily with the past surfaces when we recall Handel's confession of faith about the here and now: 'I know that my Redeemer liveth.' Like Handel, the psalmist, Isaiah, and Hosea, as we saw above, hope that the *redemptive* activity of God will be fully deployed at the end of history. I have been picking examples more or less at random. But there seem to be too many counter-examples for those who wish to associate 'redemption' primarily (or even exclusively) with the past and 'salvation' primarily (or even exclusively) with the present and the future. Are there other useful ways of distinguishing the two terms—in English and, for that matter, in their German equivalents ('Erlösung' and 'Heil')?

The classical (notorious?) slogan which goes back to the second century, 'outside the Church no salvation (extra ecclesiam nulla salus)', suggests that, for those 'outside' something complete and final is at stake.[11] A later chapter will tackle the issue of the link

[10] The confession of Jesus Christ as 'our great God and Saviour' may have also intended to dissociate itself from those in the contemporary Graeco-Roman world who confessed such deities as Zeus, Apollo, Artemis, or Asclepius as 'god [the] saviour (theos sôtêr)'.

[11] See B. Sesboüé, *Hors de l'Eglise pas de salut. Histoire d'une formule et problèmes d'interprétation* (Paris: Desclée de Brouwer, 2004). On the formation of this slogan in the writings of St Ignatius of Antioch, Origen, and St Cyprian of Carthage, see F. A. Sullivan, *Salvation Outside the Church?* (New York: Paulist Press, 1992), 18–24.

between the Church and salvation. Here I wish to note only the choice of 'salvation' over 'redemption' in this global claim, which does not run: 'outside the Church no redemption (extra ecclesiam nulla redemptio)'. Here the meaning of the English term 'salvation', like the Latin term as used in the original adage, has an unlimited, 'final' meaning: when baptized Christians die, after having maintained their faith and lived lives of moral goodness (or at least repented of sin before death), they will 'go to heaven' and thus be 'saved'. They will be saved 'from' all the dangers (moral and physical) of this world and from eternal damnation in the next world, and will be saved 'for' eternal happiness in the company of God. This meaning of 'salvation' puts the emphasis on being saved 'externally' rather than 'internally', unlike the Latin 'salus' from which the word ultimately came. 'Salus', with its associated adjectives 'salubris' and 'salvus', denoted (good) health, wholeness, welfare, well-being, being healed, being 'hale and hearty', or 'being safe and sound'. This sense is preserved in the Italian greeting (an alternative to 'buon giorno'), 'salve', or 'a good day' or 'good health to you', as in the English toast 'your good health'. Provided we reclaim the 'internal' range of meanings for 'salvation', we can recognize what it entails here and hereafter: a 'whole' life that is authentically healthy brings our true welfare in this life and in the life to come. Understood that way, 'salvation' offers nuances of meaning and an interiority that go beyond 'redemption', which suggests a somewhat external deliverance 'from'. Salvation and redemption may often function as equivalent in biblical, liturgical, and theological texts, but the former term seems richer and broader in meaning, especially in what it implies about the purposes, character, and image of God (and of the Son of God).

ATONEMENT AND RECONCILATION

Before moving to 'reconciliation', we should examine a word of Anglo-Saxon origin which once enjoyed a strong relational background: atonement. The verb 'atone' existed in Middle English; and the phrase 'at one' was used from the early fourteenth century to convey the idea of existing in interpersonal harmony or friendship. The noun 'atonement (at-one-ment)' first appeared in the early sixteenth century, and originally meant the state or condition of being at *one* with others in a harmonious unity, or the action of setting at one after discord and strife. In his translation of the NT (1525) William Tyndale rendered the noun 'katallagê' in Romans 5: 11 as 'atonement'. The Douai-Reims version of the NT (1582), when it came to Romans 5: 10–11 and 2 Corinthians 5: 18–20, consistently translated 'katallagê' and the related verb 'katallassô' as 'reconciliation' and 'reconcile'. Nearly thirty years later, in 1611, the King James Bible or Authorized Version did the same, and in those two passages used throughout 'reconciliation' and 'reconcile', except for Romans 5: 11 where it followed Tyndale's rendering: 'our Lord Jesus Christ, by whom we have now received atonement'. Clearly 'atonement' here denoted the restoration of concord and friendly relations through reconciliation, an 'at-one-ment' or personal reconciliation through Christ of two estranged parties, God and sinful human beings. By dying and rising, Christ changed the relationship between God and humanity and set them 'at one' after a situation of discord and alienation.

But gradually in the use of 'atonement' a new emphasis emerged which highlighted the *means* for restoring harmony and the *cost* entailed in reconciliation. Atonement came to denote 'making costly amends' or 'making satisfactory reparation or expiation for offences or sins'.[12] To 'atone for' meant doing something hard, so as to undo the consequences of a wrong act and so restore a relationship broken by that wrong act. Thus 'atonement' took on the narrower sense of the process which removes hindrances to reconciliation.[13]

As part of his effort to describe the effects of the whole 'Christ-event', St Paul wrote two classic passages on God's reconciling activity (Rom. 5: 10–11; 2 Cor. 5: 18–20). In using 'katallagê' and 'katallassô', the Apostle did not draw on the OT (in which there are no Hebrew or Aramaic words to express the idea) but reached for

---

[12] See the novel by Ian McEwan, *Atonement* (London: Jonathan Cape, 2001), in which the 'heroine' finds that she cannot make amends for what she did as a teenager by ruining the lives of two people in love with each other.

[13] On the history of the term see R. S. Paul, *The Atonement and the Sacraments* (London: Hodder & Stoughton, 1961), 17–32.

language out of his Graeco-Roman background. There 'reconciliation', in a secular and religious sense, denoted a change from
alienation and hostility to a relationship of friendship or even love.
Paul wrote of God or of Christ taking the initiative to reconcile sinful
human beings to himself: 'if, when we were enemies we were
reconciled to God through the death of his Son, now that we have
been reconciled we shall all the more be saved by his life. Yet not only
that; we boast in God through our Lord Jesus Christ, through whom
we have now received reconciliation' (Rom. 5: 10–11). This
reconciliation means 'bringing hostility to an end' or 'uniting those
who were formerly separated', and not necessarily 'causing to be
friendly *again*' or 'bringing *back* into harmony'. In other words, this
Pauline language does not necessarily suppose an *original* state of
harmony that was ruptured.

While the Apostle seemed to have conceived the situation as that
of human beings somehow seeing God as their enemy, God did not
see them that way. Otherwise God would not have taken the initiative
with humankind, despite being the offended party in the conflict.
Paul may also have thought of the impact of the Christ-event on the
entire cosmos, when he spoke of the 'reconciliation of the world'
(Rom. 11: 15). Reconciliation would thus touch both humanity and
seemingly the whole created world.[14]

Many people are drawn to the language of reconciliation because
of its interpersonal, relational nuances. Yet we should not ignore
some difficult or at least odd aspects of Paul's passage on reconciliation in Romans. First, he pictures our reconciliation (1) as having
already been accomplished, and (2) as effected by a third party.
As regards (1), if our reconciliation with God has already been
accomplished, it seems that we do not need to do anything.
As regards (2), one must ask how Christ has accomplished our
reconciliation with God. One can readily understand how reconciliation between alienated persons can be brought about through the
'good offices' of a third party, but it seems clear that the status of this
third party must be acknowledged by both sides. If, however, our

[14] J. A. Fitzmyer, for one, holds that this verse points not merely to human
reconciliation with God but also to a 'cosmic extension of that effect to the whole
universe'; see his *Romans*, The Anchor Bible 33 (New York: Doubleday, 1993), 612.

reconciliation has already been effected, before we were able to acknowledge the 'good offices' of Christ, in what sense was he representing our interests in the matter? One might argue that since we are the guilty party in the conflict, we have no interests to represent. But even so, it would still seem necessary that we be in some way actively involved in the process of reconciliation. If we continue to be passive while our reconciliation with God is accomplished, indeed if we remain ignorant of the event until after Christ's intervention, then 'reconciliation' is being used in a logically extended sense. Even if Christ enjoys an ontological status as the 'universal human being' and does not need to be commissioned by humankind as its representative, it would still seem necessary that individual human beings acknowledge Christ's status if they are to be reconciled with God. The 'reconciliation', spoken of here by Paul as having already been accomplished, is then reconciliation in potentiality only.

Some of these problems return and seem compounded in the other major passage from Paul: 'Through Christ God reconciled us to himself and gave us the ministry of reconciliation; that is, God was in Christ reconciling the world to himself, not counting their offences against them and entrusting to us the message of reconciliation. Therefore, we are ambassadors for Christ, with God making his appeal through us. We beg you on behalf of Christ, be reconciled with God' (2 Cor. 5: 18–20). Once again (1) reconciliation is presented as a fait accompli; it has happened before we knew or did anything about it. The conflict has already been resolved before we had even the possibility of interacting. (2) Even less than in the passage from Romans (where he fills out the 'through Christ' in terms of his death and life) Paul does not present Christ as a distinct agent. It is God the Father who emerges as the sole active protagonist and who (in and through Christ) has accomplished our reconciliation.[15] Add too (3) the plea that the Corinthian Christians 'be reconciled with God'. This seems incompatible with what has just

---

[15] As J.-N. Aletti points out, God, who was the offended party, provided the means of reconciliation by permitting his only Son to be mortally wounded by sin. Thus God reversed the roles in the reconciliation process between God and humankind; see ' "God made Christ to be sin" (2 Corinthians 5: 21): Reflections on a Pauline Paradox', in *Redemption*, 101–20, esp. 102–9. See also J. T. Fitzgerald, 'Paul and Paradigm Shifts:

been said about God having already forgiven human sin and reconciled the whole world to himself. But perhaps Paul intends to say here that, since God has forgiven and saved human beings, the Corinthians are being asked to be reconciled to this fact and to order their life accordingly. Once more, Paul is going beyond the normal Greek (and, for that matter, English) use of the term 'reconcile', which we see him using in the case of a husband and wife who were at odds with each other: 'Let her be reconciled to her husband' (1 Cor. 7: 11). In such a case, reconciliation can take place by interacting at the time of reconciliation: both parties need to be consciously and willingly involved in the very process of the restoration of the relationship between them.

Paul's statements about 'cosmic' reconciliation (Rom. 11: 15; 2 Cor. 5: 19) also invite comment. In both these passages 'kosmos' might mean the world in the sense of the whole of humanity.[16] It is not clear that the Apostle thinks that reconciliation extends beyond humanity to the entire created cosmos. A letter which may not have been written directly by Paul is, however, clear about the cosmic dimension of reconciliation: 'In him [Christ] all his fullness [the fullness of God?] was pleased to dwell, and through him to reconcile to himself all things, whether on earth or in the heavens, making peace by the blood of his cross' (Col. 1: 19–20). However we interpret 'all the fullness', our question here concerns something else: only conscious and willing agents can, properly speaking, be at enmity and then reconciled with each other in a new, peaceful situation. 'All things' here include such agents but evidently refer to more than them. It makes better sense to think of this 'reconciliation' not as primarily establishing friendly relations between personal agents but as Christ making 'all things' conform to the divine plan. There is not precisely an *interpersonal* conflict that needs to be resolved, but rather an incompatibility that needs to be dealt with and removed.

Reconciliation and its Linkage Group', in T. Engberg-Pedersen (ed.), *Paul Beyond the Judaism/Hellenism Divide* (Louisville, Ky.: Westminster John Knox Press, 2001), 241–62.

[16] V. P. Furnish argues plausibly, however, that, when Paul writes of 'the world', in 2 Cor. 5: 19 Paul intends 'us', the human objects of God's reconciling act, and that in Rom. 11: 15 Paul has in mind the Gentiles; see *II Corinthians*, The Anchor Bible 32a (New York: Doubleday, 1984), 319.

Thus Christ, through his death and resurrection, has made 'all things' peacefully *conform*, at least in principle, to the wise plan of God.

In the present time, this 'conformation' continues through a 'making peace' that goes on: through deliverance from evil (Chapter 6), cleansing by means of Christ's sacrifice (Chapter 8), transformation by his love (Chapter 9), and the activity of Christ and the Holy Spirit in the Church and in the world (Chapters 10 and 11). The 'conformation' will be definitively accomplished through the resurrection of human beings and their world (Chapter 12). Yet this conformation of all things to the plan of God is *already* taking place. Two thousand years ago, it was initiated through the union with the whole created world established by the Son of God right from his conception and birth (Chapter 5).

Many people feel instinctively drawn to the warm, relational language of 'reconciliation', as we find it in two major letters by Paul and in a wonderful hymn in Colossians (1: 15–20). Obviously it is a language that continues to communicate well. Yet, as we have just seen, we may need to remind ourselves that the NT uses such language in ways which go beyond its ordinary, secular meaning in the Greek of that time and in English usage today. Any speech drawn from human states of affairs does not simply apply to God's redemptive work towards sinful men and women. In the NT, 'reconciliation' does not point to God being changed or reconciled to human beings; rather it is God or God through Christ who effects reconciliation by changing us. This example says much about the 'character' and purposes of God. We will see other such examples: for instance, when treating 'sacrifice' and 'representation' in Chapter 8.

EXPIATION

Unlike 'reconciliation', Paul drew on the LXX for another key description of what Christ effected in his death and resurrection: 'expiation (hilastêrion)' (Rom. 3: 25), a term that is found only once elsewhere in the NT (Heb. 9: 5). 1 John writes of Christ as 'hilasmos' or expiation for 'our sins' and those of 'the whole world' (1 John 2: 2; 4: 10). 'Hilastêrion' corresponds to the verb 'hilaskomai', which turns

up twice in the NT (Luke 18: 13; Heb. 2: 17) and which in secular
Greek meant to 'appease', 'propitiate', or 'placate'. Hence some earlier
translations and commentaries rendered 'hilastêrion' as means or
place of 'propitiation' (e.g. the Douai-Reims Bible of 1582 and the
Authorized Version or King James Bible of 1611). This translation
(in English and in other languages) was obviously encouraged by
the fact that the Latin Vulgate had rendered 'hilastêrion' (and
the corresponding Hebrew 'kappôret') as 'propitiatorium'. C. E. B.
Cranfield, a classic commentator, understood Paul to present Christ
as 'a propitiatory victim', at whom God directed 'the full weight of
that righteous wrath' which sinners deserved.[17] But the scholarly tide
has turned against such interpretations. For example, the Revised
Standard Version (2nd edn., 1971) translated 'hilastêrion' in Romans
3: 25 as 'an expiation', as did J. D. G. Dunn.[18] The Revised English
Bible (1989) translated the word as 'the means for expiating sin'.
Without introducing 'sin' (which is not found in the Greek text of
Paul), J. A. Fitzmyer followed suit by rendering 'hilastêrion' as
'a means of expiation'.[19]

The shift to 'expiation' was triggered by reflection on the usage
found in the LXX and the Hebrew Bible. In the LXX version of
Exodus, Leviticus, and Numbers, 'hilastêrion' occurs twenty-one
times to designate the 'mercy seat' (Hebrew, 'kappôret') or golden
cover on the Ark of the Covenant in the Holy of Holies. On the
great 'Day of Expiation' or 'Yôm Kippûr' the High Priest smeared
blood on the 'mercy seat', which was understood to be contaminated by the sins of the Israelites. The blood was believed to cleanse
the defiled 'mercy seat', wiping away the stain of all the sins that
had accumulated over the previous year and renewing the covenant
relationship between Israel and God.[20] In Romans 3: 24–5 Paul
portrays God as having 'put forward' Jesus as the true and final

---

[17] C. E. B. Cranfield, *A Critical and Exegetical Commentary on the Epistle to the
Romans*, i (Edinburgh: T. & T. Clark, 1975), 217.

[18] J. D. G. Dunn, *The Theology of Paul the Apostle* (Grand Rapids: Eerdmans,
1998), 213–16, at 213.

[19] J. A. Fitzmyer, *Paul and His Theology: A Brief Sketch* (Englewood Cliffs, NJ:
Prentice Hall, 2nd edn., 1989), 64.

[20] See J. Milgrom, *Leviticus 1–16* (New York: Doubleday, 1991), 1009–84.

'mercy seat'. What the High Priest did year by year and only for Israel, the crucified Jesus has done once and for all in becoming through the initiative of God the place or means by which the contamination of sins has been removed for all humanity. Using a related noun, 1 John says something similar about the divine initiative: 'He (God) loved us and sent his Son to be the expiation (hilasmos) of our sins' (4: 10); and Jesus Christ is 'the expiation (hilasmos) not only for our sins but also for the sins of the whole world' (2: 2).

In the LXX 'hilaskomai' was often used to translate the Hebrew 'kippêr', which enjoyed a range of meanings, of which 'wipe away' is the meaning that is relevant here. The verb 'kippêr' sometimes had God as its subject, but never as its object. In other words, there was no question of sinners doing something in order to placate or appease God; it was God who did something—namely, by wiping away/out sin. Here LXX (and OT Hebrew) usage is decisively different from secular Greek, in which 'hilaskomai' could have as its subject human beings who propitiate someone (e.g. an offended deity). The LXX never introduces this verb or related words (e.g. 'exilaskomai') to speak of sinners appeasing or rendering favourable an offended God. It is rather God who expiates, purifies, and deals with sin (e.g. Ezek. 16: 13). Likewise in the NT it is God who is the agent or subject of expiatory activity, lovingly providing the 'hilastêrion', his only Son, who is the means and the place for wiping away the stain of sin. In his person the crucified and risen Jesus is the expiation of sin. Both Paul and John highlight the divine initiative which purifies sinners and makes them pleasing to God, so that they can receive the divine gifts (in the case of Rom. 3: 21–6 the gift of justification through faith). When Paul uses the language of Christ as 'hilastêrion' and John that of Christ as 'hilasmos', neither write of *our making amends* or atoning for our sins, still less of *our appeasing* the divine justice or propitiating an angry God. It is God who through Christ lovingly deals with our sins. This says much about the image of God we should nourish and cherish.

A later chapter will take up related issues: for instance, those concerned with the 'sacrifice' of Christ and the appropriateness of naming him our representative or our substitute. This chapter has aimed only at some preliminary clarification of several terms: redemption, salvation, atonement, reconciliation, and expiation. The proper way to use these and other terms and images will emerge, I hope, through treating in detail the whole drama of redemption, from creation to the final consummation.

2

The Creative Word and Last Adam

> Of man's first disobedience and the fruit
> Of that forbidden tree, whose mortal taste
> Brought death into the world and all our woe,
> With loss of Eden, till one greater Man
> Restore us, and regain the blissful seat...
> O goodness infinite, goodness immense!
> That all this good of evil shall produce,
> And evil turn to good; more wonderful
> Than that which by creation first brought forth
> Light out of darkness!

John Milton, *Paradise Lost*, 1. 1–5; 12. 469–73.

In completing *Paradise Lost*, John Milton (d. 1674) pictures the Archangel Michael announcing to sinful Adam the whole sweep of the future story of salvation: from Abraham, through the birth of Christ, his resurrection from the dead, and on to his final coming in glory at the end of world history. Adam reacts with astonishment at the infinite goodness of God which will 'turn' the evil of sin to something greater and even 'more wonderful' than the original creation itself. God's immense goodness has been revealed through creation and will be revealed, even more, through redemption. The divine love, both creative and redeeming, holds together the entire story which St Michael has to tell. By developing this story, Milton vividly brings to bear on his readers the work of Christ's redemption.

The Jewish scriptures highlighted the saving history through which the people experienced God's concern and powerful favour (e.g. Deut. 26: 5–9). This historical perspective prevailed over any sense of God's self-manifestation through the created world. Even the 'account of origins' provided by the opening chapters of Genesis fitted into the larger context of the salvation history of Israel. Those chapters show us how the Israelites, on the basis of specific experiences of God in their own history, thought about the origins of the world and the human race. The stories from Genesis answered the question: 'What must the beginning have been like for our past and present experiences to be what they have been and are?' Nevertheless, while the experience of God through history took precedence over any divine self-revelation through creation, the psalms indicate how salvation (whether collective or individual) and creation remained intertwined. Psalm 19 sang a hymn to God as both creator of nature and giver of the law. A wonderful hymn to God as creator (Ps. 104) ends with a 'Hallelujah (Praise the Lord)', which leads into the following psalms (Pss. 105 and 106) that gratefully recall God's saving deeds in the history of the people and steadfast fidelity in the face of their sins.

Chapters 40–55 of Isaiah, often called the Book of the Consolation of Israel, assures the people of protection by presenting God as both the 'Redeemer' (43: 14–44: 6) and the Creator of the universe (40: 12–31; 45: 9–13). The God who guides all history is the same God who creates and lovingly sustains the whole created world to achieve his purposes for it. As much as any section of the Bible, these luminous chapters indicate that an examination of redemption calls for some prior reflection on creation and the self-communicating love of God already active and revealed in creation.[1]

CREATION

In recent decades cosmologists have fascinated the general public with their findings and theories about a universe that began with an initial fireball of radiation. The very precise setting of the initial

[1] See D. Carroll, 'Creation', in J. A. Komonchak, M. Collins, and D. A. Lane (eds.), *The New Dictionary of Theology* (Wilmington, Del.: Michael Glazier, 1987), 246–58.

conditions and the exact 'fine tuning' of the four basic forces that seem to be verified everywhere in the material universe, evaluated by some statistical arguments,[2] make the whole world seem to have been planned from the beginning in view of the appearance of living, conscious observers. It all looks as if it had been designed to be completed by mind: that is to say, by the emergence of a rational species capable of observing and theorizing about the material universe. A cosmic order suggests an ultimate sufficient reason: a cosmic Orderer. Some theologians and scripture scholars like Hans Hübner have been fascinated by the Big Bang with which time started and by the mystery of what came 'before'.[3] Hübner associates the opening words of John's Gospel ('in the beginning') with the cosmologists' account of how the universe began at zero mass but with infinite density and temperature. In that enormously high initial energy do we have a hint of the transcendent power of God?

But let us bracket off cosmological and philosophical debates and ask in the light of Christian faith: What can we say about the existence and nature of the whole cosmos in general and of the human condition in particular? Where does the world come from? These questions challenge scientists and believers alike, but the latter have to deal with further, thorny issues. How can we understand the relationship between creator and creature? Does this relationship limit creaturely freedom? Sin and human weakness, while raising doubts about the goodness of God's creation, also call into question the extent to which humanity can shape and give meaning to its own existence.

In responding to these questions, this chapter will set out common Christian beliefs about creation and sin (with more to come about sin and evil in the next two chapters). Such doctrines constitute a common heritage that stems from Paul, John, Irenaeus, Augustine

---

[2] Some cite the huge statistical improbability of the passage from a non-living molecule to a living cell. The odds against our present universe and the necessary conditions for its being life-bearing are said to be much less than one in ten to the 133rd.

[3] In dialogue with Stephen Hawking, Roger Penrose, and other scientists, Hübner develops his reflections in 'Neutestamentliche Theologie und Fundamentaltheologie', in M. Petzoldt (ed.), *Evangelische Fundamentaltheologie in der Diskussion* (Leipzig: Evangelische Verlagsanstalt, 2004), 95–118, at 105–10. See also S. Singh, *Big Bang: The Origin of the Universe* (New York: HarperCollins, 2005).

of Hippo, and other ancient writers. They developed a theology of creation and sin, which served as a foundation for their beliefs in the redemption effected by Christ and the Holy Spirit.

As early as the second century, Irenaeus stated that the Christian profession of faith should begin with 'God the Creator, who made the heaven and the earth and all things that are therein' and should demonstrate that 'there is nothing either above him or after him; and that, influenced by no one but of his own free will, he created all things, since he is the only God, the only Lord, the only Creator, the only Father, alone containing all things, and himself commanding all things into existence'. The urgent need to combat the Gnostics' dismissal of material creation as defective and as the work of an inferior 'divine power' stimulated Irenaeus to present a Christian understanding of the entire cosmos: it is God's own creation (*Adversus Haereses*, 2. 1. 1).

In 325, the First Council of Nicaea articulated the Church's belief in God, the 'maker of all things, visible and invisible' (DzH 125; ND 7). The First Council of Constantinople (381) expanded this profession of faith to call the one and true God 'maker of heaven and earth, of all things visible and invisible' (DzH 150; ND 12). This was to specify in slightly greater detail how God alone is the source of all things, without exception. These two councils did no more than sum up what the Bible and early Christian writers had been saying about creation.

The NT by and large inherits, rather than develops for itself, a theology of creation.[4] But through introducing the agency of the Son (as we shall see), it does, however, decisively reinterpret the OT view of created existence. Let us see the details. The Exodus experience and God's self-manifestation at Mount Sinai had shaped the history and self-identity of God's chosen people. In understanding the way in which God had prepared a people for himself, the Israelites looked

---

[4] On creation see W. Brueggemann, *Theology of the Old Testament* (Minneapolis: Fortress, 1997), 145–64, 528–51; B. S. Childs, *Biblical Theology of the Old and New Testaments* (Minneapolis: Fortress, 1993), 107–18, 384–412; G. von Rad, *Old Testament Theology*, i (Edinburgh: Oliver & Boyd, 1962), 449–53; J. Schreiner, *Theologie des Alten Testaments* (Würzburg: Echter, 1995), 132–63. On St Paul's theology of creation, see J. D. G. Dunn, *The Theology of Paul the Apostle* (Grand Rapids, Mich.: Eerdmans, 1998), 38–42, 267–72.

back to the stories of the patriarchs (Abraham, Isaac, and Jacob), their wives (Sarah, Rebecca, Leah, and Rachel), and their families (Gen. 12–50). The Lord who led his people out of Egypt was the God who had guided Abram out of Ur and made him 'Ab-raham', the 'Father of the people'.

Around the time of David or Solomon, the 'Yahwist' theological tradition (the one that named God 'YHWH') looked even further back and expressed its belief that God's paternal guidance spanned all time and history (Gen. 2: 4–4: 26).[5] Just as David ruled over God's chosen people, so YHWH was the sovereign of the whole universe. At the time of the Babylonian captivity in the sixth century BC, the 'Priestly' tradition (Gen. 1: 1–2: 3) explored more deeply God's creative relations with all things. When creating, God calls things into being and so delivers them from 'primordial chaos'.[6] God's creative work can only be good—so concludes the opening verses of the Bible (Gen. 1: 3–2: 4a). Existence results from the very first word that comes from God, a word which he addresses to his creatures and which sustains all the subsequent words of God.

Through their encounter with Greek thought in the third and second centuries BC, some authors of the OT were to reconstrue creation from an original chaos as God's making things 'out of nothing' (2 Macc. 7: 28) and not merely, like a cosmic architect, rearranging things that pre-exist. By means of his deliberate command—free from any internal necessity or external pressure—God

---

[5] In recent years the age of the Jahwist tradition has become more controversial. Instead of dating 'J' to the time of David or Solomon, many scholars will lower the date by a century or more, and there are a number of other theories as well. See E. Zenger *et al.*, *Einleitung in das Alte Testament* (Stuttgart: Kohlhammer, 3rd edn., 1998), 108–22.

[6] Hebrew had no equivalent for 'nothing' and 'nothingness', concepts fashioned by classical Greek culture. Although the biblical authors had to make do with the idea of 'primordial chaos', they knew that the creative action of God belongs to God and to God alone. No creature can ever 'make' something the way God does—a conviction reflected by the fact that *bara*, a word for the effortless (creative and salvific) work of God, is used, in its forty-seven occurrences in the OT, almost exclusively for divine actions. Coming out of eternity and the 'beyond', God's work in creation is essentially different from human work which belongs to the space and time of this world and the 'within'. On creation, see also K. Ward, *Religion and Creation* (Oxford: Clarendon, 1996); R. Alter, *The Five Books of Moses* (New York: Norton, 2004); G. Ahn *et al.*, 'Schöpfer-Schöpfung', *TRE* xxx. 250–355.

brings into existence and sustains everything: 'Whenever you hide your face, they are dismayed; whenever you take away their breath, they die and return to their dust' (Ps. 104: 29). Were God to 'hide his face', his creation would revert to the 'pit', that is, to non-existence (Ps. 143: 7). Creation, therefore, includes that relatedness between God and all creatures, whereby the latter continually depend on the former for their existence. Thus the whole world belongs to God and reveals the radiant divine glory. The Psalms respond with praise and admiration: 'The heavens are telling the glory of God; and the firmament proclaims his handiwork' (Ps. 19: 1).

Both OT theology and Greek culture took for granted the centrality of human existence in the great scheme of things. Instead of grounding matters, as the Greeks did, in the universal qualities of being as one, good, true and beautiful, the Israelites drew their view of the human condition from faith in God as lord of history and creator of the world, with humanity as the climax of the creative work of God. The Bible opens with two distinct accounts of the 'beginning' (the Priestly and the Yahwist versions), both of which drive home the same point: human beings are the only creatures on earth which God wanted for their own sake.

Human existence, according to biblical revelation, consists in relationships—between human beings and nature, among human beings themselves, and between human beings and God. The older Yahwist account of creation (Gen. 2) portrays God placing 'man' in the garden and then providing for all his needs. The later Priestly tradition (Gen. 1) shows God preparing the earth as a 'house' or 'tent' and then bringing in the human tenants: 'male and female' (Gen. 1: 27). The 'house' belongs to the divine proprietor; humanity can only be God's steward and mouthpiece. Communication is both vertical (between God and humanity) and horizontal (among human beings themselves). The older Yahwist account of creation dwells on the fact that man needs a partner, while the later Priestly version shows God creating humankind as a community. It is to humanity as a whole that God delivers the injunction: 'Be fruitful and multiply, and fill the earth and subdue it' (Gen. 1: 28).

Human creation can respond to and collaborate with the creator—something clearly implied when God says: 'Let us make humankind in our image, according to our likeness' (Gen. 1: 26). This is to define human beings in terms of their relationship to God and their dialogue with God. The Bible speaks of one reality that is simultaneously 'image' and 'likeness'. Irenaeus and other early Christian writers developed, however, a basic distinction: the image is permanent, while the likeness is liable to change. Whatever human beings are as God's image, they are and cannot not be: if they were to cease to be God's image, they could no longer be human. The image therefore is the heart of human existence. The likeness is the image in action: it develops; it can progress and regress; it can even disappear through sin. 'Likeness', for this theology, implies a tension that lasts a lifetime.[7] Through sin those who are created in God's image wish to shape their own being, regardless of God's plan. The fundamental tragedy of sin is that, although persons remain in God's image, they exhibit something fully opposed to what they are and continue to be. In saying no to their own being, sinners deceive themselves and attempt to live a hideous illusion. We return in the next chapter to the theme of sin.

The sense of human beings as created in the divine image encourages us to understand human existence as showing forth God's glory on earth. Unfortunately, Western Christianity has frequently opted for an 'essentialist' reading of the human condition and lost sight of the aesthetic dimension. Influenced by Augustine of Hippo, it has dwelt upon a triad (memory, understanding, and love), which show how the soul reflects its creator and trinitarian prototype. Eastern Christianity has followed Irenaeus and subsequent writers: humanity is created in God's image and called to participate in God's own being. The theology of the image remains for Eastern Christians fundamental for their reflection on humanity, and yet with differences between the school of Alexandria (e.g. St Athanasius) and that of Antioch (e.g. St John Chrysostom and Theodore of Mopsuestia).

God is the prototype, since Genesis testifies that human beings are created in the very image of God. Humanity is the image that understands itself in God's own light and can find its fulfilment

---

[7] See H. Crouzel, 'Image', in A. di Berardino (ed.), *Encyclopedia of the Early Church*, i (Cambridge: James Clarke, 1992), 405–7.

only in God. In the third and fourth centuries, the Alexandrian school of theology maintained that only the soul could be the image, since both God and the soul are spiritual in nature; at best, the body somehow participates in what pertains to the soul. The Antiochene school, however, dwelt on the biblical datum that God made the whole human being in the divine image. We will return below to the Alexandrian approach.

STEWARDS OF CREATION

In the fourth century St Gregory of Nyssa summed up 'the greatness of man' as consisting 'not in his likeness to the created world but in his being in the image of the creator's nature' (*De Hominis Opificio*, 16. 2). At the same time, as the bridge between 'the divine and incorporeal nature' and 'the non-rational life of animals' (ibid., 16. 9), human beings bear a responsibility towards the natural world. The Genesis theme of men and women created in the divine image expresses not only humanity's inherent dignity but also the mission that issues from it. Human images of God manifest the divine rule on earth and have the unique mission of being God's stewards, continuing and completing God's creative work by presiding in the divine name over the rest of creation. A psalm celebrates the wonderful share in his own dignity that God has granted human beings by giving them authority over the rest of creation: 'You have given them dominion over the works of your hands; you have put all things under their feet, all sheep and oxen, and also the beasts of the field, the birds of the air, and the fish of the sea' (Ps. 8: 6–8). The Yahwist tradition of creation pictures God expressing this human dominion by bringing to the first man all the 'animals of the field' and 'birds of the air' so that he might give them their names (Gen. 2: 19–20).

In his commentary on Genesis, Claus Westermann shows how the Priestly tradition reinterprets the dominion God gives human beings over the animal world (Gen. 1: 28). At the beginning, God places human beings under a strictly vegetarian regime: seed-yielding plants and the fruit of trees (Gen. 1: 29). When the Yahwist account of the flood story ends, the Priestly tradition takes up the story and tells of the covenant that God establishes with humanity (and with all creation) through the person of Noah and his descendants. Here the Bible introduces for the first time a divine permission to eat animal flesh (Gen. 9: 2–3). According to Westermann, this concession from God takes into account the results stemming from the flood: 'animals are delivered into the hands of humans'.[8] At the same time, the Priestly tradition prohibits eating flesh with blood (Gen. 9: 4), as Leviticus 17: 10–11 will do.

Thus, from the outset, the Bible introduces norms meant to regulate the way human beings preside over the rest of creation. God, the common source of all beings, is the origin of humanity's dominion over the rest of his creatures. All come from God, even if only human beings can hear God's voice. It is only through Adam, Eve, Noah, and others in the Genesis story that the created universe can hear its creator and self-consciously find words and actions with which to respond. It is through human beings that the created world is aware of the divine self-communication and can respond appropriately. To borrow the language of St Francis of Assisi (d. 1226), humanity is to raise its voice and enter into communion with God, on behalf of 'brother sun' and 'sister moon'.

In the history of creation, God remains the one and only Lord, because nothing exists unless God constantly keeps it in existence and does not let it slip back into nothingness. That includes human stewardship as well. As St Thomas Aquinas (d. 1274) pointed out, we human stewards of God can never create energy or anything else out of nothing; we can only transform or convert what we have been given.[9] We can only be God's co-workers and collaborators; at best, our dignity lies in the fact that God calls us to be his 'co-creators'.[10]

---

[8] C. Westermann, *Genesis 1–11: A Commentary* (Minneapolis: Augsburg, 1984), 462–3.

[9] Aquinas states that when human beings make something, change occurs only in terms of 'motion according to quantity, quality, and place' (*Summa Theologiae*, 1a. 45. 2 ad 3); there is a fundamental difference between God's creative activity and the activity of creatures in 'making' something.

[10] Philip Hefner identifies the human person as a 'created co-creator': *The Human Factor: Evolution, Culture and Religion* (Minneapolis: Fortress, 1995), 35–6.

The fundamental interconnectedness of all creation means that it has only one *history*, which finds in God its source and goal. While human beings bring about the birth of *culture*, they give rise to two conflicting forces which, in the flood story of Genesis, come to a head: the one that seeks God and the other that constructs a world which allows no place for the creator. Human sin turns work into toil, and life into a burdensome struggle that battles against thorns and thistles and ekes out an existence from the soil (Gen. 3: 17–19). The flood account strikingly portrays the close link between human sin on the one hand, and creation on the other (Gen. 6: 5–8: 22). Described earlier as 'good' (Gen. 1: 25), the very earth has become 'corrupt' through human violence and aberration (Gen. 6: 11–12).

A new age opens after the flood; through the covenant with Noah, God's blessing reaches out to all creatures, both human and non-human (Gen. 9: 1–17). In Noah and his entourage, creation rediscovers its life-giving relation with its maker and readdresses itself to him. The rainbow in the sky is to be, in perpetuity, the symbol of a cosmic covenant with God (Gen. 9: 12–17). While creation and human culture are purified through the flood (in which Christians will see baptism prefigured) and reorient themselves to their creator, God restores the communion he intended from the beginning, and renews his original mission to humanity: 'Be fruitful and multiply, and fill the earth' (Gen. 9: 1; see 1: 28).

A striking recognition of God as the creator and sustainer of everyone and everything is expressed in St Paul's hope for fulfilment. He puts human beings and nature together in a common history, characterized by the interplay of two diverse forces: *one* is 'bondage to decay', and the *other* is 'eager longing' for the glorious transformation to come (Rom. 8: 18–25). Human existence is a lifelong pilgrimage towards God, the fullness of being and final goal of all creation. When the 'new heaven' and the 'new earth' come to pass (Rev. 21: 1), the whole of creation will be freed from imperfection and made new by the glory of God. A salvation effected through a very long process of creation, incarnation, and final consummation suggests the image of God as uniquely wise and patient, as well as supremely powerful.

CREATION THROUGH WISDOM/WORD/SPIRIT

By the time of St Paul, the Christian theology of creation had introduced a sea change, which is particularly relevant to our study: the Son of God, identified as Wisdom or Word, was understood to be the agent and goal of creation. This was a new step in thinking about creation; yet it enjoyed an OT background.

In the history of Israel and beyond, the OT pictured Wisdom, Word, and Spirit as personified agents of divine activity. As personifications they were not yet formally recognized as persons. Nevertheless, they operated with personal characteristics, and this was particularly so in the case of Wisdom (or Sophia).[11] Personified Wisdom became increasingly related to the creative work of God, as well as to that of providence and salvation. In the Book of Proverbs, which dates from the late sixth or early fifth century BC[12] but which has reworked some, or even much, older material, Lady Wisdom looms large in the first nine chapters. Her role in creation is announced (Prov. 3: 19), and then developed in the famous description of her primordial relationship to God and creation. 'Acquired', 'begotten', or 'created' 'long ago' as God's firstborn (Prov. 8: 22), Sophia not only existed with God before everything else but also cooperated in the divine work of creation (Prov. 8: 30–1). Delighting in God's company and then in the human community, Sophia is revealed here as profoundly related to God, to all creation, and—in a particular way—to human creatures.[13]

Among the earliest deutero-canonical books and also longest books of the Bible, Sirach contains the most extensive example of

[11] See J. L. Crenshaw, *Old Testament Wisdom: An Introduction* (London: SCM Press, 1982); D. F. Morgan, *Wisdom in the Old Testament Traditions* (Oxford: Blackwell, 1987); R. E. Murphy, *The Tree of Life: An Exploration of Biblical Wisdom Literature* (New York: Doubleday, 1990).

[12] Some scholars would lower this date by a century or two; see E. Zenger *et al.*, *Einleitung in das Alte Testament*, 326–34, where it is suggested that the final editing took place in the fourth or third century BC.

[13] See C. V. Camp, *Wisdom and the Feminine in the Book of Proverbs* (Sheffield: Almond Press, 1985); P. Joyce, 'Proverbs 8 in Interpretation: Historical Criticism and Beyond', in D. F. Ford and G. Stanton (eds.), *Reading Texts, Seeking Wisdom* (Grand Rapids, Mich.: Eerdmans, 2003), 89–101; F. Young, 'Proverbs 8 in Interpretation: Wisdom Personified', in ibid., 102–15.

Jewish wisdom literature we have. It was originally written in Hebrew around 180 BC and two generations later translated into Greek.[14] Wisdom appears at the beginning of the book (1: 1–30), at the halfway mark (24: 1–34), and at the end (51: 1–27). Sophia, according to Sirach 24: 3–7, has come forth 'from the mouth of the Most High' as divine Word, dwells like God 'in the highest heaven', and is enthroned like God 'on a pillar of cloud'. Like God, she is present everywhere ('from the vault of heaven' to the 'depths of the abyss') and has universal dominion ('over all the earth' and over 'every people and nation'). She covered 'the earth like a mist', just as the divine Spirit or Breath covered the water at creation (Gen. 1: 2).

Written a few decades before Christ's birth, the Book of Wisdom[15] yields much for our theme. Sophia is identified with spirit, a spirit that 'penetrates all things' and is thus immanent everywhere.[16] This immanence is balanced by transcendence, because Sophia is also portrayed as 'holy, unique', 'all-powerful', and all-seeing (Wis. 7: 22–4). Sublime language is used of her work in creating and conserving the world. After calling Sophia 'the fashioner of all things', the author of Wisdom celebrates her role in renewing (7: 27) and ordering all things: 'She reaches mightily from one end of the earth to the other and she orders all things well' (8: 1). That is to say, she upholds and guides creation. In short, Sophia not only 'lives with God' but is also associated constantly with all God's 'works' (8: 4).

New Testament Christians will give Jesus the title of 'Wisdom' (e.g. 1 Cor. 1: 24), and at times, without using that title, speak about Jesus being involved like Lady Wisdom in the creation and conservation of the world (e.g. Heb. 1: 1–2). We can easily guess the

---

[14] 'Deuterocanonical' is a (Catholic) name for those six books (plus further portions of other books) found in the Greek (LXX) version of the OT but not in the canon of Hebrew scriptures. The six books are Judith, 1 and 2 Maccabees, Sirach, Tobit, and Wisdom. The Hebrew text of Sirach was lost for many centuries, but about 68% of that text has now been rediscovered in Cairo, Qumran, and Masada.

[15] See H. Hübner, *Die Weisheit Salomons. Liber Sapientiae Salomonis* (Göttingen: Vandenhoeck & Ruprecht, 1999); C. Larcher, *Le Livre de la Sagesse ou la Sagesse de Salomon*, 3 vols. (Paris: Librairie Lecoffre, 1983–5).

[16] Thus Lady Wisdom not only personifies the divine activity but is a precious figure revealed when believers examine the world. She helps to overcome any sense of a divide between the transcendent otherness of God and the divine presence or immanence in creation.

reason for their belief. They knew that Jesus had brought them the *new creation* (2 Cor. 5: 17; Gal. 6: 15) of graced life through his death and resurrection, together with the coming of the Holy Spirit. The same 'power' or creative force of God deployed at the beginning in the making of the world was now revealed as the principle of the new creation or salvation offered to all (Rom. 1: 16). As agent of this new creation which was final salvation, Jesus must also be, so they recognized, the divine agent for the *original creation* of all things. What held true at the end must be true also at the beginning: eschatological claims about Christ as agent of final salvation led quickly to 'protological' claims or claims about 'first things': namely, that he was also involved in the divine act of creation. In 1 Corinthians, Paul expanded the confession of monotheism expressed in that central Jewish prayer, the Shema or 'Hear, O Israel' (Deut. 6: 4), to acknowledge a personal distinction within the godhead. The Apostle glossed 'God' with 'Father' and 'Lord' with 'Jesus Christ' to put Jesus as risen and exalted Lord alongside God the Father: 'For us there is one God, the Father, from whom are all things and for whom we exist, and one Lord, Jesus Christ, through whom are all things and through whom we exist' (1 Cor. 8: 6). Paul's redefining of Jewish monotheism involved acknowledging Christ as agent of creation, 'through whom are all things and through whom we exist'.[17] An NT christological hymn called Christ 'the firstborn of all creation', that is to say, the One who was prior to and supreme over all creation; for 'in/by him all things in heaven and earth were created, things visible and invisible . . . all things have been created through him and for him' (Col. 1: 15–16).[18] This hymn also echoes the language of Sirach 43: 26 and attributes to Christ the role of conserving creation in existence: 'in him all things hold together' (Col. 1: 17).[19]

[17] See A. C. Thiselton, *The First Epistle to the Corinthians* (Grand Rapids, Mich.: Eerdmans, 2000), 635–8.

[18] This NT hymn goes beyond the kind of language used about Wisdom. OT sapiential literature could write about things being created 'through her' but not of things being created 'for her'. Christ is not only the agent of creation but also its goal.

[19] See J.-N. Aletti, *Colossiens 1, 15–20*, Analecta Biblica 91 (Rome: Biblical Institute Press, 1981); id., *Saint Paul Épitre aux Colossiens* (Paris: Gabalda, 1993), 86–118. See also R. Bauckham, 'Where is Wisdom to be Found? Colossians 1. 15–20', in Ford and Stanton, *Reading Texts*, 129–38; M. D. Hooker, 'Where is Wisdom to be Found? Colossians 1. 15–20', in ibid., 116–28.

Sirach 43: 26 understands 'all things' to be held together by God's Word—a reminder that, in the OT, Word and Wisdom often function as equivalents in personifying the divine activity in creating and conserving things. As Solomon's famous prayer put it: 'God of my fathers and Lord of mercy, you made all things by your Word, and by your Wisdom fashioned humankind' (Wisd. 9: 1–2). 'Word' and 'Wisdom' can match each other as ways of expressing God's creative and conserving activity. In moving beyond a mere personification of God's activity to proclaiming a personal agent, the prologue of John's Gospel chose to use 'Word (Logos)', and presented the creative activity of the pre-existent Son of God: 'He (the Logos) was in the beginning with God. All things came into being through him' (John 1: 2–3).

The OT frequently uses a third way for articulating the creative and revelatory activity of God, 'Spirit'. In pre-Christian Judaism, 'spirit', 'wisdom', and 'word' were frequently synonymous ways for speaking of the divine activity. In celebrating God's creative power, the psalmist uses 'word' and 'breath (spirit)' as equivalent parallels: 'By the Word of the Lord the heavens were made, and all their host by the Breath of his mouth' (Ps. 33: 6; see Ps. 147: 18). The work of creation can be expressed in terms of God's word or in terms of the divine spirit, as Judith's prayer of thanksgiving also illustrates: 'Let your whole creation serve you; for you spoke and all things came to be; you sent out your Spirit and it gave them form' (Juditts 16: 14). In short, like 'word' and 'wisdom', 'spirit' was a way of expressing or even personifying the divine activity in the world. Thus the NT and post-NT Christian *language* for the tripersonal God flowed from the Jewish scriptures. That language was deeply modified in the light of Jesus' life, death, and resurrection (together with the outpouring of the Holy Spirit). The missions of the Son and the Spirit revealed that the personifications of Wisdom/Word and Spirit should be understood to be distinct 'persons' (to use a later term). Even if there were still centuries to go before the full-blown doctrine of God as three in one and one in three developed, the NT teaching provides a foundation and a starting point for that doctrinal development.

For this chapter what is highly significant is the way Paul, John, and other NT authors attribute to Jesus Christ a role in the divine work of creation. He is the primary agent not only in the divine work of cosmic redemption or reconciliation but also in the work of creating and conserving all things (Col. 1: 15–20).[20] Here the NT dramatically modified the OT by introducing a new way of thinking about the divine work of creation. As was to happen in the Nicene-Constantinopolitan Creed of 381 AD, the work of creation was attributed to the Son ('through whom all things were made') along with his redeeming function (what he did 'for us and for our salvation').

Here the situation was different apropos of the Holy Spirit. Paul, Luke, John, and other NT witnesses had much to say about the role of the Holy Spirit in the work of divine revelation and salvation. But no NT author says anything about the activity of the Spirit in the *creation* of the world. Here the NT does not pick up and develop what the OT presents about the creative activity of God personified as 'Spirit'. Perhaps it was too obvious to need comment. The Nicene-Constantinopolitan Creed was to call the Holy Spirit 'Lord and Life-giver', but did not repeat in the case of the Spirit the explicit language used of the Son ('through him all things were made'). Thanks to the theological thought and teaching of St Basil, St Gregory of Nyssa, St Augustine, and others, it then became clear that the Spirit inseparably operated with the Father and the Son in the work of creation as well as in that of sanctification.[21] All divine activity 'ad extra (on the outside)', starting from creation, is shared in common by the three persons of the Trinity.

But, as just said, what is very important for this chapter is the way the NT brings together the order of redemption and that of creation by understanding creation, and not merely redemption, to have occurred through the mediation of the Son of God, who is personally identical with Jesus Christ.[22] St Paul's typical greeting in his letters runs as follows: 'Grace to you and peace from God our Father and the

[20] See N. T. Wright, 'Redemption from a New Perspective? Towards a Multi-Layered Pauline Theology of the Cross', in *Redemption*, 83–4.

[21] Irenaeus had prepared the way by his image of the 'only Father' with his 'two hands', his Son and his Spirit through whom he creates (*Adversus Haereses*, 4. 40. 1).

[22] When attempting to envisage even slightly how Jesus of Nazareth could be the pre-existent mediator of creation, we need to avoid various minimalizing or maximalizing excesses: for instance, the false idea that his humanity really (and not merely in the divine intentions) existed 'before' the incarnation. Positively speaking, an appreciation of the powers Jesus used in some of his deeds (e.g. in the

Lord Jesus Christ' (Rom. 1: 7). The Apostle sets Christ, named as divine Lord, alongside 'God our Father' as the source of comprehensive *salvation* ('grace and peace'). Paul adds something crucial in the order of creation, by recasting the classic text of Jewish monotheism to include 'the one Lord, Jesus Christ' as the mediator of creation (1 Cor. 8: 6). The agency of the pre-existent Lord in creation corresponds to his central role in redemption. Jesus Christ has a unique role in both creation and redemption, which are united in the divine purpose.[23] An ancient Latin hymn, traditionally used for services in Advent, addresses Christ and begins as follows: 'Conditor alme siderum, aeterna lux credentium, Christe redemptor omnium (O bounteous creator of the heavenly bodies, eternal light of believers, Christ, redeemer of all)'. The word 'siderum', which denotes the sun, moon, and stars, recalls the creation of light and of the sun and other heavenly bodies (Gen. 1: 3–5, 14–19). Christ, the *eternal* light and not merely the light of the passing world, has not only brought that light to believers forever, but also has come as the redeemer of all.

A painting by Caravaggio (d. 1610) kept in the Church of St Louis in Rome, *The Calling of Matthew*, brilliantly illustrates the connection between creation and redemption. The outstretched arm of Christ recalls that of Adam in Michelangelo's portrayal of creation in the Sistine Chapel. The light on the face of Matthew shows how he has recognized and accepted the divine Light who has come into the world (John 1: 9; 9: 5). Above and behind the extended hand of Christ is an open window, its woodwork in the form of a cross. Caravaggio superbly brings together, in the one person of Christ, creation, incarnation, and redemption.

This kind of coupling of redemption and creation with the mediation of Christ, a coupling that is firmly based in the NT,[24]

---

multiplication of the loaves and fishes and the raising of several dead persons) could help us here. The causative powers involved in such deeds belong to the creator. See G. O'Collins, *Incarnation* (London: Continuum, 2002), 13–25.

[23] In pondering Christ's creative mediation in the cosmos, one might specify some wide-reaching parallels between the cross and creation: for instance, things die that new life can come. See John 12: 24. The created world suffers its 'crucifixion' through decay and death, but it will be liberated, transformed, and made new (Rom. 8: 18–27).

[24] Ephesians 1: 9–10 states clearly that creation was planned with the coming of Christ in mind.

makes it puzzling that many Christian theologians over the centuries have separated or even opposed redemption and creation. Often alleging that human sin gave a decisively new direction to God's plan, they failed to see how creation and the story of salvation were united in the Son of God from all eternity. This was to ignore what the Letter to the Ephesians had to say about the redeemed being 'chosen in Christ' to be God's people even 'before the foundation of the world' (Eph. 1: 4).[25] To be sure, the order of redemption does not bring a *mere* restoration of the order of creation. But there is continuity in the newness, above all through the one plan of God and the one figure of the creative Word who is also the Redeemer. Without creation, there could not have been an incarnation and the redemption it brought. The creation of the world and humankind provided the possibility for the Son of God to assume a human nature.

Happily there have also been those like St Irenaeus (d. around 200), St Maximus the Confessor (d. 622), Blessed John Duns Scotus (d. 1308), and others who in various ways maintained the biblical vision of creation and redemption as two distinguishable but inter-connected moments in God's one saving plan for all humanity and the whole cosmos. Such outstanding poets as Dante Alighieri (d. 1321) and John Donne (d. 1631) used the Mother of Jesus to associate creation with the redemption. In *The Divine Comedy* Dante opens canto 33 of the *Paradiso* by calling Mary the 'virgin mother, daughter of your Son'. In conceiving and giving birth to the Redeemer, Mary became the 'maker' of her creator, who through the 'eternal plan' of God 'nourished his love in her womb' on the way to redeeming humanity and the world.[26] John Donne also appreci-ated the paradox of Mary being the human maker of her Maker and mother of her Father, with Christ being understood to be 'father'.

[25] See A. T. Lincoln, *Ephesians*, Word Biblical Commentary 42 (Dallas: Word Books, 1990), 23–4.

[26] To quote the words of Dante: 'Vergine madre, figlia del tuo figlio,/ Umile ed alta più che creatura,/ Termine fisso d'etterno consiglio,/ Tu se' colei che l'umana natura/ Nobilitasti si, che 'l suo fattore/ Non disdegnò di farsi sua fattura./ Nel ventre tuo si raccese l'amore/ Per lo cui caldo nell'etterna pace/ Così è germinato questo fiore' (canto 33, 1–7). A twelfth-century Marian antiphon, 'Alma Redemptoris Mater (Bountiful Mother of the Redeemer)', expresses the same paradox: 'tu quae genuisti/ Natura mirante, tuum sanctum Genitorem (you who, to the astonishment of nature, gave birth to your Maker)'.

Donne's poem 'Annunciation' revelled in the paradox of the infinite Son of God accepting a finite existence through the incarnation. Even before time was created, the One whom Mary was to conceive in time had conceived her in the divine mind and intentions. After his human conception, the Light of the world was shut up and confined within the holy but dark cloister of Mary's womb.

> Salvation to all that will is nigh,
> That All, which always is All everywhere,
> Which cannot sin, and yet all sins must bear,
> Which cannot die, yet cannot choose but die,
> Lo, faithful Virgin, yields himself to lie
> In prison, in thy womb; and though he there
> Can take no sin, nor thou give, yet he will wear
> Taken from thence, flesh, which death's force may try.
> Ere by the spheres time was created, thou
> Wast in his mind, who is thy Son and Brother,
> Whom thou conceiv'st, conceived; yea thou art now
> Thy Maker's maker, and thy Father's mother,
> Thou hast light in dark; and shutst in little room,
> Immensity cloistered in thy dear womb.

Apropos of the incarnation of the Son of God, Maximus wrote: 'This is the great and hidden mystery; this is the blessed end on account of which all things were created. This is the divine purpose foreknown prior to the beginning of created things' (*Ad Thalassium*, 60). Thus Maximus brings together creation and the redemptive incarnation. Over two centuries earlier, Athanasius of Alexandria made a similar link. God has created humankind in and according to the Word (Logos). Here Athanasius took up a theme already introduced by Origen: a human being is *logikos*, which means both 'rational' and 'made according to the Logos'. Since God has created us in Christ, Athanasius argued, we must be images (lower case) of the perfect Image (upper case) of the Father, Christ himself. This set up Athanasius' characteristic way of understanding the incarnation: 'The Word of God came in his person, so that, as he was the Image of the Father, he could create afresh humankind after the image' (*De Incarnatione*, 13. 7).

Well over a century earlier Tertullian was more vivid in bringing together the coming of Christ and the formation from the dust of the earth of the first human being (Gen. 2: 7–8): 'in all the form which was moulded in the clay, Christ was in his [God's] thoughts as the human being who was to be' (*De Carnis Resurrectione*, 6). Even before Tertullian, Irenaeus had associated creation and incarnation. He blessed God for the incarnation: it enabled human beings to understand the original dignity with which the Father had created them in the beginning. 'In no other way could we have learned the things of God, unless our Master, existing as the Word, had become man. For no other being had the power of revealing to us the things of the Father, except his own proper Word' (*Adversus Haereses*, 5. 1. 1). Characteristically Irenaeus fashioned his unified vision of creation and redemption by also drawing on the comparisons and contrasts Paul made between the first Adam and the last (or second) Adam (Rom. 5: 12–21; 1 Cor. 15: 21–2, 45–9). Here we reach a second great link the NT and the Christian tradition has acknowledged between creation (in terms of the creation of the first human being) and redemption, and this time the link focuses on the created, human condition which Christ assumed rather than on his divine power as mediator of creation. In associating the first Adam and the last Adam, artists and writers have left us various visual and verbal images that play an important role in linking the past to the present and showing how redemptive actions in the past have their saving impact in the present.

THE SECOND ADAM

The paintings on the walls of the Brancacci Chapel in Florence show Masaccio (1401–28) at his artistic and spiritual best—not least in the way he links Adam and Eve with Christ. Driven from the Garden of Eden, our first parents are in despair. Weeping and weighed down with terrible pain and loss, they move along a path of sorrows. But the same path brings them to the next scene: Christ on the shores of Lake Galilee surrounded by his apostles, who will found the Church. In his own brilliant fashion, Masaccio follows a tradition that reaches back to St Paul, the connection and contrast between two corporate figures: the first Adam, who triggered the whole story of human sin, and the New or Second Adam who has brought the blessings of grace and eternal life. The connection and contrast initiated by Paul is the second major link that Christianity established between redemption and creation.

Paul seems to have drawn on Jewish traditions and the Hebrew scriptures to develop in his own striking way the 'New' or 'Last Adam' doctrine of Christ (or Christology) to be found in 1 Corinthians and Romans. Joseph Fitzmyer gathers the evidence that 'the incorporation of all human beings in Adam' is an idea which 'seems to appear for the first time in 1 Corinthians 15: 22'. He likewise offers evidence that allows him to qualify as 'novel teaching' Paul's argument in Romans 5 about the way in which Adam's sin had a 'maleficent influence on all human beings'.[27] But the blessings brought by Jesus Christ, the man foreshadowed by Adam, went far beyond the measure of Adam's wrongdoing (Rom. 5: 15–17). Before spelling out how Paul's Adam Christology, by linking the doctrine of redemption with the original creation, illuminates wonderfully the former, let us recall how successful Paul's contribution has proved in the life of Christianity.

Not only Irenaeus but also such writers as Clement of Alexandria (d. around 215), Origen (d. around 254), Hilary of Poitiers (d. 367/8), Ambrose of Milan (d. 397), Gregory of Nazianzus (d. 389/90), and Gregory of Nyssa (d. around 395) enriched Christian theology by reflecting on Jesus as the New/Second Adam.[28] By referring twice to Adam, an ancient and classic liturgical text, the *Exultet* or Easter Proclamation, sung during the Easter Vigil, implied Christ's role as Last Adam. Adam and Christ featured frequently in popular medieval drama. The 'Mystery Plays' highlighted the connection between the two Adams by the practice of having the same actor

---

[27] J. A. Fitzmyer, *Romans*, The Anchor Bible 33 (New York: Doubleday, 1993), 136, 406, 412.

[28] Some connected Adam (from whose side God formed Eve according to Gen. 2: 21–2) with Christ as the New Adam by interpreting the piercing of Christ's side on the cross (with the subsequent flow of water and blood that symbolized baptism and other 'mysteries') to constitute the birth of the Church. Just as Eve was formed from the side of Adam while he was in a deep sleep, so the Church was formed from Christ while he was in the sleep of death. See e.g. St John Chrysostom (d. 407), *Catecheses*, 3. 13–19.

portray both Adam and Christ.[29] A contrast between the damage done by the First Adam and the gifts of the Second Adam entered the Council of Trent's 1547 decree on the justification of sinful human beings (DzH 1524; ND 1928). Right down to the twenty-first century, images of Adam and Christ are still joined in icons used in the official worship of the Eastern Christian tradition and in the decoration of its churches.

This iconographic tradition links creation, which reached its climax with the making of the original Adam and Eve, to the redemption effected by the Second Adam. The human condition in its glory and misery is symbolized by Adam and Eve. After being created in the image and likeness of God, they lapsed into sin and lost paradise. Eastern icons show the last Adam descending into the dark pit of the underworld and releasing from their long bondage Adam, Eve, and innumerable others waiting for redemption in the 'limbo of the Fathers'. In some of these icons Christ carries the wooden cross on which he has died, and so can remind Christians of the tree from which Adam and Eve took the forbidden fruit. Even more explicitly, a hymn by the Latin poet Venantius Fortunatus (d. around 610), *Crux Fidelis* ('faithful cross'), links the tree of life with the tree of death in the one great drama of creation, fall, and redemption. The preface for the feast of the Holy Cross or Exaltation of the Cross (14 September), a feast which goes back at least to the seventh century, declares: 'Death came from a tree, life was to spring from a tree.' Some imaginative writers and artists have linked Adam with the Second Adam through the symbol of the garden: from the garden of Eden, to the garden of Gethsemane and the garden where Christ was buried and after his resurrection met Mary Magdalene (John 19: 41–2; 20: 11–18), and on, finally, to the garden of the heavenly Jerusalem which Christ as the risen Lamb will illuminate (Rev. 21: 23; 22: 1–2).

In connecting Adam and Christ, no work of literature has surpassed 'Hymn to God my God in my Sickness' by John Donne:

---

[29] See further R. Woolf, *The English Mystery Plays* (Berkeley, Calif.: University of California Press, 1980); and B. Murdoch, *Adam's Grace: Fall and Redemption in Medieval Literature* (Cambridge: D. S. Brewer, 2000).

> We think that Paradise and Calvary,
> Christ's Cross and Adam's tree, stood in one place;[30]
> Look, Lord, and find both Adams met in me;
> As the first Adam's sweat surrounds my face,
> May the Last Adam's blood my soul embrace.

Another outstanding reference to the Second Adam turned several decades later in *Paradise Regained* by John Milton. After expanding the Genesis story of Adam and Eve into the twelve books of *Paradise Lost*, Milton focused the four-book sequel entirely on the temptation in the wilderness. Unlike Adam and Eve, Jesus, the Second Adam, succeeds in resisting temptation.

The images of Adam and Eve and the image of Christ as the New Adam have been linked in church teaching, art, liturgical traditions, literature, and legends to associate redemption with creation. To be sure, considering Christ as the New or Second Adam is not the only way to understand and interpret what he did for human beings through his life, death, and resurrection. But it is one way which has proved enduringly successful, from St Paul down to John Henry Newman's 'Dream of Gerontius' ('a second Adam to the fight and to the rescue came') and beyond. It serves to shed light on redemption, and does so in three particular ways.

First, the Adam/Christ contrast vividly reminds us that human beings are saved not merely through the divine power 'from the outside'. By the loving 'condescension' of God's plan, they are also saved 'from the inside', through the incarnate Son of God, who is their brother. The two figures in Masaccio's pitiless scene appear to have lost paradise forever. But they are on a path that leads to another human figure, that of Christ, the second Adam who will heal and transform human destiny for all eternity.

Second, this contrast shows the deep link between the whole of creation, in which Adam and Eve are the high point and God's

---

[30] An old and enduring legend told the story of the tree from which Adam and Eve took the forbidden fruit and how it came be used as the tree of Calvary on which Christ died. According to a related legend, Calvary was the place where Adam was buried; Christian artists at times placed his skull, and occasionally even his skeleton, at the foot of the cross. Some artists have pictured Adam and Eve standing together in a sarcophagus under the cross. A few representations have the figure of Adam holding a chalice to receive the first drops of blood falling from Christ on the cross.

intended stewards, and redemption. What Christ does in his glorious resurrection from the dead involves the whole created world and human stewardship for the earth. Eastern icons of Christ's descent to the dead hint at this link. Huge rocks, which have been shattered to open Christ's passage down into the 'limbo of the Fathers', suggest that the Easter transformation includes, even here and now, the whole world.

Third, Eastern icons depicting Christ's meeting with Adam and Eve—such as the sublime one in the monastery of Chora (Istanbul)—show large crowds of people standing behind them. In liberating and raising Adam and Eve, the Second Adam raises all humanity. This way of representing Christ's redemptive work differs dramatically from a familiar painting of the resurrection by Piero della Francesca (d. 1492) to be found in San Sepolcro (Tuscany) and acclaimed by Aldous Huxley as 'the finest picture in the world'. The victorious Christ stands majestically alone above the prostrate soldiers who have been guarding his tomb. No one else is present. The Eastern icons do much better theologically by introducing Adam, Eve, and their companions to indicate vividly that the resurrection is not only an individual victory but also the saving event for all the world. As corporate figures, Adam and Eve[31] foreshadow Christ, *the* corporate figure par excellence, whose commitment to the work of redemption already has its impact on the entire human race and the cosmos.

Through the sequence of his frescoes in the Brancacci Chapel, Masaccio pointed Adam and Eve in the direction of Christ, the Second Adam. He drove home the connection by placing diagonally opposite the tormented figures of Adam and Eve a scene of St Peter baptizing a group of neophytes. The shame and loss of the fall into sin do not have the last word. Incorporation through baptism into the final Adam, now risen from the dead, brings the new life of present grace and future glory. But, before taking up in detail the

---

[31] Adam and Eve also prefigure all human families which, while seldom including one son (Cain) who murders another (Abel), are always in various ways dysfunctional and in need of redemption. The future of the human race depends on the health of marriage and the family. The Book of Genesis pictures marriage and the family not only as coming from the creative hand of God but also as needing redemption from sin and evil.

story of Christ's redemptive achievement, we need to reflect further on the fall into sin and the human misery that calls out for a Redeemer. The deep suffering that afflicts us highlights the aspect of love in our image of God, who through the incarnation personally takes on suffering and enters into a profound solidarity with human beings in their pain.

3

The Human Condition

People are religious to the extent that they believe themselves to be not so much *imperfect*, as *sick*. Anyone who is half-way decent will think himself utterly imperfect, but the religious person thinks himself *wretched*.

> Ludwig Wittgenstein, *Culture and Value* (Oxford: Blackwell, rev. edn., 1980), 51e.

I leave it to you to say why it is
that every moment we are awake we do not weep.

> Allen Afterman, 'Pietà'.

Talk of redemption or salvation inevitably raises the question: What is the problem? What needs to be fixed? The scriptures, Christian tradition, and contemporary experience converge in their response: everywhere disorder and unhappiness afflict men and women. Human beings are sinful, suffering, and mortal. Often deep human desires are not being met. We are not what we would like to be and are not where we would like to be. All manner of discontents pervade the world. Even, or especially, those whose material resources allow them to dedicate their lives to constant gratification and the avoidance of suffering at all costs suffer from a fatally flawed perception of human existence; they are doomed to deep disappointment. But can mainstream Christian tradition sum up the human predicament in one word? Drawing on such key witnesses as St Paul in Romans, it sees the central problem not as unsatisfied desires, false consciousness, or anything else, but as sin.

SOME OBJECTIONS

Such an answer faces some important objections. First, can we have an adequate view of sin *before* we understand and appreciate salvation? Surely we should begin by reflecting on the astonishing events and blessings of redemption, and then we will be in a better position to grasp the evil of sin?[1] Christian preachers, theologians, and spiritual writers have often made the valuable observation that we cannot 'really know' the malice of sin until we deeply appreciate how our salvation came through the suffering and death of Christ. Nevertheless, St Paul establishes universal sinfulness (Rom. 3: 23) *before* he presses on to spell out the new life 'in' Christ and 'through' the Spirit. He wants to show how 'all are guilty' *before* he develops various dimensions of redemption: righteousness or justification (Rom. 3: 24–5: 21), God's saving act through Christ (Rom. 8: 1–4), life according to the Holy Spirit (Rom. 8: 5–17), and the rest. The example of Paul in his longest and most mature letter convinces me that we should begin by probing the sinful human condition and then move to examine various aspects of redemption.[2] Beyond question, an appreciation of the redemptive deeds of Christ will throw further light on the nature of human sinfulness. But we need at least a provisional insight into sin and evil[3] before exploring redemption. The case of the Samaritan woman in John's Gospel exemplifies this

[1] B. Sesboüé, *Jésus-Christ l'unique médiateur. Essai sur la rédemption et le salut*, i (Paris: Desclée, 1988), 25–7. (A second edition of 2003 has different pagination and a new cover, but it does nothing else but add one footnote (251, n. 46), as well as make a handful of insignificant corrections.) For a more nuanced presentation of this issue, see K. Rahner, *Foundations of Christian Faith* (New York: Seabury Press, 1978), 93.

[2] The movement of Dante's *Divine Comedy* is instructive. After taking the reader through hell and the sins for which people have been condemned, he constructs a long climb up the mountain of purgatory around seven terraces on which sinners are being cleansed from the seven deadly sins, which begin with the worst (pride) and end with the least serious (lust). It is only after this long treatment of sin that Dante moves into heaven and expounds the workings of redemption; see e.g. the account of Anselm's theology of satisfaction in canto 7 of *Paradiso*.

[3] The Christian tradition has distinguished between the *moral* evil of sin and various forms of *physical* evil. It is not only sin but also the limited conditions of all created beings that give rise to evil: e.g. the suffering which is built into the created order.

point. It is only *after* she has been gently reminded of her immoral situation and begins to 'feel' her need for forgiveness (John 4: 16–18) that she can recognize who Jesus is and become the means of bringing the people of Sychar to acknowledge him as 'the Saviour of the world' (John 4: 29, 39, 42).

A second objection has frequently come from theologians of Eastern Christianity: the West begins with sin and correlates liberation from sin with the cross, forgetting the essential role of the resurrection (along with the coming of the Holy Spirit) in bringing human beings to share in the divine life (2 Pet. 1: 4). Eastern theologians (a) rightly require that redemption be not reduced to freedom from sin through the impact of Christ's suffering and death, (b) correctly respect the central importance of the resurrection and the outpouring of the Holy Spirit, and (c) use 'divinization' as a suitable expression for God's redemptive activity. In this book I will attempt to honour these three requirements. Nevertheless, that is not to exclude approaching redemption by first reflecting on sin. Unless sin is dealt with, any calling to share in the divine life will remain frustrated. Hence it seems appropriate to examine sin before moving to spend chapters on various themes connected with redemption.

A third objection recalls how deeply and universally suffering affects human life.[4] Is it primarily suffering that makes us candidates for salvation? Would it be more accurate to sum up redemption as deliverance from (physical and mental) pain and other forms of suffering? Undoubtedly, talk of 'redemption from suffering' sometimes has too strong a psychological tone and almost suggests that *the* human problem is interior, mental suffering. It can gloss over the fact that human beings suffer from a whole range of evils, including undeserved and horrendous injustice. Over and over again we see hatred and monstrous cruelty inflicting on innocent people the worst that human beings can do to each other.

---

[4] See F. Young, 'Suffering', in A. Hastings, A. Mason, and J. Pyper (eds.), *The Oxford Companion to Christian Thought* (Oxford: Oxford University Press, 2000), 687–9; M. McCord Adams, 'Evil, Problem of', in E. Craig (ed.), *Routledge Encyclopedia of Philosophy*, iii (London: Routledge, 1998), 466–72; J. Scharbert *et al.*, 'Leiden', *TRE* xx. 669–711. In various essays Johann Baptist Metz (b. 1928) has expounded redemption as coming to those who suffer and remember suffering: see e.g. his 'The Future in the Memory of Suffering', *Concilium* 9 (1972), 14–25.

Yet some forms of suffering, as the OT witnesses (e.g. Deut. 8: 5;
Wisd. 11: 9–10) and NT (e.g. Heb. 12: 5–13; 1 Pet. 1: 6–7), can prove
learning experiences that further the personal growth of human
beings. Deliverance from such suffering would be loss rather than
gain. Some suffering may be necessary for spiritual growth—'the
price of personal progress', so to speak. Nevertheless, such an 'edu-
cational' model has its obvious limits, once we reflect on the excessive
amount of suffering that afflicts innumerable people. Their enormous suffering seems quite out of proportion to any individual or
personal growth that it might bring.

At times, to be sure, one can recognize a fairly straight line between
sin and suffering. Some sins—for instance, deliberate and large-scale
fraud that is detected and leads to a prison sentence—show how
one's own suffering can result from sin. In many, tragically numerous, cases the greed, fear, hatred, or downright selfish indifference of
powerful persons cause the immense suffering and even death of
millions of others. Yet at other times—for instance, the death of a
much-loved child through a brain tumour—the awful pain of individuals can hardly be understood to be the consequence of some
sin(s) of the parents and other family members. Much suffering
wears a mysterious, inexplicable, and even apparently pointless face.

Some modern thinkers have reopened the issue of the passibility of
God. In place of the traditional view of God as impassible, they have
argued, on various grounds, for the view that God suffers in his
creation. Such a view has radical consequences for their accounts of
what suffering means and what then constitutes the story of the
divine salvation of suffering human beings and their world.[5] While
sincerely respecting this alternative view, I find it very difficult to
envisage God as both suffering (essentially and even eternally?) and
also saving us from our suffering and sin. But this is not to play down
the terrible suffering involved in the passion and death of the incarnate Son of God. His love made him appallingly vulnerable and put
him in the hands of merciless sinners (see Chapters 8 and 9 below).

---

[5] For a very good summary of the issue and bibliography, see P. S. Fiddes,
'Suffering, Divine', in A. E. McGrath (ed.), *The Blackwell Encyclopedia of Modern
Christian Thought* (Oxford: Blackwell, 1993), 633–6.

In making his case for the all-pervasive reign of sin, St Paul frequently specifies or at least implies the disastrous suffering that sin brings (e.g. Rom. 1: 29–31). Yet he attends primarily to sin which has spread its deadly reign throughout the whole world before grace, life, and peace came with Christ and the Holy Spirit (Rom. 8: 1–11). In short, sin and suffering are radically connected, as we shall see. But it is above all the power, pollution, and alienation of sin that calls for the redemption of human beings and their world.[6]

A fourth objection highlights the hungers of the human heart. We crave a life that is utterly full and will never end. We search for meaning that will light up everything. We hunger for a perfect love that will prove totally and enduringly satisfying. Where love is concerned, our hearts are a 'bottomless gorge', as William Blake (1757–1827) put it. Such longings point to God who is total Life, Meaning, and Love. Or else we can express these longings in terms of the human thirst for the fullness of truth, goodness, and beauty, to be found ultimately and only in God who is Truth, Goodness, and Beauty itself. As St Augustine of Hippo classically said when addressing God, 'you have made us for yourself, O Lord, and our hearts find no rest until they rest in you' (*Confessions*, 1. 1). In this context one can also appeal to Karl Rahner's reflections on human beings as dynamically oriented towards the 'absolute Mystery', the 'transcendent Ground' of their existence.[7] Is redemption then primarily or exclusively a matter of satisfying fully and finally our radical human hunger? To be sure, the ultimate goal of salvation is just that: a totally fulfilling union with God through Christ. But Augustine knew very well how sin stops us from responding to God's call and receiving the divine gifts. (We will take up below his reflections on sin.) Rahner dedicated pages to the possibility of human beings deciding against God and freely closing themselves against the

---

[6] See R. C. Cover and E. P. Sanders, 'Sin, Sinners', *ABD* vi. 31–47; A. McFadyen, 'Sin', in the *Oxford Companion to Christian Thought*, 665–8; 'Sin', in F. L. Cross and E. A. Livingstone (eds.), *Oxford Dictionary of the Christian Church* (Oxford: Oxford University Press, 3rd edn., 1997), 1505; G. von Rad, *Old Testament Theology*, i (Edinburgh: Oliver & Boyd, 1962), 154–65; J. Schreiner, *Theologie des Alten Testaments* (Würzburg: Echter, 1995), 245–77; D. Sitzler-Osing *et al.*, 'Sünde', *TRE* xxxii. 360–442.

[7] See K. Rahner, *Foundations of Christian Faith* (New York: Seabury Press, 1978), 44–89.

'absolute Mystery', who has created them and on whom they constantly depend.[8] Hence, before coming to the nature and goal of salvation, we must spend time reflecting on sin.

SIN IN STORY AND HISTORY

The richly symbolic language of the opening chapters of Genesis pictures God as creating all things 'good', with humanity forming the climax of the divine work of creation. 'The man' and 'the woman' of Genesis 2 transgressed God's command, ate the forbidden fruit, and lost both their innocent relationship with each other and their trusting relationship with God. The story vividly portrays their loss of innocence and urge to redress their self-image: 'The eyes of both were opened, and they knew that they were naked; and they sewed fig leaves together, and made loincloths for themselves' (Gen. 3: 7). They now 'knew' through their experience the difference between 'good' and 'evil' (Gen. 3: 5). In their guilt they tried to hide 'themselves from the presence of the Lord God' (Gen. 3: 8). They had hoped that eating the forbidden fruit would make them even more 'like God' (Gen. 3: 5), but now they anxiously attempt to get away from God. Sin has disrupted their basic relationship with their divine Lord.

The story of the first sin brilliantly presents what everyman and everywoman do: their instinct is to put the blame on someone else. The man blames the woman and even God: 'the woman whom you gave to be with me, she gave me fruit from the tree' (Gen. 3: 11). The woman blames the crafty serpent who tempted her: 'the serpent tricked me, and I ate' (Gen. 3: 13). But the man and the woman have deliberately disobeyed the divine will and must suffer the consequences.

The Genesis story picturesquely tells what follows the sinful loss of their first innocence, when the man and the woman were unashamedly naked (Gen. 2: 25)—in a guiltless relationship to one another and to God, which traditional language was to call 'original justice'. The biblical text appeals to an ancient explanation for the pain of

<hr />

[8] Ibid., 90–106.

childbirth, when God says to the woman: 'I will greatly increase your pangs in childbearing; in pain you shall bring forth children' (Gen. 3:16). In place of an ideal relationship of joyful equality and mutual dependence intended by the creator (Gen. 2: 18–23), the woman finds herself 'ruled over' by her husband (Gen. 3: 16) and named by him 'Eve' (Gen. 3: 20). Where pain now characterizes the woman's experience of giving life through childbearing, something similar holds true of the man. His work in cultivating the garden should have been normal and natural (Gen. 2: 15), but sin turns work into distressing toil (Gen. 3: 17–19). When bringing forth life, in this case by gaining bread from the ground and its crops, the man too will have to suffer pain. In language that is as fresh as ever, the Genesis story drives home the point: far from enhancing their life, sin leaves the man and the woman less than they should really be, and ushers in destructive consequences.

The most distressing consequences concern not only a loss of familiarity with God but also the nature of death. Fashioned from dust (Gen. 2: 7), the man and the woman are by nature mortal. Their death should have been like that of Abraham, who was to die surrounded by his family in 'ripe old age'—a death that peacefully completes a life spent in faithful obedience to God (Gen. 25: 1–11).[9] But disobedience to God has changed the experience of death for sinful human beings; death has become a troubling, inexorable fate (Gen. 3: 19), a grievous sign of sin. Flanked by suffering and pain, death signals the radical change that sin has brought to the human condition.

Having made a decision unworthy of those created in the divine image (Gen. 1: 26–7), the man and the woman are banished from the garden of Eden into a foreign place. Cherubim and a flaming sword now guard the entrance to the garden and 'the way to the tree of life' (Gen. 3: 24). Other books of the Bible will use exile and suffering in a foreign land to symbolize sin and the lot of sinners: for instance, the

---

[9] According to the Yahwist tradition (which Genesis 25 draws on), physical death is humanity's return to dust and the handing back of one's life's breath to God. The OT expresses a firm belief in afterlife only in post-exilic times. On death, see H.-P. Hasenfratz *et al.*, 'Tod', *TRE* xxxiii. 579–638: K. H. Richards and N. P. Gulley, 'Death', *ABD* ii. 108–11.

Babylonian exile in Second Isaiah.[10] Jesus' parable of the lost son pictures the dissolute sinner as leaving his parental home for 'a distant country' (Luke 15: 13). The last book of the Bible will portray final damnation as 'the second death' to which the damned will be banished (Rev. 20: 10, 14) and final redemption as entering a heavenly Jerusalem and receiving abundant blessings from the 'tree of life'. For humanity, paradise regained will mean re-entering the garden and being given access to the ultimate 'tree of life', watered by the river of the water of life coming from the Lamb (Rev. 22: 1–2).

The Genesis story sees the disobedience of Adam and Eve as initiating an avalanche of sin. Cain murders his brother; this fratricide opens the way for a terrifying increase of violence and the unbridled revenge killings practised by Cain's descendant, Lamech (Gen. 4: 8, 23–4). Violence also brings a breach of boundaries between heaven and earth. 'Beings of the heavenly court' take human wives even though their offspring remain mortal and do not become semi-divine (Gen. 6: 1–4). Whatever the source of this fragment of mythology, lustful practices contribute to the steady advance of sin that degrades the human condition. Once called 'good', the earth itself is now corrupted through the wicked deeds of human beings (Gen. 6: 11–13). In their colourful way, the opening chapters of Genesis show human beings opting against God and one another. Evil decisions coalesce and shape a whole situation of sin, which needs 'cleansing' to allow for a new beginning (Gen. 9: 1–7).

Although God's judgement takes the form of a catastrophic flood, the merciful love of God still operates. Earlier in the Genesis story, God provides garments of skin to replace the flimsy clothing of fig leaves, and fittingly dresses up the man and the woman after they sin (Gen. 3: 21). He puts a 'mark' on the first murderer, so that no one would kill Cain (Gen. 4: 15). Then, the Bible uses Babylonian traditions of prehistoric floods to highlight God's faithful mercy that sharply contrasts with the stubbornness and the sinful inclinations of the human heart. At the flood, God respects human freedom and offers all people the option of avoiding the impending doom. He

---

[10] N. T. Wright has expounded repentance from sin as homecoming from exile. But see the misgivings expressed by C. Seitz, 'Reconcilation and Plain Sense Witness', in *Redemption*, 25–42.

then rescues Noah and a remnant of human beings and animals: they are the ones who have taken up God's offer (Gen. 6: 5–8: 22).

Notwithstanding the new beginning marked by God's covenant with Noah, the history of sin continues. The story of the tower of Babel expresses an arrogant attempt to overreach human limitations (Gen. 11: 1–9). The attempt ends in an insuperable breakdown in human communications: the people are scattered over the face of the earth and their one language is broken up into many. The biblical text takes an old legend about the origin of different language groups and uses it to symbolize a proud desire to procure fame and security, something that quickly proves self-destructive (Gen. 11: 4).

Genesis thus illustrates how sin advances gradually, steadily, and inexorably. It has a 'history': the sum of many individual, free, and concrete choices that merge to alienate humanity from God. Despite the attempts of the man and the woman of Genesis 3, sin cannot be blamed on 'the serpent' or on some other obnoxious source. Humanity chooses to become 'like God' and to experience existentially ('to know') the difference between good and evil (Gen. 3: 5). The avalanche effect of sin, before and after the flood, continues to account for the progressive separation sin brings between the creator and humankind. The sum of so many single evil options forms a wedge that pushes God and humanity further apart. The cherubim with the flaming sword at the door of the garden (Gen. 3: 24) symbolize the need for repentance, conversion, and purification. Only thus can humanity enjoy again access to its creator.

The opening chapters of Genesis present the sinfulness that emerged at humanity's origins and left an enduring heritage of evil in options against God, oneself, other human beings, and created nature. Christians came to express that legacy in terms of inherited 'original sin', a doctrine that owes much to St Paul and St Augustine of Hippo. I postpone to the next chapter a treatment of original sin. The present chapter continues its sketch of the human condition by examining personal sin or the sinfulness that results from the misuse of freedom.

But first let me add something about the status of the Genesis stories: from Adam to Noah. These stories, as we have just seen, express the perennial human condition. But what *kind* of stories are they? What is their historical status? Traditionally the Adam story has been understood, as in the classical treatment by John Milton's *Paradise Lost*, to present an initial period of perfection in creation and an original innocence that ended with a 'one-point' event, the fall of Adam and Eve into sin. Yet the Adam story need not be interpreted as necessarily entailing the first human couple (monogenism) spoiling a state of primordial happiness by one spectacular sin. It could also apply to a number of original human beings (polygenism), who, right from the start of their existence, through sin drifted away from what God intended for them and so left to their descendants a world which lacks what God wanted, a world in which manifold evil hampers the proper exercise of freedom. As for the Great Flood, it has been traditionally interpreted as God judging and punishing human beings 'from the outside', so to speak. Yet it could (and should) be understood as a powerful symbol of the intrinsic self-destructiveness of human sin. In that case the divine 'judgement' in the story would point to God's allowing the natural consequences of sin to work themselves out.

PERSONAL SIN

(1) *Prophets and Sages* God's covenant with Noah recalls the conviction that human beings have been created in the divine 'image' (Gen. 9: 6). Yet the biblical narrative rarely loses sight of the sinful failures and even slavery to sin that plague humankind. The Ten Commandments sum up various duties towards God and neighbour (Exod. 20: 2–17; Deut. 5: 6–21; Lev. 19: 1–37). The Deuteronomic version, in particular, goes on to insist that obedience to these commandments will bring real welfare and rich blessings (Deut. 6: 1–3).[11] The divine commandments spell out the conditions for human well-being, but they also hint at persistent iniquity. Human beings lapse into idolatry by setting up false gods. They murder other people, commit adultery, steal, and bear false

---

[11] On the Decalogue, see B. S. Childs, *Old Testament Theology in a Canonical Context* (London: SCM Press, 1985), 63–83; G. von Rad, *Old Testament Theology*, i. 190–219; 'Commandments, The Ten', *Oxford Dictionary of the Christian Church*, 382–3.

witness. The OT repeatedly condemns these and other sins as rebellion against the Lord, as foolishness, and as infidelity to the covenant relationship with God.

The great OT prophets denounce human crimes and offences. In the name of God, Isaiah inveighs against the people's religious superficiality (Isa. 1: 10–20); they must learn to 'rescue the oppressed, defend the orphan, and plead for the widow' (Isa. 1: 17). Amos warns Israel against trampling on the poor, pushing aside the needy, and taking bribes (Amos 5: 11–12). Through the prophet Hosea, God indicts Israel. Sin brings suffering and death to the whole of creation: 'Swearing, lying and murder, and stealing and adultery break out; bloodshed follows bloodshed. Therefore the land mourns, and all who live in it languish; together with the wild animals and the birds of the air, even the fish of the sea are perishing' (Hos. 4: 2–3). Israel must learn again to 'seek' God and 'live' (Amos 5: 4). Sin has repudiated God's offer of life and love.

Personal responsibility for sin is by no means absent in the Genesis story: Adam, Eve, and Cain, for example, are pictured as personally culpable. The free misuse of personal responsibility accounts for the heinous nature of sin and the outrageous disruption it brings about in God's order of creation. However, Jeremiah (31: 27–30) and, even more clearly, Ezekiel (18: 1–32) underscore personal responsibility. Human beings are prone to blame others (e.g. parents and ancestors), instead of recognizing their personal guilt that brings misfortune. God is not powerless or deaf; it is the contamination of sin that wrecks people's lives (Isa. 59: 1–21). Sins are free choices made from the heart; God wants to change wicked human hearts and turn sinners into obedient people (Ezek. 11: 19–21).

The *Miserere* (Ps. 51), understood as King David's prayer after his sins of adultery and murder (2 Sam. 11: 1–27), sums up OT thought on the evil of sin. In the first place, sin is a personal offence against God: 'Against you, you alone, have I sinned, and done what is evil in your sight' (Ps. 51: 4). David has committed terrible injustice against Uriah the Hittite, Bathsheba's husband, but the fundamental evil of sin consists in a ruptured relationship with God. Sin is a clear sign of the absence of true wisdom and of a joyless heart (Ps. 51: 6). The *Miserere*, along with the parable of the prodigal son (Luke 15: 11–32), has shaped profoundly the way Christians understand sin—not as a merely ethical evil, let alone as only a regrettable mistake, but as a personal offence against a loving God for which one must take responsibility and ask forgiveness. Like David in the psalm, the prodigal acknowledges his sins to be first and foremost an offence against God ('I have sinned against heaven') and only then an offence against his father (Luke 15: 18, 21).

The *Miserere* (and, behind it, the story of David's adultery and murder) and Jesus' parable of the prodigal son have also moulded the way Christians *react* to their sins.[12] In recognizing their guilt and asking pardon from God, they follow ideally a middle path between (a) a pathological scrupulosity, which compulsively detects sin where none exists or tortures itself over past sins long forgiven by God, and (b) a laxity, which refuses to accept one's culpability and dismisses even grave sins as minor 'mistakes' or blemishes on one's record caused by unfortunate circumstances and/or the failure of others. We return to this theme below.

Before leaving the OT, let me add a word about the Wisdom of Solomon, the most theological of all the deutero-canonical works (see Chapter 2 above). Written only a few years before the birth of Jesus, it pictures poignantly the reasoning of sensual and ungodly sinners (Wisd. 1: 16–2: 24). They think of themselves as being 'born by mere chance' and of death as the end of their existence. Life has no long-range meaning for them, and they give themselves to sensual satisfaction—even at terrible cost to others. Wisdom allows us to overhear their talk and thoughts: 'Let us oppress the righteous poor man; let us not spare the widow or regard the grey hairs of the aged. But let our might be our law of right' (Wisd. 2: 10–11). The OT prophets denounce the oppression of helpless, righteous people. But the Book of Wisdom goes further in depicting dramatically the way in which wicked sinners urge each other to live frivolously and persecute mercilessly. Their wickedness has blinded them; their sin clouds and corrupts their reasoning; they know neither God nor 'the secret purposes of God' (Wisd. 2: 21–2).

---

[12] On the prodigal son, see D. Brown, 'Images of Redemption in Art and Music', in *Redemption*, 314–19. The *Miserere* enjoys some notable settings, such as those by Gregorio Allegri (d. 1652) and Christopher Willcock (b. 1947).

(2) *The NT and Beyond* Jesus and his followers kept up the Jewish teaching on sin while adding some new accents. Jesus saw that sin comes from within a person (e.g. Mark 7: 20–3; Matt. 5: 27–8). Like the author of Wisdom, he knew that something goes wrong in the human mind and heart even before sinners commit evil actions. Jesus upheld the Ten Commandments (Mark 10: 19) and followed the prophets in stigmatizing social injustice, especially the failure to act justly and lovingly towards those in terrible need (Luke 16: 19–31). Jesus went so far, according to one tradition, as to make the Final Judgement depend simply on our practical concern for the hungry, the sick, prisoners, homeless persons, and others in great need (Matt. 25: 31–46). This pushed beyond even the highest OT standards, with Jesus teaching something no prophet had taught: he identified himself with all in terrible need. This corresponded to the table fellowship with the pariahs of his society—something no OT prophet had ever practised. Jesus also broke new ground by linking together the command to love God and love our neighbour (Mark 12: 28–34). This was to turn all sins into failures to follow the love-command.

The NT authors normally do not add much to the OT teaching on sin. James, for instance, stigmatizes abuses committed by the wealthy (2: 1–7; 4: 13–17; 5: 1–6). Yet many of these warnings not only have their background in the OT prophets and wisdom traditions but also echo sayings of Jesus about the dangers of wealth. But the Johannine literature and the Pauline letters introduce new themes when writing about sin.

The striking Christocentrism of John entails representing sin as choosing darkness, hatred, and falsity, rather than light, love, and truth. Thus sin becomes a refusal to 'come' to Christ and believe in him. This very Christocentric perspective on faith and sin also includes introducing its counterpoint, the devil, 'a murderer from the beginning' and 'the father of lies' (John 8: 44). Sinners are 'children of the devil' (1 John 3: 8).

Even more than John, Paul almost personifies sin itself.[13] Sin is a cosmic force of evil that enters into human beings through their

---

[13] For Paul on sin, evil, and death, see J. D. G. Dunn, *The Theology of Paul the Apostle* (Grand Rapids, Mich.: Eerdmans, 1998), 79–161.

submission to it. Along with death, its fearful consequence and expression, sin has exercised dominion over human beings and made them its slaves (Rom. 5–8). Believers cease to be the slaves of sin when they become God's slaves (Rom. 6: 15–23). Another strong emphasis from Paul, as we have seen above, is his teaching that 'all have sinned' (Rom. 3: 23), and suffer the tragic consequences of sin: Jews by offending against God's written law and Gentiles by not following what they could know through the visible things God has made and through the law written in their hearts (Rom. 1: 18–3: 20). Early Christian formulas confessed that Christ died 'for our sins' (1 Cor. 15: 3). Paul agrees, and adds: 'Sin is universal.'

In many ways, Paul illustrates how sin threatens the life of the Church, especially when believers turn back to the lifestyle of their 'old self' that they have renounced at baptism (Rom. 6: 6; see Col. 3: 9). Sin can manifest itself as instability in the profession of faith, or the acceptance of a 'different gospel' (Gal. 1: 6). Believers can become 'lazy', 'fainthearted', 'weak' (1 Thess. 5: 14), envious, and quarrelsome (1 Cor. 1–4). Some bring civil cases against other Christians 'before the unrighteous', instead of turning for help to 'the saints' (1 Cor. 6: 1). Paul enjoins Christians to 'deliver to Satan for the destruction of the flesh' anyone guilty of illicit sexual relationships (1 Cor. 5: 1–5). Some of the Corinthian Christians abuse the eucharistic assemblies (1 Cor. 11: 17–30), or accept 'false apostles, deceitful workmen', who disguise themselves as 'apostles of Christ' (2 Cor. 11: 13). Paul admits that he is afraid to visit the Corinthians a third time, since he may encounter 'quarrelling, jealousy, anger, selfishness, slander, gossip, conceit, and disorder' (2 Cor. 12: 20).

In the post-NT situation, St Augustine developed three definitions of sin. First, sin is 'any deed, word, or desire against the eternal law' (*Contra Faustum*, 22. 27), a definition that in a different order prompted many later writers to call sin any thought, word, or deed against the will of God. Augustine explained eternal law as 'the divine order or will of God, which requires the preservation of the natural order and forbids its violation' (ibid.). Speaking of sin as disobedience to the *will of God* (rather than simply 'against the natural law'), Augustine made it clear that sin is no mere breach of an impersonal law but a personal act of rebellion disrupting our relationship with God.

Augustine's second conception of sin centred around an egoistic love of self, associated with a deep unwillingness to love God. Quoting Sirach 10: 13 as 'pride is the beginning of sin', Augustine asked: 'And what is pride but the craving for undue exaltation? And this is undue exaltation, when the soul abandons him to whom it ought to cleave as its end, and becomes a kind of end to itself' (*De Civitate Dei*, 14. 13). Augustine distinguished between two cities shaped by two distinct loves: 'the earthly by the love of self, even to the contempt of God; the heavenly by the love of God, even to the contempt of self. The former, in a word, glorifies in itself, the latter in the Lord' (ibid., 14. 28).

Third, Augustine also defined sin as a 'turning away from God and a turning toward creatures' (*De Libero Arbitrio*, 2. 53). Sin, as 'aversion', or turning away from the contemplation of God and 'conversion', or turning toward creatures, brings about 'a disorder and a perversity', because sinners distance themselves from the creator, the highest good in person, and turn towards inferior, created realities (*Ad Simplicianum*, 1. 2. 18). Augustine considered such a lapse of the will to be evil, 'because it is contrary to the order of nature, and an abandonment' of the good 'which has supreme being, for some other thing which has lesser good' (*De Civitate Dei*, 12. 8). Augustine's Neoplatonist background supported this third version of sin: on the hierarchical scale of existence, the sinner freely decides to move downwards rather than upwards. Augustine emphasized the fact that sin proceeds from a deliberately free decision on the creature's part to discard God's plan and determine one's own actions. The creature turns to selfishness as opposed to interdependence and interconnectedness, two fundamental characteristics of God's creation (see *De Civitate Dei*, 14. 11).

The Christian tradition has oscillated between a 'legal' and a relational understanding of sin (Augustine's first and second definitions): sin is a decision against God's eternal law or the disruption of the creature's relationship with the creator. Those who favour the former approach often explain sin as being an offence against 'the natural law', the objective, moral order intended by God for all human beings and their world as the path to their flourishing and fulfilment. In recent years Christian teachers and theologians have explored in greater depth the personal and relational implications of

sin (Augustine's second definition). Thus in a 1984 apostolic exhort-
ation John Paul II described sin as 'the radical cause of all wounds
and divisions between people, and in the first instance between
people and God' (*Reconciliation and Penance*, 4). He underlined the
fact that 'sin, in the proper sense, is always a personal act, since it is
an act of freedom on the part of an individual person and not
properly of a group or community'. Then, he added that 'to speak
of social sin means . . . to recognize that, by virtue of human solidarity
which is as mysterious and intangible as it is real and concrete, each
individual's sin in some way affects others'. To the 'ascending' solidarity that is 'the profound and magnificent mystery of the communion of saints', there corresponds another, perverse and 'descending'
solidarity a 'communion of sin, whereby a soul that lowers itself
through sin drags down with itself the Church and, in some sense,
the whole world'. Thus John Paul II revived Augustine's third definition of sin and, without watering down personal accountability, he
also highlighted the 'structures of sin' that result from many individual sins (ibid., 16).

A THREEFOLD EVIL

Thus far this chapter has retrieved some key insights about sin and
evil from the scriptures and from subsequent Christian teaching.
Bondage, corruption, and a failure to love serve to organize much
of this material.

So far from proving life-giving, sin is a lethal force that threatens
humans' well-being and subjects them to forces they cannot control.
Sin takes the form of idolatry or worshipping false gods which
enslave people and dominate their entire existence. In the Western
world we repeatedly see how such idols as the drive to possessions,
success, and power can take over the lives of people and become the
shrine at which they worship. These idols take the place of God; it is
all too easy to submit to such 'gods' which rob us of our freedom and
keep us in permanent slavery. The Ten Commandments open by
warning against idolizing false gods. Those gods have not disap-
peared; they have taken other forms, which also include the cult of

the body and obsession with sport; the warning remains as important as ever.

Or else the bondage of sin may show up as 'inner demons', the various compulsions and addictions that take over the lives of many persons. Locked into patterns of destructive behaviour, they can become hopelessly dependent on drugs, alcohol, and sexual promiscuity. Such compulsions override what reason and rational decisions propose. As if possessed by these cravings, people can seem helpless in the face of unmanageable forces, lose control of their existence, and suffer the tragic results of their compulsive and addictive behaviour. More victims than perpetrators of evil, they see their lives spiralling out of control and feel themselves powerless to break the destructive patterns that engulf and enslave them. The inner demons may take the form of haunting fears, depression, paranoia, and a consuming bitterness that broods over the past. Injuries and failures from the past can constantly fill our minds. Or else the prospect of coming death can turn into a terrifying threat that dominates our waking hours. We can become obsessively concerned with security and maintaining our good health.

Sinful bondage may arise from various economic, social, and political forces. At times organized evil, over which we seem to have little or no control, appears embedded in the structures of society. After living in Italy for over thirty years, I am all too sadly aware of the demonic power of the Mafia, the Camorra, and the 'n'drangheta'. They continue to resist persistent government attempts to dismantle them, and form a network of monstrous evil from which so many Sicilians, Neapolitans, and Calabrians cannot escape. On the world scene, the drug trade, the arms trade, internet pornography, and trade in human beings provide evidence of a sinful greed that enslaves and destroys millions of people almost everywhere.

In the last few paragraphs I have picked dramatic examples to demonstrate how sin brings bondage and damages or even destroys human beings and their world. Over and over again, St Paul pictures or almost personifies sin as a demonic force ('Sin' in upper case) that dominates human beings and brings destructive consequences (Rom. 5–8). As we saw above, in its own picturesque way the Book of Genesis spells out the tragic aftermath of sin. The radical choice is between becoming slaves to God or remaining slaves to sin and so suffering the awful consequences (Rom. 6: 15–23). No one has surpassed Paul in picturing the powerful and sinister dominion exercised by 'Sin' that 'dwells within' like an enemy entrenched in 'my' life. Hence 'I do not do the good I want, but the evil I do not want is what I do' (Rom. 7: 17, 19).

Corruption provides a second way of organizing what needs to be said about sin. Genesis yields a graphic account of how sin degrades and defiles human beings and corrupts their environment (see above). Those first chapters of the Bible vividly picture an epidemic of evil that follows the first sin and that contaminates and pervasively pollutes the life of human beings and their world. The Holiness Code of Leviticus 17–27 offers no compromise between the holiness of God and the religious impurity of human beings. Strictly speaking, only God is truly (and indescribably) holy, absolutely pure, the 'utterly Other', and the 'awesome and fascinating mystery (mysterium tremendum et fascinans)' (Isa. 6: 3, 5). The Code requires the Israelites to be holy because their God is holy (Lev. 19: 2; 20: 26). They are called to be sanctified and purified so as to be rendered fit to be consecrated to God and stand in the divine presence. The problem goes beyond Israel: 'Everybody is liable to be defiled and to defile. Impurity is universal.'[14] The disorder of sin pollutes, corrupts, and soils human life everywhere.

In the third place, sin embodies a refusal to love and live through the gift of divine love. All sin is a failure to respond to love and to practise the command of love: love towards God and towards our neighbour. In Augustine's terms, sin means 'love of self, even to the contempt of God'. It involves a self-chosen alienation or estrangement from God and others, a turning away from those who would bring us life, God and our neighbours. Martin Luther memorably depicted what that sinful condition looked like: 'a human being bent in on himself (homo incurvatus in seipsum)'.[15] No one has surpassed John's Gospel in its distressing picture of what a failure to love

[14] Mary Douglas, *In the Wilderness: The Doctrine of Defilement in the Book of Numbers*, Journal for the Study of the Old Testament Supplement Series 158 (Sheffield: Sheffield Academic Press, 1993), 25.

[15] *Luther's Works*, xxv: *Lectures on Romans* (St Louis: Concordia, 1972), 291, 313, 345.

involves: hatred, darkness, and falsity. Here the choice, love or hatred, is even starker than what we find in Leviticus (between holiness and pollution).

INNOCENT OR IRREDEEMABLE

This chapter began with a reflection from Ludwig Wittgenstein about what different people believe themselves to be. His observation deserves to be expanded, at least by drawing attention to the two extremes: those who ignore or deny sin in their lives and feel no need of salvation, and those who think of themselves as too bad to be redeemed.

All those who think of themselves as essentially innocent[16] and have little consciousness of sin are simply not in a position to hope and pray to be delivered from the predicament of sin. They feel that there is nothing essentially wrong with them. They believe that they are fundamentally all right and do not need any redemption. Hence they cannot share Paul's anxious question: 'Wretched creature that I am, who is there to rescue me?' (Rom. 7: 24). They want to run their own lives and think of themselves as being in control of their lives. They can realize themselves and their own possibilities.[17] Utterly self-reliant, they are led by optimistic confidence in the open-endedness of human achievement. If something goes wrong, they can save themselves. They are self-sufficient and consider themselves perfectly capable of finding their own way, until, sooner or later, time runs out on them.[18]

---

[16] Albert Camus (1913–60) classically expressed in one of his novels what he called 'the most natural idea of a human being', that of one's own innocence: 'We are all like that little Frenchman at Buchenwald who insisted on registering a complaint with the clerk, himself a prisoner, who was recording his arrival. A complaint? The clerk and his comrades laughed: "Useless, old man. You don't lodge complaints here." "But you see, sir," said the little Frenchman, "my case is exceptional. I am innocent." We are all exceptional cases' (*The Fall*, trans. J. O'Brien (London: Penguin, 2000), 60).

[17] On systems of self-realization see S. T. Davis, 'Karma or Grace', in *Redemption*, 235–53.

[18] See R. Kiely on the idea of the individual's ability to redeem himself or herself: ' "Graven with an Iron Pen": The Persistence of Redemption as a Theme in Literature', in ibid., 277–94.

Self-denigration, low esteem, pessimism, and even despair characterize the opposite extreme. People can feel that there is so much basically wrong with them that nothing and no one can set it right. Their existence seems pointless and even absurd. They feel enslaved to hostile powers, hopelessly corrupted, and quite alienated by the tragedy of broken relationships. They are too bad to be redeemed. Fallen and helpless, they surrender to failure and take themselves to be irredeemably evil. Literature and life offers endless examples of tragic, seemingly irredeemable situations that appear beyond salvation. In Eugene O'Neill's *Long Day's Journey Into Night* Mary Cavan Tyrone is a morphine addict, her husband and elder son are alcoholics, and the younger son suffers from tuberculosis. She cries out in her pain: 'Let's . . . not try to understand what we cannot understand, or help things that cannot be helped—the things life has done to us we cannot excuse or explain.'[19] This extreme may enjoy one blessing or redeeming feature, the conviction that a mere human being cannot break our chains, cleanse our pollution, and reorder our relationships with God and others. The mediator of creation must come in person to enable that to happen and so ensure that the divine project for humankind and the world reaches its goal.

Such then is the human condition: sinful, suffering, mortal, and incapable of self-redemption. We need Someone beyond ourselves to heal all our alienations and lead us to new life. But before taking up the redemptive work of Jesus Christ, I want to spend a chapter on the heritage of evil that we are born into (or what goes by the name of 'original sin') and something never explored by those who write on redemption: the witness of children to our human condition.

---

[19] Act II, Scene ii. See also E. Stump, 'Narrative and the Problem of Evil: Suffering and Redemption', in *Redemption*, 207–34.

4

Original Sin and Children

Childhood itself has a direct relationship to God...
[The love of God] endures despite the fact that sin rose to power in history right at the origins of the human race...
All childhood in heaven and on earth derives its name and its origin from that one childhood in which the Logos itself receives its own nature in the act of eternal generation by the Father.

Karl Rahner, 'Ideas for a Theology of Childhood', *Theological Investigations*, viii.

Before taking up the redeeming work of Christ, I want to fill out my account of the human predicament by examining (a) an enduring legacy of evil which has been widely named 'original sin' and from which (as many Christians believe) babies are delivered by baptism, and (b) the witness to the human condition offered by children themselves. The former theme has triggered over the centuries much reflection, teaching, writing, and controversy. The latter theme has been widely neglected; Karl Rahner seems to be the only major modern theologian to have written (albeit briefly) on childhood and the way children are willing to be absorbed by the mystery of God.

BAPTISM AND ORIGINAL SIN

Christians have always understood baptism to be the means by which God frees human beings from sin, brings them a rebirth, and makes them through the Holy Spirit a new creation in Christ (Rom. 6–8). By appropriating symbolically the death and resurrection of Jesus (Rom. 6: 3–4), baptism strikingly illustrates how events in the past enjoy a saving impact in the present. In every generation, the crucified and risen Christ was experienced as 'the cause of eternal salvation' (Heb. 5: 8) for all who were baptized into him. Baptism was and remains the basic ritual of initiation through which his work of salvation publicly reaches human beings.

In the course of the second century, or perhaps even earlier, Christians started baptizing children and infants, as well as continuing to baptize adults. From the third century, theologians had to come to terms with an issue that is still controversial today: does baptism always remit sin, even in the case of infant baptism? Adults become sinners, and obviously do so through their own free choice. But what about infants and children who have not yet reached the age of reason and are too young to have consented to sin? If baptism always remits sin, what could that sin be in the case of infants? In this way reflection on 'original sin' developed out of established practice and came to a head in the late fourth century, in the controversy between Augustine of Hippo and the disciples of Pelagius.[1] A theologian and biblical scholar from the British Isles, Pelagius taught in Rome in the late fourth and early fifth centuries before heading down to North Africa when Rome became menaced by the Goths.

Pelagius and his followers (the Pelagians, as they came to be known) maintained a 'do-it-yourself' version of Christianity which held that we can freely move towards salvation, and that we do not rely right from the start on divine grace or transforming help lovingly given by God. Because of their nature created by God, human beings, Pelagius argued, always have the power to choose good. The Pelagians explained original sin as no more than the bad example of Adam and Eve, which had not interiorly harmed their descendants and, in particular, had left intact the natural exercise of free will. Hence human beings could achieve salvation through their own

---

[1] See 'Original Sin', *Oxford Dictionary of the Christian Church*, 3rd edn., 1195–7; K. Rahner, 'Original Sin', in *Foundations of Christian Faith* (New York: Seabury Press, 1978), 106–15.

sustained efforts.[2] Babies, they argued, are born quite sinless and unaffected by any pre-existing corruption; hence their baptism serves only to insert them into the Church.

Before setting out the teaching on original sin developed by Augustine and others, we must first summarize the drift of a key passage from Paul: Romans 5: 12–21. The Apostle, who understands all human beings to be enslaved to sin and death, ascribes this universal misery not only to Adam as humanity's first parent but also to all human beings, since they ratify their present, ungraced state by their own personal sins. Paul considers Adam to be the initial cause of humanity's sinful and mortal condition: through him 'sin entered into the world' (Rom. 5: 12a) and death was the direct consequence (Rom. 5: 12b). Then Paul adds the conclusion that 'death spread to all, because all sinned' (Rom. 5: 12c–d). Paul presumes Adam to be an historical figure like the rest of us, and holds that we all sin through the bad exercise of our human freedom. In the wake of Adam's evil influence, we continue promoting a universal situation of slavery to sin and death.

But where Adam initiated and headed the age of universal sin and death, Christ heads the age of grace and life that God offers to all (Rom. 5: 14). Paul is concerned with something greater than the mere remission of sins: he deals with the full inheritance that will be ours in Christ at the end of time. Paul repeatedly insists in Romans 5 that Christ's benefits prove incomparably more extensive than all the harm caused by Adam, Eve, and their descendants. Christ gives life in a superabundant way, which far surpasses the deadly impact of sin. Thus, in dealing with the whole history of sin, the Apostle compares and contrasts what has come from Adam and what comes from Christ; it is only in and through Christ that anyone can be justified. Lastly, we should add that Paul does not address some of the questions that Augustine and the Pelagians were to raise in the fourth century: sin's transmission from one generation to the next, the

---

[2] See 'Pelagianism', in *Oxford Dictionary of the Christian Church*, 1248–9. Over the centuries Pelagianism has surfaced again and again, e.g. under modern forms of secular humanism, which, while reducing 'salvation' to this-worldly success, understand such success as a goal to be reached by one's own work and efforts.

particular question of infant baptism, and children's need to be delivered from an inherited sinfulness.[3]

Long before Augustine, Tertullian (d. around 225) and Cyprian (d. 258)—both of Carthage in North Africa—tried to explain and justify the Church's baptismal practice.[4] They believed that we are all born into this world carrying a 'wound' or bearing a 'wounded inheritance'. Since this 'inherited sin' does not result from any deliberate act of our own against God, it can never bar our way to the divine mercy. When writing about baptism, Cyprian distinguished its effects. First and foremost, baptism restores humanity to full communion with God the Father in Christ and through the Holy Spirit; its secondary effect is to remit sin: 'the Father sent the Son to preserve us and give us life, in order that he might restore us' (*De Opere et Eleemosynis*, 1).

Augustine resisted the Pelagians on two grounds.[5] First, the long-standing practice of baptizing infants and doing so for the remission of sins meant that infants come into the world in some kind of inherited sinful state. Second, since God sent his Son to save the whole of humanity, everyone must somehow be under the reign of sin and consequently in need of baptism. Without being baptized into the life of Christ, no one could have access to God. Given that everyone needs salvation, then baptism must be required of and available to all human beings, including children. Since baptism is necessary for salvation, Augustine had to conclude that those children who died without baptism could not inherit eternal life, and suffered what he called 'the lightest possible condemnation', the nature of which he could not 'define' (*Contra Iulianum*, 5. 44). He also drew the conclusion that refusing to baptize a child constituted an act of injustice and cruelty toward that child (*De Gratia Christi et de Peccato Originali*, 2. 5. 5). Children and babies, as well as adults, have the right to be 'born from water and the Spirit', so that they may enter the kingdom of God (John 3: 5).

Unable to read the NT easily in the original Greek, both Augustine and before him Ambrosiaster (an otherwise unknown fourth-century

---

[3] See J. A. Fitzmyer, *Romans*, The Anchor Bible 33 (New York: Doubleday, 1993), 405–28.

[4] See 'Baptism', in *Oxford Dictionary of the Christian Church*, 150–2.

[5] On the mindset of Pelagius and his followers, see Peter Brown, *Augustine of Hippo: A Biography* (Berkeley, Calif.: University of California Press, new edn., 2000), 462–4.

writer who commented on Paul's letters and was for a long time confused with St Ambrose of Milan) understood the Old Latin translation of Romans 5: 12c ('in whom all sinned') to mean that we are all born sinners 'in Adam'. Being incorporated in advance in Adam, all men and women have already sinned en bloc in the very person of Adam. When discussing Romans 5: 12b ('death spread to all'), Augustine interpreted 'death' as bodily death. The classical philosophy of his day encouraged Augustine to understand death simply as an imperfection and threat: it has to be God's punishment and a direct consequence of Adam's sin.

Challenged by the Pelagians, Augustine led the other bishops at the Sixteenth Council of Carthage (AD 418) in upholding the following positions: first, physical death is the direct consequence of sin; second, the universal and constant Catholic tradition is that of baptizing children 'for the remission of sins'; and, third, whoever dies in 'original sin'—i.e. without receiving baptism—is condemned to eternal damnation (DzH 222–4; ND 501–2). Even though incapable of committing personal sins, children have inherited from Adam 'original sin, which must be expiated by the bath of regeneration' (DzH 223; ND 502). The doctrine of damnation for those who die 'in original sin' or without baptism reflects the extreme importance that early fifth-century Christians attached to the basic sacrament of Christian initiation. Yet this doctrine can also suggest a harsh and demanding God, ready to condemn forever even infants and young children who are personally quite innocent.[6] Moreover, once infant baptism became almost universal, some or even many parents took an almost magical view of the sacrament, especially when the memory faded of the long catechumenate in which adult candidates received a thorough instruction in doctrinal and moral principles.

In the controversy with the Pelagians, Augustine insisted that human beings suffer greatly from the consequences of Adam's sin; their created condition of freedom is deeply impaired, though not destroyed. Against Pelagius and his followers Augustine rightly asserted that whatever belongs to our human condition cannot be a matter of individual choice and that, at all times, human beings

---

[6] Very many Christians no longer support Augustine's view, that a failure to baptize means denying children salvation.

truly need God's grace to participate in Christ's redemption. Augustine also understood that in challenging the reality of original sin, the Pelagians called into question the meaning of baptism itself and of our rebirth in Christ as the necessary requirement for salvation.

Although earlier theology had formulated original sin as a statement about the uniqueness of Christ's mediation and his redemption of our humanity, after Augustine and the Pelagian controversy it became also an assertion about the corrupt nature of our human condition. Irenaeus had shown how in Christ we should understand our existence as created in the image of God (see Chapter 2 above). Augustine and the Sixteenth Council of Carthage added: only in Christ do we reach newness of life and a full communion with God. In Christ, we can come to know and welcome God's original plan for humanity and, in the same Christ, we can more than recover the treasures lost through sin.

The teaching on original sin, as developed in the fifth and sixth centuries, expressed the sinful condition of all human beings: we may be free, but we are all born sinners. The Second Council of Orange (AD 529) was to condemn Pelagius posthumously for holding that through Adam's sin 'the freedom of the soul remained unharmed'; Adam's 'fall' damaged all his descendants and, in particular, their 'freedom of soul' (DzH 371–2; ND 504–5). They are all born deprived of the life of grace that they ought to have possessed and would have possessed but for Adam's sin. Bodily death continued to be considered the primary sign and consequence of original sin (ibid.). Thus official teaching emphasized the need for spiritual rebirth through baptism: the fullness of life and grace is no natural right or personal achievement but God's free gift through Christ. Hence 'original sin' refers not only to our human solidarity in sin but also to our call to a new, supernatural life in Christ. Far from being merely a depressing statement about the wounded or deficient nature of our inherited human condition, the doctrine of original sin underlines humanity's need for Christ's grace: there is no way to true fulfilment and eternal life except through him.

In the Middle Ages official teaching and theology added only a few footnotes to the beliefs on original sin that came down from the patristic period. In a letter of 1201, Pope Innocent III distinguished personal sin from original sin. Unlike personal sin, original sin is simply inherited and does not involve any deliberate offence against God. Consequently, in the case of infants, who are not yet capable of personal sin and personal conversion, original sin can be 'forgiven' through baptism alone. Innocent added that, whereas those infants who die in the state of original sin will not enjoy the beatific vision or face-to-face vision of God, hell is a punishment reserved for those adults who have sinned gravely and deliberately against God (DzH 780; ND 506). The Pope thus settled an issue, raised already by Augustine: do unbaptized infants merit hell? Medieval theologians proposed the existence of 'limbo', appealing to later teaching that had been falsely attributed to the Sixteenth Council of Carthage (DzH 224), and that spoke of 'a certain middle place', which was neither heaven nor hell. I will return in a later chapter to the question of the final destiny of the unbaptized.

The sixteenth-century leaders of the Protestant Reformation reopened the issue of original sin, but at the other extreme from any Pelagian optimistic minimalizing of the damage caused by the sin of Adam and Eve. Martin Luther, John Calvin, and other Reformers looked pessimistically at the human condition as being corrupted by the sin of our first parents. But whatever we say here, we should not set out too starkly the differences between the Roman Catholic and the Reformed/Protestant views of the justification of sinnners and the role of human beings in the process of justification.[7] It would be a false caricature to represent the Protestant views as maintaining that when human beings are baptized for the remission of (original and personal) sin, they receive justification as if they were merely passive puppets. Likewise it would be a false caricature to present the Roman Catholic position as holding that human beings can earn justification, as if God were simply responding to some human actions. Both sides held and hold that God's gift of justification is truly a free gift;

---

[7] The 1999 'Joint Declaration on the Doctrine of Justification', which contains forty-four common statements covering basic aspects of justification, was accepted by the Catholic Church and the World Lutheran Federation, and was signed on 31 October 1999. The full text is found in *Origins* 28 (1998), 120–27; key extracts are found in ND 2000k–2000s. See C. S. Evans, 'Catholic–Protestant Views of Justification: How Should Christians View Theological Disagreements?', in *Redemption*, 255–73. In 1987 the Second Anglican–Roman Catholic International Commission published an agreed statement, which is called *Salvation and the Church* and contains significant material on justification (nos. 12–24).

we do not save ourselves. Both sides, albeit with different emphases, agreed and agree that God requires a response from us as part of his redemptive project. God saves by grace, to which the human response is faith, a 'faith that works itself out in love' (Gal. 5: 6).[8] As regards historical details, let me limit myself to what the Council of Trent said about original sin and justification.

In its fifth session (1546) the Council of Trent produced a decree on original sin that, while largely reaffirming earlier teaching, added some insights and emphases. The grace of justification can be understood only in relational terms: it is God's gift to humanity, while the process of conversion forms the human response to the same gift. Trent, in refusing to interpret original sin as a constitutive element of our human condition, made five points. First, through the merits of Christ baptism truly remits the guilt of original sin and makes the baptized 'the beloved children of God'. Second, baptism restores the 'holiness and justice' lost through sin.[9] Third, original sin is transmitted through 'propagation', something the Council refused to specify further. Fourth, concupiscence remains in the baptized as an 'inclination to sin'; even though concupiscence 'comes from [Adam's] sin and inclines to [personal] sin', it is not 'sin in the true and proper sense'. Fifth, Trent understood 'death' as referring to the 'captivity in the power of...the devil' that draws upon itself 'the wrath and indignation of God' (DzH 1510–15; ND 507–12). Consequently, the effect of original sin is spiritual rather than bodily death.

The emphasis of this teaching on original sin is positive rather than negative: it stresses 'the grace of our Lord Jesus Christ' rather than the depravity of human beings. Original sin allows us to understand that

---

[8] When assessing St Paul's various metaphors for redemption, Gordon Fee properly pays attention to 'justification', but without allowing this metaphor to dominate ('Paul and the Metaphors for Salvation', in *Redemption*, 62–6). It is a significant metaphor, which stands in continuity/discontinuity with the OT's notion of God's saving justice and the merciful fidelity of God to the covenant. The OT also speaks of the human justice of those who devoutly try to fulfil their side of the covenant. Yet the scriptures are aware that 'nobody is righteous before God' (Ps. 143: 2). Paul moves beyond such a statement of *fact* to one of *principle*: 'no one will be/can be justified in the sight of God by deeds prescribed by the law' (Rom. 3: 20; Gal. 2: 16). Self-justification or self-salvation is impossible.

[9] The Council of Trent, *Decree on Original Sin* (DzH 1511, 1515; ND 508, 512). Trent chose the words 'holiness and justice' as biblical terms that could express God's gift to humanity before the fall.

evil cannot be a power or an actual *being* that exists on some kind of par with God; evil is the direct result of some action (a *doing*) on the part of God's creatures, whether angelic or human. This teaching also indicates that evil does not necessarily characterize our universe: although sin and evil can lord it over history, the final say always belongs to God. Such teaching reflects the *Exultet*, a hymn of praise sung during the Easter Vigil, which goes back at least to the seventh century and calls original sin the 'happy fault' that merited for us such a Saviour.

The twentieth century brought new support and fresh challenges for the doctrine of original sin. Some scientists have aimed at reducing to mere psychological and physical determinism any phenomena associated (by Augustine, Luther, and others) with original sin. Yet the doctrine of original sin seems to make a secular reappearance in the neo-Darwinian views of such writers as Richard Dawkins. He pictures us human beings as prisoners of the 'selfish genes of our birth' and rebelling against the genetic lineage that determines us.[10] One might see some parallel between the 'selfish' genes ruthlessly bent on survival and the ingrained selfishness to which the doctrine of original sin has been understood to witness. Beyond the world of science works of modern fiction and history keep talk of original sin alive. Some readers understand that way the beautiful, powerful, and evil ring which holds together the story line in J. R. R. Tolkien's *The Lord of the Rings*. The corrupting inheritance of the ring easily calls to mind original sin and its legacy.[11] In the area of contemporary history, a critic of the foreign policy of the current US government presents the 2003 invasion of Iraq as an 'original sin' from which more mistakes (or 'sins') ineluctably followed.[12] What is to be said?

First, writers like G. K. Chesterton (1874–1936) and Reinhold Niebuhr (1892–1971) who dealt directly with the theological notion

[10] For a careful and critical evaluation of Dawkins' thought, see A. McGrath, *Dawkins' God: Genes, Memes, and the Meaning of Life* (Oxford: Blackwell, 2005).

[11] On original sin, see Stratford Caldecott, *Secret Fire: The Spiritual Vision of JRR Tolkien* (London: Darton, Longman & Todd, 2003), 60–1, 79, 104–5. Caldecott interprets the ring as the source of temptation, a theme which is not too far from that of original sin. In any case Caldecott recognizes that the symbolism of Tolkien's story can mean different things to different people. The story is not an allegory, in which there are simple and even straightforward answers to the meaning of the ring.

[12] L. Diamond, *Squandered Victory: The American Occupation and the Bungled Effort to Bring Democracy to Iraq* (New York: Times Books, 2005).

were famous for their comments that original sin is probably the most credible and even obvious article of Christian belief. When born into this world, babies are normally welcomed with love but also inherit a sinful situation for which they are not personally responsible. At least partly, they are at the mercy of a legacy of evil which stretches back to the beginning of human history. The doctrine of original sin supplies a plausible account for a situation that every newcomer on the human scene must face: the shadow side of human history and a certain ingrained predisposition to sin.

Second, a modern awareness of the human *solidarity* expressed in doing good and committing evil encourages a more comprehensive understanding of original sin.[13] We experience this solidarity for good (in the new life brought by Jesus Christ) and for evil (in a stubborn propensity to sin that the baptized must confront even after the deepest personal conversion). To be human is to share with other human beings in a history that is sinful and in a universal need to be redeemed by Jesus Christ. Thus the doctrine of original sin vividly expresses the basic condition and need of all human beings.

Third, polygenism, the view that the human race does not derive from an original pair of ancestors but from many, seems to threaten the doctrine of original sin and its transmission to all the descendants of 'Adam and Eve'. In a 1950 encyclical *Humani Generis*, Pope Pius XII warned that polygenism may not be clearly reconcilable with belief in original sin and its transmission (DzH 3897; ND 420). Some Christians turn to the Bible to take a stand for monogenism and against polygenism. But this is a thoroughly modern issue: neither the authors of Genesis nor Paul could have taken a position on something they knew nothing about. While theology discusses the possibility of polygenism, some molecular biologists entertain the idea that our race may not derive from many, but from one original couple.[14]

---

[13] Various modern authors have developed helpful insights into the essentially *social* nature of human beings and their existence-in-relationship. For relations between 'the self' and 'the other' (and the world), see e.g. J. Macmurray, *The Self as Agent* (London: Faber, 1957); id., *Persons in Relation* (London: Faber, 1961); J. Zizioulas, *Being as Communion: Studies in Personhood and the Church* (New York: St Vladimir's Seminary Press, 1985).

[14] *Homo sapiens* seems to have first appeared in East Africa around 200,000 years ago; the oldest anatomically modern human fossils yet recovered seem to be about

INFANT BAPTISM

As regards infant baptism, Augustine felt it to be his pastoral duty to 'labour on behalf of those children who, though under the protection of parents, are left more destitute and wretched than orphans'. He was speaking about the unbaptized children of Christians, babies who were still 'unable to demand for themselves' the grace of Christ that their parents 'denied them' (*De Peccatorum Meritis*, 3. 13. 22). In response to Pelagius, Augustine wrote: 'Let him grant that Jesus is Jesus even to infants ... He shall, indeed, save his people; and among his people surely there are infants ... In infants, too, there are original sins, on account of which he can be Jesus, that is, Saviour, even unto them' (*De Nuptiis et Concupiscentia*, 2. 35. 60). For many centuries after Augustine, the baptism of infants was understood not only as deliverance from original sin but also as strictly necessary for their salvation if they were to die before reaching 'the age of reason'. Even though he recognized that the original sin which infants inherit could not be considered to be their personal sin (as was the case with the original guilt of Adam and Eve), Augustine characterized the refusal to baptize infants as denying them salvation. He was unconditionally concerned that through the sacrament of baptism the 'work' of Christ's redemption should also be 'accomplished' for infants.

Nowadays, many believers do not share Augustine's view that infants who die before being baptized are excluded from enjoying eternal happiness through the vision of God. Moreover, numerous Christians have retrieved the ancient sense of Christian initiation as a process in which the moment of baptism plays a part but is not in itself total sacramental initiation. Hence some hold that baptism might be validly placed at different points in this process of initiation, either very early or later in the journey of an individually appropriated faith—that is to say, as very young infants or as adult believers.

195,000 years old. See I. McDougall, F. H. Brown, and J. G. Fleagle, 'Stratigraphic Placement and Age of Modern Humans from Kibish, Ethiopia', *Nature*, 17 February 2005, 733–6.

However, one should recall here not only Western traditions of baptism but also the tradition of Eastern Christianity which confers the entire rite of initiation on infants. In this tradition they are baptized, confirmed, and receive Holy Communion in one ceremony. Eastern Christians do not postpone to a later stage any of the elements in the threefold process of initiation.[15] The practice of Eastern Christians in joining baptism and the Eucharist forcefully illustrates that not only baptism but also the Eucharist *makes present* and *accomplishes* the redeeming work of Christ. His past saving act also comes to bear here and now, when infants are baptized and share in the Eucharist.

Serious reflection on the practice of infant baptism involves us in pondering the nature of original sin itself. First, since as such it is not voluntary, personal sin or sin in the primary sense, we do better to put inverted commas around the term and so indicate that 'original sin' is sin by way of analogy. Some Christians speak of 'original sin' as involving *collective* guilt inherited from the sin of the first human beings. To be sure, it is important to recall how the whole human race, right from birth, is afflicted by the presence of evil. Yet here also it is advisable to use inverted commas, since any such 'collective guilt' which we inherit simply by being born into the world does not entail the *personal* responsibility and guilt (or guilt in the primary sense) of newborn children. Second, Christians have often spoken of 'original sin' as a taint or stain which is transmitted biologically through human history and from which baptism washes us clean. It could be better to lay the emphasis on what human beings *lack* at birth and on the *context* into which they are born. We are born lacking the incorporation into Christ (or life 'in Christ') and the indwelling of the Holy Spirit (e.g. Rom. 6: 11, 23; 5: 5; 1 Cor. 3: 16) to which we are called but which we do not yet enjoy. Furthermore, our full freedom and spiritual growth are circumscribed and hampered by the manifold presence of evil in the world into which we come. This lack and

---

[15] On different approaches to baptismal initiation, see *One Baptism, One Eucharist, and a Mutually Recognized Ministry*, Faith and Order Paper 73 (Geneva: World Council of Churches, 1975), no. 14 ('The Baptism of Infants and Believers'); and *Baptism, Eucharist and Ministry*, Faith and Order Paper 111 (Geneva: World Council of Churches, 1982), nos. 11–14.

this context translate and summarize more convincingly what 'original sin' entails.

When parents ask for their children to be baptized, they show their own faith that baptism brings the one meaningful existence they know. Christian parents know that in baptism they themselves have been united with Christ, and that through the life of the Spirit they have been reborn into the community of the Church. Having now shared human life with their children, they wish also to share with them the new life of baptism which provides the power required to resist sin and move to the fullness of salvation. Even if infants must wait some years before making their own personal commitment, they matter equally to God and should matter equally to Christian believers and to other human beings. Hence adult believers bear the responsibility of hearing what children reveal about the human condition in need of salvation.

THE WITNESS OF CHILDREN

All the studies I have ever read on redemption seem to share the same silent presupposition: adults are the only witnesses to the human condition to be heard. It is in terms of adults that we should examine and measure redemption, our common need for redemption, and its impact. The vivid influence of love on children (as also the sad damage they suffer when unloved) makes them prime witnesses for what Chapter 9 will present on redemption as transforming love. If children enter the picture at all, they are recalled as human beings on the way to adulthood, without importance in themselves and having value because one day they will become adults. Maria Montessori (1870–1952), Karl Rahner (1904–84), and Robert Coles (b. 1929) disagree with such a reductionist view and insist that children are much more than beings in transition.

Maria Montessori appreciated and honoured children as religious persons who experience the profound meaning of human existence, have their own spiritual lives, and are deeply contemplative. She advocated a child-centred approach to education in which children set the pace and are guided through play and a variety of sensory materials. Her method has become an integral part of modern nursery and infant-school education.[16] But modern theologians have ignored the lead she gave by her insights into the witness children offer to the human predicament and its remedy. Rahner appears to be the sole exception, with his essay 'Ideas for a Theology of Childhood'.[17] He never knew the poetry of Dylan Thomas (1914–53), but he approached the theme of childhood in a somewhat similar way—through memory.

In such poems as 'Poem in October' (a reminiscence on his thirtieth birthday) and 'Fern Hill' (another poem that recalls his childhood), Thomas evoked the ways in which children can give themselves to the mystery around them. He mulled over the spiritual insights that he felt he had lost. He knew how as a child he was engaged by the unseen and the intangible: 'the parables' that come with the 'sun light', and 'the legends of the green chapels' that belonged to the 'forgotten mornings when he walked with his mother' and 'the mystery sang alive' for him ('Poem in October').

Like Dylan Thomas, Rahner looked back on the experiences of childhood and invited others to do so. Rahner set his face against interpreting childhood as 'a mere provisional conditioning for the shaping of adult life in its fullness', as if it 'should be left behind as quickly and completely as possible and vanish into unreality'.[18] Particular, full individuals in 'a direct relationship' with God from the outset,[19] children exhibit, Rahner wrote, not only a basic orientation to God but also a trust, an open readiness to be controlled by another, and 'the courage to allow fresh horizons' which privilege their response to divine grace.[20] Childhood is and reveals 'a basic condition which is always appropriate to a life which is lived aright'. Hence 'for our existence to be sound and redeemed . . . childhood

---

[16] M. Montessori, *The Montessori Method* (New York: Schocken Books, 1964); id., *The Discovery of the Child* (Notre Dame, Ind.: Fides, 1965).

[17] K. Rahner, 'Ideas for a Theology of Childhood', *Theological Investigations*, viii (London: Darton, Longman & Todd, 1971), 33–50.

[18] Ibid., 36.

[19] Ibid.

[20] Ibid., 48. Rahner adds on the same page: 'The mature childhood of the adult is the attitude in which we bravely and trustfully maintain an infinite openness in all circumstances and despite the experiences of life which seem to invite us to close ourselves.'

must be an intrinsic element in it'.[21] 'In a child', Rahner declared, 'a human being begins who must undergo the wonderful adventure of remaining a child forever, becoming a child to an ever-increasing extent.'[22]

Rahner appreciated deeply what the trusting openness of children reveals about the human condition. Yet he also knew that from the beginning of their existence they must cope with the human condition, shaped by 'a history of guilt, of gracelessness, of a refusal to respond to the call of the living God'. The effects of original sin affect 'radically and interiorly' their situation, even before they are born. At the same time, from the very outset children are 'encompassed by the love of God through the pledge of that grace' which comes to everyone 'from God in Jesus Christ'. Rahner refused to see childhood as an 'innocent arcadia' that then becomes 'muddied'. It is a mystery of redemption, open to and enfolded by God who is utter mystery.[23] But, unlike Robert Coles, Rahner never attempted to describe in detail how children experience the early years of their lives.

Through more than thirty years of research into the lives of children, Coles published a unique series of eight books that record how children speak about their lives. That research began with the sick and often dying children whom as a young doctor he got to know in the Children's Hospital in Boston and who shared with him their spiritual concerns. 'I found in them', he recalled, 'a kind of moral inwardness, not to mention a spiritual yearning that nothing in my training prepared me for'.[24] Over the years Coles learned to absorb the complexity of children's lives. At the end of three decades of work with them, he realized that he had avoided exploring the religious and spiritual components with which children had confronted him early in his medical career. He went back to his records, wrote *The Spiritual Life of Children*,[25] and showed how, with

[21] Ibid., 47.   [22] Ibid., 50.   [23] Ibid., 39–40.
[24] J. Woodruff and S. C. Woodruff (eds.), *Conversations with Robert Coles* (Jackson, Miss.: University Press of Mississippi, 1992), 13–14.
[25] Boston: Houghton Mifflin Company, 1990; see also J. W. Fowler, 'Strength for the Journey: Early Childhood Development', in D. A. Blazer (ed.), *Faith Development in Early Childhood* (Kansas City: Sheed & Ward, 1989), 1–36; F. James, 'Children and Childhood in the New Testament', in S. C. Barton (ed.), *The Family in Theological Perspective* (Edinburgh: T. & T. Clark, 1996), 65–85; D. Hay and R. Nye, *The Spirit of the Child* (London: HarperCollins, 1998); and a special supplement on children's spirituality in *The Way* 1996.

surprising feeling and subtlety, children ponder the great questions about the human predicament: 'Where do we come from? What are we? Where are we going?' These were the eternal questions asked by Leo Tolstoy (1828–1910) and the post-impressionist painter Paul Gauguin (1848–1903), who wrote them out on a great triptych he completed shortly before his death in Tahiti.[26] Along with all their differences in circumstances and personalities, children shared in common the ability to reflect on the deepest spiritual questions, to feel regret for bad actions, and to show compassion for the sufferings of others.

Children spoke to Coles of their own suffering and the suffering of those whom they loved. They thought about the point and purpose of their lives. They wondered about God's existence and attitude towards human beings. Connie, an eight-year-old girl, helped to influence the way Coles understood and practised his role as psychoanalyst. She chided him for being interested only in her problems and not in her religious faith. When he did take up her faith, he found how she pondered the deep questions of good and evil, admitted that she herself was 'a real troublemaker', was convinced that God watched over her, and recognized how she needed faith to help her along in her everyday life.[27] Tony, an eleven-year-old whose life was in the balance, talked to Coles about God, about the suffering his illness brought his family, about all the mistakes he had ever made. He did not want to die, but he also knew that he might not survive: 'A lot of the time I'm thinking to myself—if you go, Tony, then where will you go to? I ask and ask. I know I'll never get the answer until I go, and I don't want to go, not until I'm as old as grandpa! But I might, so I should be wondering, I guess. Better to wonder than just lie here and feel lousier and lousier.' Tony, in fact, recovered and left hospital—after facing death, reviewing every aspect of his life, and wondering about its purpose.[28] He had grown spiritually, through confronting a key issue of redemption: 'the last enemy' who is 'death' (1 Cor. 15: 26). Another boy, twelve-year-old Eric, told Coles of how questions of God, the divine will, and 'What's it all about?' became more pressing after he saw a woman who had been

---

[26] Coles, *The Spiritual Life of Children*, 37.   [27] Ibid., 10–19.
[28] Ibid., 101–9.

killed in an accident caused by a drunken driver being extracted from her car. Then a truck killed his cousin who was crossing a street. Eric admitted: 'I'm thinking that I'm here now, but one day I'll be gone. That's far off, I hope, but it could be tomorrow.'[29]

Coles has much to report about the place of prayer in the lives of children, Christian, Muslim, and Jewish. Some heard the encouraging and enlightening voice of God—often through their scriptures. At times in their prayer they had to endure the silence of God. One boy asked God for help not only for himself but for all the suffering people whom he saw on television; he was sure that God cares deeply about those who suffer.[30] Those who read Coles's work may well make other choices. But for me his most moving report came from Margarita, a girl who suffered under the terrible deprivations of life in one of the favelas in Rio de Janeiro. Her mother, who continued to work in a luxury hotel to support her seven children, suffered from tuberculosis and was soon to die of the disease. Margarita told Coles about what crossed her mind when she looked at the statue of Christ that dominates Rio: 'I shouldn't blame Jesus! I do, though, sometimes. He's right there—that statue keeps reminding me of him. And the next thing I know, I'm talking with him, and I'm either upset with him, or I'm praying for him to tell me why the world is like it is.' She said that Jesus talked with her, but not when she talked with him. He would take her by surprise: 'I think I go walking to find some strength, and just when I give up, he's there. He tells me to remember his own life—it was full of trouble. I try to remember what he said what his life was like. When I hear Jesus talking to me, I wish I knew more about him.'[31]

In pursuing his study of the spirituality of children, Coles encouraged them to draw pictures of God and used their drawings to persuade them to speak further about God. In particular, their pictures of the divine 'face' helped them to describe their ideas of God. Often children drew many pictures of God, and the differences between the drawings caught some of the complex dimensions of their view of God and his relations to human beings. Coles found those drawings of God's face and the conversations about them

[29] Ibid., 280–9, at 283–5.   [30] Ibid., 69–90.   [31] Ibid., 90–7, at 91, 94.

revealed a whole range of divine 'attributes': eternity, grandeur, power, love, and vulnerability.[32]

Despite (or maybe one should say because of?) his deep commitment to children and their welfare, Coles never became naive or sentimental about them. As he put it, 'from the same children who spoke of God and pilgrimage I've heard quite other sorts of language—curses and worse: offhand insensitivity, outright callousness, even cruelty, as one observes in children anywhere'. For all that, children allowed Coles to glimpse their deeper selves and their spiritual lives. 'How young we are', he reflected, 'when we start wondering about it all, the nature of the journey and of the final destination.'[33] Significantly Coles reached for the language of pilgrimage, a classic human and Christian image for our existence and story. Dante used the image to open the *Divine Comedy* ('in the middle of life's road I found myself in a dark wood—the straight way ahead lost'); the spiritual transformation of the pilgrim will take him through hell and purgatory to heaven. The image reinforces the consciousness of the whole of life (from childhood on) as a spiritual journey, a preparation for death and eternal life.

In one chapter, 'Christian Salvation',[34] Coles moved beyond the witness of children to the human condition and drew together the insights into salvation offered by Christian children. Repeatedly they spoke of the 'visit' of Jesus and his 'promise' to us—a visit and a promise that affect everyone. They pictured him as 'the One who survived childhood and later suffering, and is still very much present'.[35] His cross shaped their sense of faith in him, but it was the whole story of Jesus, from the beginning to the end, which entered into their sense of him as Saviour. They saw his saving work encompassing everything, from his coming on 'visit' right through to his ceaseless work for us now and the welcome home in the afterlife when he will be 'glad to see us'. This broad view of what made up and makes up the redemptive 'achievement' of Jesus provides the agenda for my next chapter.

---

[32] *Coles, The Spiritual Life of Children*, 40–68.   [33] Ibid., 331, 335.
[34] Ibid., 202–24.   [35] Ibid., 209.

5

The Whole Story of Redemption

> God made Jesus Christ our wisdom, righteousness, sanctification, and redemption.
>
> St Paul, 1 Corinthians 1: 30.

> Man stole the fruit, but I must climb the tree.
>
> George Herbert, 'The Sacrifice'.

> And all alone, alone, alone
> He rose again behind the stone.
>
> Alice Meynell, 'Easter Night'.

The fathers of the Church shared *two basic convictions*. First, the situation of fallen humanity was so desperate that any effective saviour of humanity must be divine; only the personal presence of the Son of God among us could have brought salvation. This raises the questions: how might we understand a particular man, Jesus of Nazareth, not only to possess all the essentially human characteristics but also to be truly divine in his person? And why is this personal identity vital for the story of redemption?

Here we need to endorse the conviction that persons are *persons-in-relationship*.[1] The human life of Jesus transposed to the level of human beings and their history the unique, filial relationship that exists eternally between Father and Son within the divine life. It was not the divine substance or nature as such that was incarnated or took on the human condition. Rather it was a person-in-relationship,

---

[1] See e.g. J. Macmurray, *Persons in Relation* (London: Faber, 1961); G. O'Collins, *Christology: A Biblical, Historical and Systematic Study of Jesus* (Oxford: Oxford University Press, rev. edn., 2004), 224–49; id., *The Tripersonal God* (Mahwah, NJ: Paulist Press, 1999), 174–80.

the eternal Son of God, who assumed fully our human condition and lived out a genuine human history. Thus the Son–Father relationship revealed in the life of Jesus and, particularly in his ministry and death (see below), was identical with the Son–Father relationship that exists eternally (in and through the Holy Spirit) within the life of the tri-personal God. This same relationship was involved when the Word/Wisdom of God mediated the creation and conservation of all things. From the Son–Father relationship revealed in the history of Jesus, the early Christians drew the conclusion: that same relationship operated in the mediation of all creation (see Chapter 2 above).

This Son–Father relationship in the Spirit, played out dramatically in human history, accounts for the unique value and efficacy of what Jesus did, suffered, and achieved for the salvation of human beings and their world. Some of his actions, such as touching a leper, taking children into his arms, and breaking bread with his friends, needed only human powers. Other actions, such as miraculously curing the sick and handicapped, required divine powers. But, due to his Son–Father relationship, all his actions enjoyed a unique value and efficacy. It was his personal identity-in-relationship which meant that he could achieve what the fathers of the Church repeatedly highlighted: namely, deliver us from sin and death and bring us forever as adopted sons and daughters into the divine family.

Second, the fathers of the Church understood that all the stages of his incarnate history effected human redemption, and not merely his death on the cross.[2] They did not belittle the climax of redemption in the crucifixion and resurrection, but rather placed these events in the whole story of Christ's saving activity. St Gregory of Nyssa, for instance, listed some of these events and their characteristics: 'the human birth, the advance from infancy to manhood, the eating and drinking, the weariness, the sleep, the grief, the tears, the false accusations, the trial, the cross, the death, and the putting in the tomb'.[3]

In their own popular way Christmas carols make a similar point, by presenting the birth of the Saviour in terms of (1) what went

---

[2] See B. Daley, ' "He Himself is Our Peace" (Ephesians 2: 14): Early Christian Views on Redemption in Christ', in *Redemption*, 149–76.

[3] *Oratio Catechetica*, 36. 21–37. 2.

before (his eternal pre-existence with the Father and work in creating all the universe) and of (2) what followed the story of the nativity: the life, death, and resurrection of Christ and even his coming at the end of history. As regards (1), 'Adeste Fideles' draws on the language of the Creed to state the eternal identity of the Christ Child: he is 'God of God, light of light, very God...begotten, not created (Deum de Deo, lumen de lumine...Deum verum, genitum, non factum)'. Some carols recall that without the tiny Christ Child there could be no world at all. 'See amid the winter's snow' expresses amazement: 'Lo, within a manger lies / he who built the starry skies'.

As regards (2), 'The first Nowell the angel did say' looks in two directions, not only back to creation but also forward to the redemptive death of Christ: 'Then let us all with one accord / sing praises to our heavenly Lord, / that hath made heaven and earth of nought, / and with his blood mankind has bought.' Why should the carol refer to the redemptive death which the Christ Child will accept and undergo? Since myrrh was used to embalm corpses, Christian tradition consistently took that gift brought by the Magi to symbolize Christ's death. Hence carols which introduce the Magi and their gifts look ahead to the violent death of the Child. 'The first Nowell', which dedicates half of its verses to the 'three wise men', ends with such a reference to Christ's sacrificial death. Another carol, 'We three kings of Orient are', concentrates from the start on the Magi, their journey, and their three gifts, each one of which enjoys a separate verse. The next-to-last verse spells out the meaning of the third gift: 'Myrrh is mine, its bitter perfume / breathes a life of gathering gloom; / sorrowing, sighing, bleeding, dying / sealed in the stone-cold tomb.' But the carol does not stop with the future death and burial of the Christ Child. It presses on to complete the story with his resurrection: 'Glorious now behold him arise, / King and God and sacrifice; alleluia, alleluia, / earth to heaven replies.' 'Once in royal David's city' looks even further ahead, to 'when our eyes at last shall see him'—not 'in that poor lowly stable, / with the oxen standing by', but 'in heaven, / set at God's right hand on high, / when like stars his children crowned / all in white shall stand around'.[4]

---

[4] For further examples see H. Keyte and A. Parrott (eds.), *The New Oxford Book of Carols* (Oxford: Oxford University Press, 1992).

Chapter 2 above illustrated connections between the coming of Christ and what went before in the creation of the world. This present chapter will sketch the redemptive dimensions of his conception and birth and of what followed: in his 'advance from infancy to manhood' (Gregory of Nyssa), the ministry, the passion and death, the 'descent to the dead', the resurrection, the outpouring of the Holy Spirit, and the final coming of Christ in glory. I will be concerned to show, where necessary, connections between these stages and their salvific import. Subsequent chapters will reflect in greater depth on something more difficult and controversial: the nature of the redemption conveyed through this whole story.

CONCEPTION AND BIRTH

Through his conception and birth, the Son of God took on the human condition and personally became part of human history, with all its spiritual and material components. The whole of created reality is interconnected, not least the mental and spiritual—a relationship expressed over the centuries by various sayings such as the Chinese proverb, 'the right man sitting in his house thinking the right thought will be heard five hundred miles away'. Modern science has shown how radically our bodies insert us into the material world. We become part of the cosmos and the cosmos part of us. Once upon a time people often naively assumed a far-reaching autonomy and stability for the human body. They had not yet discovered that our life is constituted by a dynamic process of constant circulation between our bodies and our material environment. Xavier Léon-Dufour put it this way: 'In our universe there circulates a total body of "materials" which are the object of unceasing exchanges.' He drew the conclusion: 'My body is the universe received and made particular in this instant by myself.'[5] To adapt the words of John Donne, no body is an island. An isolated bodily person would be

---

[5] X. Léon-Dufour, *Resurrection and the Message of Easter* (London: Geoffrey Chapmn, 1974), 239.

a strange anomaly. Our bodies make us share in and incessantly relate to the universe.

The world's wisdom and modern science vindicate the conviction of Gregory of Nyssa and other church fathers that through his conception and birth Christ entered into a kind of physical contact with the material universe in general and humanity in particular. Athanasius of Alexandria clearly took this line (*De Incarnatione*, 8–10, 17–32). But it was the identity of the One who was conceived and born that was uniquely important for Athanasius, Gregory, and the others. The whole human race and the whole created order were transformed by something unprecedented, the personal presence in the world of the Son of God. Add too the way in which Irenaeus and other church fathers appreciated the corporate function of Christ as the 'last' Adam, the new head of the human race who reversed the failure of the first Adam. In a typical passage of his *Adversus Haereses*, Irenaeus wrote: 'The Son of God . . . was incarnate and made man; and then he summed up in himself the long line of the human race, procuring for us a comprehensive salvation, that we might recover in Christ Jesus what in Adam we had lost, namely the state of being in the image and likeness of God' (3. 18. 1).

Irenaeus, Gregory of Nyssa, and other church fathers, while not isolating Christ's coming into the world from the whole story that followed, saw it as initiating an entire process of transformation and divinization.[6] From Irenaeus (*Adversus Haereses*, 3. 19; 4. 20) on to its high point in the writings of Gregory of Nazianzus and Gregory of Nyssa and beyond, we find the theme of the 'wonderful exchange (admirabile commercium)': 'It was God who became human that we humans might become divine.' In the seventh century, Maximus the Confessor celebrated the unifying and transforming work of God inaugurated by the very fact of the union of divinity and humanity in the incarnate Son of God. Christ 'initiated a universal unification of all things with himself, by beginning with our divided selves, and became a complete human being, from our stock, for our sakes, in our way—possessing completely what is ours except for sin'. So he

[6] See J. Gross, *The Divinization of the Christian according to the Greek Fathers* (Anaheim, Calif.: A. & C. Press, 2002). For Augustine's treatment, see G. Bonner, 'St. Augustine's Concept of Deification', *Journal of Theological Studies* 37 (1986), 369–86.

'summed up all things in himself and revealed that all creation is one' (*Ambigua*, 41).

When locating the redemptive value of Christ's conception and birth *within a complete redemptive story*, the fathers of the Church had the authority of the scriptures behind them. All four Gospels handle in that fashion their strikingly different ways of presenting the coming and life of Christ. Sometimes they do so with real subtlety. Mark begins his Gospel at the ministry of John the Baptist and the baptism of Jesus, and not at the conception and birth of Jesus. This Gospel opens with the only quotation from the OT that does not belong with the sayings of Jesus: 'Behold I am sending my messenger before your face, who shall prepare your way (hodon); the voice of one crying in the wilderness: "Prepare the way (hodon) of the Lord, make his paths straight"' (Mark 1: 2–3). John the Baptist who prepares 'the way' will soon meet his violent death (Mark 1: 14; 6: 14–29). For Jesus himself 'the way (hê hodos)' will turn out to be the way of the cross (Mark 10: 32, 52). Right from his opening chapter, Mark subtly relates the appearance of Christ to his coming passion and death.

So too does Matthew, and he does so in various ways: for instance, through an 'inclusion'. The question of the Magi, 'Where is he who has been born king of the Jews?' (Matt. 2: 2), receives an extended answer towards the end of the Gospel when Jesus is condemned, mocked, and crucified as 'the King of the Jews' (Matt. 27: 11, 29, 37, 42). Thus the birth of Jesus anticipates his death, a death which will redeem all people, Jews and Gentiles alike. Right in his opening chapters Matthew delicately suggests salvation for all, not only through the exotic orientals who arrive with their gifts for the newborn Jesus but also through the genealogy of Jesus (Matt. 1: 1–17). The list includes four women who were regarded as foreigners; they illustrate how even in his ancestry Jesus was already redemptively related to Gentiles. Once again we can spot an 'inclusion', since the theme of salvation for all will recur in Matthew's final chapter and the command to 'make disciples of all nations' (Matt. 28: 19).

Writing before the composition of any of the Gospels, St Paul also places the coming of Christ within the unfolding process of salvation. In his Letter to the Galatians, he writes of God in the 'fullness of time' sending his Son to be 'born of a woman' and born into Jewish society ('born under the law'). But at once the Apostle adds that the incarnation took place in order to redeem those who were in bondage under the law and to bring Jews and Gentiles alike into the divine family as adopted sons and daughters, by sending the Holy Spirit into their hearts (Gal. 4: 4–7). To be sure, Paul does not write much about God sending his Son or about the birth of the Son. But whenever he does so, he links that coming and birth forward to what is going to happen, the saving mystery of the crucifixion, resurrection, and gift of the Spirit (e.g. Rom. 1: 3–4; 8: 3–4).

The liturgical feasts that follow Christmas Day also play their role in interpreting redemptively the nativity. On 26 December comes the feast of the first Christian martyr, St Stephen, a feast celebrated on that day since the fourth century. The first reading recalls the dying words of Stephen ('Lord Jesus, receive my spirit' and 'Lord, do not hold this sin against them'), words which clearly evoke what Jesus himself had said in Luke's account of the crucifixion (Acts 7: 59–60; Luke 23: 34, 46). The readings for the feast of St John Apostle on 27 December evoke the incarnation of the One who came to share with us eternal life (1 John 1: 1–4) and his resurrection from the dead (John 20: 2–8). Those readings cast light on the saving link between the birth of Jesus and the Easter mystery. On 28 December in Western Christianity (on 29 December in Eastern Christianity), the feast of the Holy Innocents recalls the massacre ordered by Herod the Great when he heard of the birth of the King of the Jews (Matt. 2: 16–18). Once again the liturgy joins with Matthew's Gospel in seeing the shadow of the cross falling upon the birth of Jesus.

Lastly, from the middle of the sixth century Christians began celebrating the feast of the Circumcision on 1 January (see Luke 2: 21). Many modern Anglican liturgies call the feast the Naming of Jesus (because it was the day when he received his name); since 1969 the Roman Catholic calendar has called it the Solemnity of Mary, the Mother of God. The change in the designation of the feast can shift attention from something often treasured in the past by theologians, popular writers, and painters: the pain and tiny loss of blood suffered by Jesus when he was circumcised. They understood that episode to initiate his bloody sacrifice for the expiation of the sins of the world. Some theologians reflected that, given his divine identity, even the slightest loss of blood could have saved all humanity. In the words of a hymn by St Thomas Aquinas ('Adoro te devote'), 'one drop could save the whole world from every crime (cuius una stilla salvum facere totum mundum quit ab omni scelere)'. Four centuries later, in his poem 'Upon the circumcision' John Milton (1608–74) presented Christ's circumcision as the first step towards expiating human sin: the Baby 'now bleeds to give us ease./ Alas, how soon our sin/ Sore doth begin/ His infancy to seize!' In reporting the circumcision of Jesus on the eighth day after his birth, Luke's Gospel made it possible to establish a liturgical and theological connection between the nativity and the atoning death of the Redeemer.

Down the centuries Christian preachers, poets, and artists have concurred with the NT writers in setting the conception and birth of Christ within a broad redemptive setting. For his Christmas Day sermon of 411 or 412 St Augustine of Hippo spelled out the intended aftermath of the nativity: 'The Creator of man has become man that the Ruler of the stars might suck at the breast of a woman; that the Bread might be hungry; the Fountain thirst; the Light sleep; the Way be wearied with the journey; the Truth be accused by false witnesses; the Judge of the living and the dead be judged by a mortal judge . . . the Foundation be hung upon a tree; Strength be made weak; Health be wounded; Life die' (*Sermo*, 191. 1). On a Christmas Day in the seventeenth century, John Donne had a similar message to preach: 'the whole life of Christ was a continual Passion . . . His birth and death were but one continual act, and his Christmas Day and his Good Friday are but the evening and morning of one and the same day.'[7]

Like preachers, such poets as St Robert Southwell (1561–95), John Milton, and T. S. Eliot (1888–1965) have recalled the purpose of Christ's birth, the salvation of the human race. In 'The Burning Babe' Southwell describes a vision on 25 December of 'a pretty Babe all burning bright', who tells of his desire to wash sinners in his blood and purify them through the fire of his love. In 'On the Morning of Christ's Nativity' Milton dwelt mainly on the paradox of God being born as an infant. But in verse 16 he introduced a reference to the saving passion of Christ: 'The Babe lies yet in smiling infancy/ That

---

[7] J. Donne, *The Showing Forth of Christ: Sermons of John Donne*, selected and edited by Edmund Fuller (New York: Harper & Row, 1964), 78.

on the bitter cross/ Must redeem our loss.' When the Magi return home in Eliot's 'The Journey of the Magi', they are left with the anguishing question: 'Were we led all that way for/ Birth or Death?' Such details in the account of their journey as 'three trees on a low sky' have already alerted the reader to the death Christ would suffer on a cross flanked by criminals on two other crosses.

A fourteenth-century artist, Master Bertram of Minden, painted a scene of the Annunciation in which, despatched from the hand of God the Father, the tiny figure of the Son of God carries a wooden cross as he flies down towards Mary. The artist introduced right there at the conception of Christ a blatant link with his coming death. In a picture attributed to a fifteenth-century Perugian painter, Benedetto Bonfigli, the adoration of the Magi has been dramatically juxtaposed with a scene of the crucifixion. The direct juxtaposition of the two episodes, from the beginning and the end of Christ's earthly story, expresses the idea that he was born in order to die for the salvation of humanity. In a painting of the Child Jesus, Bartolomé Esteban Murillo (d. 1682) depicts him as sweetly innocent and almost completely nude; he rests on a little cross as he sleeps alone and clasps under his right arm a skull. Two small angels look down from above and invite the viewers to join them in contemplating the Christ Child in his future suffering and death.

'ADVANCE FROM INFANCY TO MANHOOD'

The scriptures, the liturgy, Christmas carols, Christian writers, preachers, and artists have felt little difficulty not only in relating the birth of Jesus to the further story of his saving activity but also in showing how a redemptive impact was already being exercised by the Christ Child. Those who people the infancy narratives of Matthew and Luke, such as Mary, Joseph, Zechariah, Elizabeth, the shepherds, the Magi, Simeon, and Anna, count among the first witnesses to what the newborn Jesus was already doing as Saviour of the world. As regards the redemptive significance of 'the human birth' of Christ (Gregory of Nyssa), the opening chapters of Matthew and Luke have shaped forever Christian imagination and faith. The saving force of

Christ's coming pervades these chapters and emerges with startling clarity in such passages as the three prayers provided by Luke: the 'Magnificat', the 'Benedictus', and the 'Nunc Dimittis' (Luke 1: 46–55, 68–79; 2: 29–32). But what of the next stage, those thirty or so years before he was baptized and began his public mission, or those years which Gregory of Nyssa called the 'advance from infancy to manhood'? Can we manage to identify the redemptive value of Christ's 'hidden life' at Nazareth? The Gospels of Matthew, Mark, and Luke can help us here.[8] We might reply in general and say that Jesus embodied the message of the divine kingdom before preaching it. His life at Nazareth expressed in advance the hidden, humble quality of the kingdom. But can we say anything specific?

Luke twice speaks of the Christ Child growing up and becoming older, bigger, wiser, and more blessed by God (Luke 2: 40, 52). Even such an unchallengeable defender of Christ's divinity as St Cyril of Alexandria (d. 444) took Luke at his word and recognized how Jesus followed the normal laws of human growth in advancing from childhood to manhood (*Quod unus sit Christus*, 760). This growth made Jesus the sublime Mediator of salvation that we see him to be at his fully mature and adult stage. Through his hidden years, his life of faith developed strongly and clearly, so that the Letter to the Hebrews was able to sum up his human story as that of One who had begun and run perfectly the race of faith (Heb. 12: 1–2). In his public ministry he showed himself to be unconditionally committed to the service of the reign of God which was breaking into the world. When he spoke about faith, his words reflected the kind of faith that

[8] For some of what follows, see R. E. Brown, *The Birth of the Messiah: A Commentary on the Infancy Narratives in the Gospels of Matthew and Luke* (New York: Doubleday, new edn., 1993). When I draw on the Gospels, (1) I accept the widely accepted scheme that there were three stages in the transmission of Jesus' deeds and words: the initial stage in his earthly life; the handing on, by word of mouth or in writing, of traditions about him; the authorial work of the four evangelists. (2) I also agree that one can use such criteria as multiple witness in arguing that the accounts of certain deeds and words go back substantially to the first stage: i.e. to Jesus himself. (3) When I draw on the Gospels I will indicate whether I understand some passage to report what Jesus did or said at stage one, or whether I use the passage to illustrate what a particular evangelist at stage three (and/or the tradition behind him at stage two) understood about Jesus' work or identity. (4) I cannot stop every time to justify why we can hold some deed or saying to have its historical origin in what Jesus said and did, but I will cite only examples for which such justification is possible.

lay behind his life of service: e.g. 'if you had faith as a grain of mustard seed, you could say to this mulberry tree, "be rooted up and be planted in the sea", and it would obey you' (Luke 17: 6).[9] He had grown in an intense faith that put him uniquely at the disposition of God. When he assured the father of the epileptic boy, 'all things are possible to him who believes', that was an invitation to share his own faith. He promised that those who keep asking in prayer will be heard (Matt. 7: 7–12 = Luke 11: 9–13). In this and other ways he spoke about faith as an insider, who knew personally what the life of faith was like and wanted to share it with others. His self-surrender to God showed itself in, and was fed by, the life of prayer he assiduously practised (e.g. Mark 1: 35; 6: 46; 14:12–26, 32–42). Praying like that expressed a deep sense of dependence and trust—in other words, a strong, even intimate relationship of faith in God. The 'advance from infancy to manhood' brought Jesus to that uniquely robust faith which underpinned his saving ministry.[10]

Luke helps us further in our quest for the redemptive significance of the hidden years in Nazareth through a story about Christ as a boy (visiting the Temple in Jerusalem) that he received and adapted (Luke 2: 41–52).[11] We find the kernel of the tradition Luke received in the question: 'Did you not know that I must be in my Father's house [or 'involved in my Father's affairs' or even 'among those belonging to my Father']?' From stage three (Luke) we can move back to stage two (a pre-Lukan tradition). But it is difficult to move further back to stage one, and hazard any guesses about what the twelve-year-old Jesus might have done and said. Such tests as multiple witness do not apply; there is no comparable story, for instance, in Matthew. What we can be more confident about is seeing how Luke (1) recognizes that, already as a boy, Jesus was the Son of God, and (2) wants to develop initially some redemptive themes. First, the journey to Jerusalem for the Passover feast anticipates the later journey Jesus will make with his disciples to Jerusalem (Luke 9: 51–19: 28). Luke presents Jesus as the Saviour on *pilgrimage* to the holy place. Second, Mary and Joseph find the Boy Jesus among the teachers in the Temple, the sacred setting

---

[9] Like others I hold that 'mulberry tree' goes back to Jesus, and that 'mountain' (Mark 11: 23; Matt. 17: 20) is a secondary development.

[10] For more on the faith of Jesus, see G. O'Collins, *Christology*, 250–68.

[11] See R. E. Brown, *The Birth of the Messiah*, 471–95.

where Luke begins his Gospel (1: 8–22) and the sacred setting where his Gospel will end: after the ascension of Jesus the disciples return to Jerusalem and spend time in the Temple praising God (24: 52–3). Luke introduces a clear inclusion to suggest how Jerusalem and its Temple create the central point in the whole history of salvation. Third, the whole story of the finding of the Boy Jesus leads up to the 'punch line' in which Luke provides the first words of Jesus. They take the form of a question: 'Did you not know that I must be in my Father's house?' It is no longer Gabriel, Simeon, or anyone else who pronounces on the identity of Jesus; he himself does so and reveals an intimate relationship of obedience to 'my Father'. He says about himself what the heavenly voice will say at his baptism (Luke 3: 22). For the first time Luke introduces 'must (dei)', a Greek word which will turn up eighteen times in his Gospel and twenty-two times in Acts and conveys a sense of events and persons being in conformity with the divine will. In the drama of human salvation, Jesus was to show himself unreservedly at the disposal of God who is his Father. His visible obedience to Mary and Joseph (2: 51) on their return to Nazareth symbolized his radical obedience to the invisible God.

A further way in which the Gospels, this time Matthew, Mark, and Luke, (unwittingly) fill in the redemptive value of the 'advance from infancy to manhood' comes through their reports of the preaching of Jesus, which followed after his baptism and period in the wilderness. The content of that preaching discloses something of what had been happening in the imagination, mind, and heart of Jesus during his hidden years in Nazareth. He had been building up a rich store of images and full-blown parables that were to characterize the vivid presentation of the saving reign and rule of God. His preaching of salvation took its shape during the thirty or so years before Jesus began his public ministry. Joachim Jeremias hints at this when he writes: 'the pictorial element of the parables is drawn from the daily life of Palestine'.[12] If we were to gather together all the images of Jesus' sayings and parables and put them together, we would have a broad picture of daily life in ancient Galilee. As he was growing up, Jesus obviously had a keen eye for his environment, and what he saw or heard would feed into his preaching of the kingdom.

---

[12] J. Jeremias, *The Parables of Jesus* (London: SCM Press, rev. edn., 1963), 11.

Jesus was to speak of stewards running large households for absentee landlords, burglars ransacking households, judges administering the law, fishermen sorting out their catch, merchants in search of precious pearls, robbers beating up travellers on lonely roads, farmers harvesting their crops, sick beggars starving outside rich households, women mixing yeast into the flour, young men leaving home and family for a more 'cheerful' life elsewhere, children playing games and sometimes quarrelling in the village squares, and neighbours arriving home late at night and looking for food. He had noticed women using the right kind of material when they mended torn clothes, rich people throwing big parties, businessmen unable to repay loans, landowners building bigger granaries to hold bumper harvests of grain, lilies growing in the fields, and young people playing their parts when friends got married. He knew that sheep could easily stray into the wilderness, that farmers fatten calves for special feasts, and that donkeys and oxen should be taken every day to water. At times these animals could fall down wells and need to be rescued at once, even on the sabbath day. Jesus noted that cultivating the soil and adding fertilizer could revitalize barren fig trees. Farmers might buy up to five yoke of oxen. Gentile farmers kept pigs and fed them on pods. Jesus became familiar too with forecasting weather and the approach of summer, the market-price of sparrows, the skins used for different brands of wine, and the safe places above the floodline for constructing large buildings.

Certain of these images came from the rich storehouse of the Jewish scriptures or had clear associations with them. For instance, the language of Jesus about vineyards, harvests, feasts, and a merchant in search of fine pearls had its OT roots. He had prayed over such images for himself and heard them read in the synagogue. That also tells us about the preparation for his ministry of salvation during the hidden years in Nazareth. Yet he gave those inherited images his own special 'twist'. The language he was to use later illustrated how, as he grew to mature manhood, Jesus was deeply sensitive to the people and the things around him—from kings going to war, farmers piling up manure heaps and growing mustard plants, right through to tiny sparrows falling dead to the ground. Everything spoke to him of God and what God wanted to do for human beings. His teaching during his public ministry revealed how responsive he had been to all that was happening around him and how he saw it all as alive with God and the divine desire to share the fullness of life with us. Such commonplace scenes as farmers sowing seed on variable terrain had suggested to him God's coming close to human beings and the problems they meet in responding to the powerful presence of the One who was always actively and lovingly attentive to them. During the years in Nazareth Jesus had been intensely alive to his world and what was happening between human beings and their constantly loving God. When he began preaching, he wanted to infect others with that perspective on life, a perspective that could bring their conversion and open them to the grace of the divine kingdom.[13]

THE PUBLIC MINISTRY

Nowadays it is hardly controversial to insist on the importance of the ministry of Jesus in the whole drama of redemption. In the past, however, many theologians neglected the human story of Jesus and moved straight from the birth of Christ to the crucifixion when developing their version of the salvation he brought.[14] This was to ignore the essential role played by his proclamation of the divine kingdom in the story of human redemption. Gregory of Nyssa selected some features of the public ministry when he wrote of 'the eating and drinking, the weariness, the sleep, the grief, [and] the tears'. 'The eating and drinking' presumably refer to a response Jesus made to his critics over his lifestyle in the service of sinners: 'The Son of Man has come eating and drinking, and you say: "Behold a glutton and a drunkard, the friend of tax collectors and sinners"' (Luke 7: 34 = Matt. 11: 19). The 'weariness' and 'sleep' recall times when the Gospels report Jesus as weary (John 4: 6) and sleeping through a storm at sea (Mark 4: 37–8). 'The grief' and 'the tears' came from the episodes when Jesus 'wept' over Jerusalem (Luke 19: 41) and the

[13] The baptism of Jesus, with his anointing by the Holy Spirit, marks the transition from his 'hidden life' to his public ministry. In Chapter 10, we will consider something of the redemptive relevance of the baptism.

[14] See e.g. J. A. de Aldama *et al.*, *Sacrae Theologiae Summa*, iii (Madrid: Editorial Catolica, 4th edn., 1959).

death of his friend Lazarus (John 11: 35). The items Gregory picked out highlight the true humanity of the Saviour. But we need to add something about the proclamation of the kingdom of God, which was utterly central in Jesus' saving work.

Jesus spent his brief ministry announcing the royal reign of God, as both already present (e.g. Matt. 12: 28 = Luke 11: 20; Luke 17: 20) and as coming in the future (e.g. Mark 1: 15; Matt. 6: 16 = Luke 11: 2). On Jesus' lips 'the kingdom' was tantamount to talking of God as Lord of the world, whose decisive intervention would liberate sinful men and women from the grip of evil and give them a new, final, and lasting age of salvation. The parables, miracles, and other works of Jesus belonged integrally to his message of the present and coming kingdom. The parables mediated the kingdom with its challenge and grace, by calling their hearers to repentance, enacting the divine forgiveness, and effecting a religious transformation. They conveyed deliverance from the satanic forces (e.g. Mark 3: 27) and *life* in abundance: a gift expressed by the silent but powerful growth of tiny seeds (e.g. Mark 4: 26–32); by the immeasurably valuable treasure that breathes new life into someone's existence (Matt. 13: 44); by the wonderful banquet that will last forever (Matt. 8: 11). Jesus opened up new possibilities of life by forgiving sinners and healing the sick. His longest and greatest parable, that of 'the prodigal son' but better called 'the merciful father' (Luke 15: 11–32), spoke of a divine mercy that brought someone who was spiritually lost and morally dead to a fresh life of joy.

Matthew, Mark, and Luke (the Synoptic Gospels) recall not only that Jesus worked miracles but also that his miraculous deeds were powerful signs of the kingdom, inextricably bound up with his proclamation of divine salvation. His healings and exorcisms were compassionate gestures, the first fruits of the presence of the kingdom which manifested God's merciful rule already operative in and through his person. Matthew edited a traditional saying to present Jesus as saying: 'if it is by the Spirit of God that I cast out demons, then the kingdom of God has come upon you' (Matt. 12: 28).[15] His exorcisms, in particular, manifested the strength of the Spirit

[15] Luke seems to provide the original version of the saying: 'if by the finger of God I cast out demons...' (Luke 11: 20); see J. P. Meier, *A Marginal Jew: Rethinking the Historical Jesus*, ii (New York: Doubleday, 1994), 407–23.

(Mark 3: 22–30), which empowered Jesus' ministry for the kingdom, right from his baptism by John. His miracles served the cause of life, not least the feeding of the five thousand in the wilderness. This episode was reported not only by the Synoptic Gospels but also by John, who developed from it the theme of Jesus as 'the bread of life' (John 6: 22–58), the giver of life in abundance (John 10: 10), Life in person (John 11: 25; 14: 6).

Both in his preaching and in his miraculous deeds, Jesus himself was inseparably connected with the arrival of the divine kingdom. In his person and presence, God's rule had come and was coming. As speaker of the parables, for example, Jesus belonged to the kingdom and effected its powerful presence. Mark and then Matthew and Luke clearly saw Jesus and his activity in that way. A saying about God's kingdom coming with power (Mark 9: 1 = Luke 9: 27) could easily be applied to Jesus himself as the Son of Man coming in his kingdom (Matt. 16: 28). High implications about Jesus' saving function and identity emerge from the way the Synoptic Gospels portray his role for the kingdom. But how did Jesus himself think of himself and his mission?

He seems to have conceived his mission as that of one who had been sent by God (e.g. Mark 9: 37; 12: 6), to break Satan's power (e.g. Luke 10: 17–18), and to realize the final rule of God (Matt. 12: 28 = Luke 11: 20). At times Jesus went beyond a prophetic 'I was sent' to say 'I came' (e.g. Mark 2: 17; Matt. 11: 19). He presented himself as something 'greater than' a prophet like Jonah or the classically wise king, Solomon (Matt. 12: 41–2 = Luke 11: 31–2). Despite evidence that he distanced himself from talk of being 'the Messiah' or promised deliverer sent by God (e.g. Mark 8: 27–31; 15: 2), it is quite implausible to argue that Jesus was oblivious of performing a messianic mission. He gave some grounds for being perceived to have made such a claim (Mark 11: 1–11). Otherwise it is very difficult to account both for the charge against him of being a messianic pretender (Mark 14: 61; 15: 2, 9, 18, 26, 32) and for the ease with which his followers began calling him 'the Christ' immediately after his death and resurrection. He had also betrayed a messianic consciousness by a key saying about his miraculous activity (Matt. 11: 2–6 = Luke 7: 18–23), and implied something about himself when contrasting 'mere' Davidic descent with the higher status of being the Messiah (Mark 12: 35–7).

Instead of dwelling directly on Jesus' awareness of his messianic mission, it may be even more illuminating to fill out what realizing the present and final rule of God entailed for him. Jesus so identified himself with the message of God's kingdom that those who responded positively to this message committed themselves to him as disciples. To accept the coming rule of God was to become a follower of Jesus. With authority Jesus encouraged men and women to break normal family ties and join him in the service of the kingdom (Mark 10: 17–31; Luke 8: 1–3). By relativizing in his own name family roles and relationships, Jesus was scandalously at odds with the normal expectations of his and other societies.

The personal authority with which Jesus taught and performed his miracles was blatant. Unlike normal miracle workers in Judaism, he did not first invoke the divine intervention but simply went ahead in his own name to heal or deliver people from diabolic possession. He likewise spoke with his own authority, prefacing his teaching with 'I say to you' (Matt. 5: 21–44) and not with such prophetic rubrics as 'thus says the Lord' or 'oracle of the Lord'. It was above all the 'objects' over which he claimed authority that were startling. Either by what he said or by what he did (or both), Jesus claimed authority over the observance of the sabbath (Mark 2: 23–8; 3: 1–5), the Temple (Mark 11: 15–17) and the law—three divinely authorized channels of salvation. A unique sacredness attached to that day (time), place, and code. Let me briefly recall some aspects of the attitude towards the law and the Temple that Jesus showed in his saving mission.

He took it upon himself not only to criticize the oral law for running counter to basic human obligations (Mark 7: 9–13) but also to set aside even the written law on such matters as retribution, divorce, and food (Matt. 5: 21–48; Mark 7: 15, 19). It is admittedly difficult to establish precisely Jesus' original temple-saying (Mark 14: 21–48; Acts 6: 13–14). But it involved some claim that his mission was to bring a new relationship between God and the people, which would replace the central place of their current relationship, the Temple in Jerusalem.[16] His mission was to replace the Temple and its cult with something better ('not made with human hands'). At

---

[16] See N. T. Wright, *Christian Origins and the Question of God*, ii: *Jesus and the Victory of God* (London: SPCK, 1996), 489–519.

least on a level with Jesus' astonishing assertion of personal rights over the time, place, and law of Jewish life was his willingness to dispense with the divinely established channels for the forgiveness of sins (temple offerings and the priestly authorities) and to take on God's role by forgiving sins in his own name—either by word (Mark 2: 1–12; 3: 28; Luke 7: 47–9) or by table-fellowship with sinners (e.g. Luke 15: 1–2).

Thus, in proclaiming salvation through the present divine rule, Jesus repeatedly claimed or at least implied a personal authority that can be described as setting himself on a par with God. Since he gave such an impression during his ministry, one can understand members of the Sanhedrin charging Jesus with blasphemy; they feared that Jesus was a false prophet and was even usurping divine prerogatives (Mark 14: 64).[17]

But what of Jesus and the *final* rule of God? Apparently, he saw his ministry not only as embodying the climax of God's purposes for Israel (Mark 12: 2–6) but also as involving his own *uniquely authoritative role* in bringing others to share in the eschatological kingdom: 'I assign to you as my Father assigned to me, a kingdom that you may eat and drink at my table in my kingdom, and sit on thrones judging the twelve tribes of Israel' (Luke 22: 29–30; see Matt. 19: 28). Here Jesus testified to himself as critically significant in the full message of the coming kingdom. His testimony to himself was an essential part of that message. Other such claims to be decisive for our final relationship with God got expressed in terms of 'the Son of Man': 'I tell you, every one who acknowledges me before men, the Son of Man will acknowledge before the angels of God. But he who denies me before men will be denied before the angels of God' (Luke 12: 9–10 = Matt. 10: 32–3). The future and final salvation of human beings was understood to depend on their present relationship with Jesus.[18]

I suggested above that deliverance and the gift of life in abundance sum up much of what Jesus intended when proclaiming the saving

---

[17] See A. E. Harvey, *Jesus and the Constraints of History* (Philadelphia: Westminster, 1982), 170–1. E. P. Sanders, however, argues that Jesus merely gave the impression of being ambitious for kingship: *Jesus and Judaism* (London: SCM Press, 1985), 317–18. On some aspects of Jesus' claim to authority, see B. Chilton, 'Amen', *ABD* i. 184–6; G. F. Hasel, 'Sabbath', *ABD* v. 850–6, at 854–5; H. Weder, 'Disciple, Discipleship', *ABD* ii. 207–10.

[18] On 'Son of Man', see O'Collins, *Christology*, 61–8.

kingdom of God. He understood that life to be mediated through the new family of God which he was establishing; becoming through dependence on Jesus his brothers and sisters, men and women could accept a new relationship with God even to the point of addressing God as their loving and merciful 'Abba (Father)' (Mark 3: 31–5; Matt. 6: 9; Luke 11: 2). Jesus himself seemed to be conscious of his own unique divine sonship (Matt. 11: 25–30; see Luke 10: 21–2), an intimate filial relationship with 'Abba' which gave him a unique knowledge about human salvation and a unique right to invite others to enjoy the loving and life-giving fatherhood of God.[19] In other words, that relationship underpinned what we would call his role as *the* Revealer and *the* Saviour in creating this new family.

His family was to be all-inclusive. He appreciated the spontaneity, openness, and trust of children, which made them models in receiving the reign of God. Jesus wanted them also to belong to his new family (Mark 9: 33–7; 10: 13–16). In the rural society of ancient Galilee, children were low on the social and religious scale, but in Jesus they found their special friend. He associated with and made disciples among women, persons also considered inferior in social and religious status. To have women among his travelling companions was startling and even scandalous (Luke 8: 1–3). His new brotherhood and sister-hood was open to all humanity. Even if he preached to the chosen people, he called humanity as such to decision. He addressed his Jewish audiences as human beings, inviting them to accept the good news, repent, and be saved. He spoke to them in parables, the language of every day and not the special religious language of some 'holy' people. It was for both Jews and Gentiles alike that Jesus expected and prepared the future kingdom of God (Matt. 8: 11).

FACED WITH DEATH

Next we come to that highpoint in Christ's redemptive story which Gregory of Nyssa called 'the false accusations, the trial, the cross, [and] the death'. Later chapters will take up the question of the

---

[19] On Jesus as Son of God, see ibid., 113–35.

impact of Christ's passion and death on human salvation. It is
difficult for many today to recognize any redemptive possibilities in
suffering. But what is beyond controversy is the fact that from the
start of Christianity believers accepted that Christ 'died for our sins'
(e.g. 1 Cor. 15: 3). Here I wish only to say something about the
redemptive intentions of Jesus himself when his passion and death
loomed up. Did he not only anticipate his violent death but also in
some sense understand that it would bring God's final reign and
prove salvific for the human race? Did he intend to offer an atoning
sacrifice for all? There are indications that this was so, and hence that
there is some continuity between what he intended and the early
Christian interpretation of his death.

Before reviewing those indications it is important to emphasize
that we should not suppose that those intentions—or rather what we
can establish about them—provide the *only* reason for acknowledging that Jesus died to save sinful men and women and for deciding
how that death for others worked or works. There could have been
and can be more meaning and efficacy in his death than he fully and
clearly realized when he accepted that death. The value of what
rational agents decide, do, and suffer can go beyond, at times far
beyond, their conscious intentions. Nevertheless, we normally expect
the value of important human actions to stem at least partly from the
conscious intentions of the agent in question.

Many among those who discuss the intentions of Jesus when faced
with death never raise the issue that has just been raised in the last
paragraph. Among the few who have done so was Joachim Jeremias,
but he took a maximal position on the role of Jesus' intentions. He wrote:

The very heart of the kerygma, that 'Christ died for our sins in accordance
with the Scriptures' (1 Cor 15: 3), represents an interpretation of a historical
event: this death happened for us. But this raises the question whether this
interpretation of the crucifixion of Jesus has been arbitrarily imposed upon
the events, or whether there was some circumstance in the events which
caused this interpretation to be attached to it. *In other words*, we must ask:
Did Jesus himself speak of his impending death, and what significance did he
attach to it?[20]

[20] J. Jeremias, *The Problem of the Historical Jesus* (Philadelphia: Fortress, 1964), 13;
emphasis mine.

The implication of Jeremias's position must be clearly stated. If we cannot establish historically that Jesus himself attributed a redeeming significance to his impending death, this interpretation of his crucifixion deserves dismissal as 'arbitrarily impressed'. Nothing short of such proof would apparently have satisfied Jeremias. Seemingly the only reason why he was ready to accept Jesus' death as having happened 'for us' and 'for our sins' was the actual demonstration that Jesus himself interpreted his coming death that way. If we do not join Jeremias in his maximal position, what can be said?

First things first. At some point Jesus began to anticipate and accept his violent death. He saw his ministry as standing at least partially in continuity with the prophets. In his prophetic role Jesus expected to die a martyr's death and apparently expected that to happen in Jerusalem (e.g. Luke 11: 47, 49–51; 13: 34–5; Mark 12: 1–12). Not only past history but also contemporary events had their lesson to teach. The violent death of John the Baptist showed how perilous a radical religious ministry was in the Palestine of that time. Jesus would have been extraordinarily naive not to have seen the danger. Before his final Passover in Jerusalem, opposition had already built up against him. His mission for the kingdom had provoked various charges: of violating the sabbath, working miracles through diabolic power, rejecting the purity regulations, showing contempt for the divine law, acting as a false prophet, and expressing blasphemous pretensions. Then his entry into Jerusalem and protest in cleansing the Temple, if they did happen at the end of his ministry (Mark 11: 1–19 parr.) and not at the beginning (John 2: 13–25), were a final, dangerous challenge to the religious authorities in the city and the power they exercised through the Temple.

In the light of such (and further) material from the Gospels, we can reasonably conclude that at some point Jesus realized that he would lose his life violently and yet went ahead in obedience to his God-given mission. On the eve of his death, the last supper and the agony in the garden strikingly exemplified this free obedience to the Father's will (Mark 14: 17–42 parr.). There are notorious difficulties in settling the details of those episodes. The Synoptic Gospels, not to mention John and Paul on the last supper, do not provide uniform evidence. Nevertheless, it seems reasonable to accept some historical core for the story of Jesus' agonizing decision to accept his destiny. Centuries later some medieval Christians represented this decision through the theme of Christ climbing the cross; sometimes they even pictured him as using a short ladder to do so. George Herbert (1593–1633) in 'The Sacrifice' maintained the medieval image: 'Man stole the fruit, but I must climb the tree.'[21] Whatever the image we prefer, the question remains. But did he understand his suffering and death to be salvific? If so, in what sense and for whom?

The theme of God's kingdom can help us here. Jesus' message of the kingdom entailed a future suffering ordeal: a time of crisis and distress which was to move towards 'the day' of the Son of Man (Mark 13 parr.), the restoration of Israel (Matt. 19: 28 par.), the banquet of the saved, and the salvation of the nations (Matt. 8: 11 par.). Thus the arrest, trial, and crucifixion of Jesus dramatized the very thing which totally engaged him, that rule of God which was to come through a time of suffering. At the last supper Jesus linked his imminent death with the divine kingdom: 'Truly I say to you, I shall not drink again of the fruit of the vine until the day when I drink it new in the kingdom of God' (Mark 14: 25 par.). It is widely agreed that this text has not been shaped by the eucharistic liturgy of the early Church, but comes from Jesus himself at his last meal with his friends. The argument is this: since Jesus interpreted his death in terms of the coming kingdom, he saw that death as a saving event; for he had consistently presented the equation: the kingdom = human salvation. He integrated his death not only into his surrender to his Father's will but also into his offer of salvation to human beings. It is hardly surprising that Jesus would have made such a positive integration between the coming kingdom and his death. As we have seen, the message about the divine reign was inseparable from the person of Jesus. This essential connection between the message of Jesus and his person meant that the vindication of his person in and through death[22] involved the vindication of God's kingdom and vice versa.

At the last supper, the 'words of institution', if taken at their face value, show Jesus defining his death as a sacrifice which will not only representatively atone for sins but also initiate a new and enduring

---

[21] See J. A. W. Bennett, *Poetry of the Passion* (Oxford: Clarendon Press, 1982), 15–17.
[22] On the way Jesus expected to be raised from the dead and so vindicated by the Father, see O'Collins, *Christology*, 70–2.

covenant with God. But here we must reckon with the question: How far have the sources of Paul, Mark, and the other evangelists been shaped by liturgical usages in early Christian communities? In 1 Corinthians 11: 23–5 we read: 'The Lord Jesus on the night when he was betrayed took bread and when he had given thanks, he broke it and said, "This is my body which is for you. Do this in remembrance of me." In the same way also the cup, after supper, saying, "This cup is the new covenant in my blood. Do this, as often as you drink it, in remembrance of me." ' In Mark's version of the last supper, however, the double instructions to perform the Eucharist ('Do this in remembrance of me', and 'Do this as often as you drink it, in remembrance of me') are missing. And—what is more significant for the issue under discussion—the qualification of 'my body' being 'for you' is also missing. However, unlike the Pauline tradition, Mark describes the blood as being 'poured out for many'. His version runs as follows: 'He took bread, and blessed, and broke it, and gave to them, and said, "Take; this is my body." And he took the cup, and when he had given thanks he gave it to them, and they all drank of it. And he said to them, "This is my blood of the covenant, which is poured out for many" ' (14: 23–4).

Confronted with the differences between the Pauline tradition (to which, apart from adding, apropos of 'my blood', 'which is poured out for you', and not including, apropos of the cup, 'do this in remembrance of me', Luke 22: 19–20 approximates) and the Markan tradition (which is more or less followed by Matthew 26: 26–8 (who qualifies the 'poured out for many' as happening 'for the forgiveness of sins'), some writers back away from relying too much on the words of institution as accurate sources for settling the way Jesus understood his death. Whom did Jesus believe to be the beneficiaries of his sacrificial death? The 'for you' of the Pauline and Lukan tradition indicates the companions of Jesus at the last supper. Of course, in that case he may well have intended them to represent others. Mark (followed by Matthew) has Jesus speaking of his blood 'poured out for many' (= all). But in that case did Jesus mean not merely all Jews but also all Gentiles? At the same time, one may not overlook the convergences between the traditions. The Pauline–Lukan tradition ('new covenant') and the Markan–Matthean tradition ('the covenant') both report Jesus as speaking of a covenant instituted through his 'blood' and as echoing key OT passages (e.g. Exod. 24: 3–8; Jer. 31: 31–4). Ultimately, the pressure on us to establish precisely what Jesus said and intended at the last supper can be eased in three ways: by (1) recalling his *characteristic attitudes*, (2) pointing to *contemporary ideas*, and (3) noting *an implication* in early Christian convictions about Jesus' atoning death.

(1) In general, *the characteristic ways* in which persons act and speak can fill their deaths with meaning, even when they have no chance at the end to express their motivation and make an explicit declaration of intent. In the case of Jesus, even if he never explicitly designated himself as 'the Servant of the Lord', he consistently behaved as one utterly subject to his Father's will and completely available for the service of those who needed mercy and healing. His words and actions brought divine pardon to those who felt they were beyond redemption. He never drove away lepers, children, sinful women, taxation agents, and those crowds of 'little people' who clamoured for his love and attention. A straight line led from his serving ministry to his suffering death. Even if the community (stage two) or Mark himself (stage three) added the words 'to give his life as a ransom for many', there was a basis in Jesus life (stage one) for the saying 'the Son of Man came not to be served but to serve and to give his life as a ransom for many' (Mark 10: 45). He who had shown himself the servant of all was ready to become the victim for all. And, as some writers have insisted, that service was offered especially to the outcasts and the religious pariahs.[23] Part of the reason why Jesus' ministry led to his crucifixion stemmed from the fact that he scandalously served the lost, the godless, and the alienated of his society. The physician who came to call and cure the unrighteous (Mark 2: 17) eventually died as their representative. His serving ministry to the reprobates ended when he obediently accepted a shameful death between two reprobates. His association with society's outcasts and failures led to his solidarity with them in death. In these terms, the passion of Jesus became integrated into his mission as a final act of service. In death, as in life, he served and sacrificed himself for others.

Whom did Jesus take to be *the beneficiaries* of his suffering and death? While Jesus understood his fellow Jews to be the primary

---

[23] See e.g. J. Moltmann, *The Way of Jesus Christ* (London: SCM Press, 1990), 112–16.

beneficiaries of the divine salvation mediated through his mission (Matt. 15: 24; see 10: 5–6), his vision was universal; he addressed his Jewish audience as human beings, and required from them a realistic love towards other human beings in need, a love which was willing to cross racial frontiers (Luke 10: 25–37) and include everyone, even one's enemies (Matt. 5: 43–8 parr.). He called for a new brotherhood and sisterhood which denied any sacrosanct value to family or tribal bonds within Israel: 'Whoever does the will of God is my brother, and sister, and mother' (Mark 3: 35 parr.). This statement has a universal ring, which we also find in the parable of the tax-collector and the Pharisee (Luke 18: 9–14). There Jesus highlighted the extent of God's generosity; the divine pardon was offered to all.

By rejecting purity regulations (Mark 7: 14–23 par.) which preserved the boundaries between Jews and Gentiles, Jesus implied that this distinction had no ultimate significance before God. Hence Jesus' vision of Israel entailed 'many coming from the east and west to sit at table with Abraham, Isaac, and Jacob in the kingdom of heaven' (Matt. 8: 11 par.). The restoration of Israel (Matt. 19: 28 par.) or Israel's being superseded (Mark 12: 9 par.) meant salvation for the nations. Having lived and preached such a universal vision, at the end, Jesus, one can reasonably suppose, accepted in some sense that he would die for all people.

(2) *Contemporary ideas* also serve as pointers to his intentions in the face of death. The experiences of the Maccabean martyrs in the second century BC helped to promote an idea which was in the air at the time of Jesus. The suffering and violent death of just persons could expiate the sins of others. The martyrdom of even one individual could representatively atone for the sins of a group: someone could die 'for' his city or his people.[24] Once the threat of violent death loomed up, it would have been strange if Jesus had never applied to himself this religious conviction of his contemporaries. It may be that Jesus envisaged the vicarious suffering of the Suffering Servant (Isa. 52: 13–53: 12) as foreshadowing and illuminating his own impending death. But we do not need to make our case simply in terms of this one passage. Expiating the sins of others by suffering

---

[24] See M. Hengel, 'The Atonement', in *The Cross and the Son of God* (London: SCM Press, 1986), 189–284.

'for' them was an idea widely reflected in the Maccabean literature and elsewhere.

(3) We can also point to the *implication* of a very early Christian tradition that Jesus' crucifixion was a death 'for us', which representatively atoned for human sin (e.g. 1 Thess. 5: 10; Rom. 4: 25). These formulations enshrine a conviction which has no background in Jewish expectations. At the time of Jesus popular messianic hopes did not include a suffering Messiah. Moreover, to proclaim a crucified Messiah (who had then been vindicated by being raised from the dead) was an awful and profound scandal (1 Cor. 1: 23). Crucifixion was seen as the death of a criminal who perished away from God's presence and in the place and company of irreligious men (Gal. 3: 13; Heb. 13: 12–13). Hence the early Christians proposed something utterly offensive when they announced that the crucifixion of someone who had been executed as a messianic pretender was in fact a sacrificial death which atoned representatively for the sins of all.[25]

How can we account for this understanding of Jesus' crucifixion as the vicarious atoning death of the Messiah, a death that had universal impact? Would the disciples' encounters with the risen Jesus and reception of the Holy Spirit have been sufficient to trigger this interpretation? They went much further than trying to modify messianic expectations in order to proclaim Jesus as a martyred prophet like John the Baptist and others before him. They recognized in Jesus' crucifixion the representative death of the Messiah which atoned for human sin. They could hardly have done so, unless the earthly Jesus had already in some way claimed to be Messiah and also indicated that his coming death would have such an atoning value. The disciples needed, so to speak, all the help they could get if they were to cope with the scandalous idea that his death on the cross had representatively atoned for the sins of all.

What I have argued for here is that, when faced with death, Jesus in some way interpreted it as a representative service for others. Later chapters will need to fill out matters. Here my purpose was to 'place' the passion and death of Jesus in the whole redemptive story which began with his conception and birth.

[25] See ibid., 93–185; G. O'Collins, 'Crucifixion', *ABD* i. 1207–10.

THE DESCENT TO THE DEAD

Gregory of Nyssa moved from the death of Christ to his being 'put in the tomb'. The Apostles' Creed likewise confesses '[Jesus Christ] died and was buried', and presses on at once to say 'he descended to the dead'. Essentially the 'descent to the dead' or 'descent into hell' (as it was traditionally called) expressed Christ's stay among the dead after his death on the cross and his victory over death, often represented in Eastern icons by his liberation of Adam and Eve. All four Gospels tell of the burial of Jesus and of his tomb being discovered empty on the third day by Mary Magdalene either alone (John) or accompanied by one or more other women (Mark, Matthew, and Luke). Occasionally the NT portrays his resurrection as a deliverance from the underworld (e.g. Matt. 10: 40; Rom. 10: 7) and from the corruption of the grave (Acts 2: 24–32). Some words of the risen and exalted Jesus in the Book of Revelation ('I have the keys of death and Hades'—1: 7) imply that for the first time the gates of the underworld have been opened for someone to leave and that, in rising from the grave, Christ has gained power over death and Hades. But there is not yet any clear sense of his having won a victory *in* the underworld. For his account of the death and burial of Jesus, Matthew may have drawn on a popular tradition about many OT saints being released from the underworld by Christ (Matt. 27: 52–3). But he used the tradition not to introduce any activity of Christ in Hades but rather to express part of the significance of the crucifixion: the power of death has now been broken.[26]

In early Christianity, from the beginning of the second century, a fuller scenario began to develop of Christ's descent to the underworld. He was presented as having descended to break open the gates of the underworld, defeat, and trample underfoot Death and Hades (which imprison the dead in the underworld). During his stint in Hades he announced to the dead the salvation he had achieved, and then brought the righteous out of captivity and up to heaven. Those to whom he preached and whom he delivered were first understood

[26] See R. E. Brown, *The Death of the Messiah*, ii (New York: Doubleday, 1994), 1118–33, 1137–40.

to be the saints of the OT; they had been hoping so long for his coming. Then some Eastern writers included righteous pagans in the picture as also being beneficiaries of Christ's descent to the underworld. Eventually Christ was pictured as having broken the power not simply of death (see 1 Cor. 15: 44–5; Rev. 20: 14) but also of Satan and the forces of evil. By that time Adam and Eve also had often gained a central prominence. Whenever Christians portrayed Christ releasing Adam and Eve from Hades, they gave fresh power to the Adam/New Adam motif which holds together superbly the deep link between the creation story, in which Adam and Eve are the high point, and the story of redemption (see Chapter 2 above).[27]

In the twentieth century Hans Urs von Balthasar developed a 'dramatic' version of the story of redemption in which the theology of Holy Saturday was central and involved Christ being estranged from God.[28] As I will indicate below (Chapter 7), I find it hard to accept a view of Christ as being alienated from God and under divine judgement.

THE RESURRECTION, THE SPIRIT, THE FINAL AGE AND THE PAROUSIA

Christ's resurrection from the dead was the decisive moment in the drama of human salvation. St Paul had received an original consensus articulated in such confessional formulas as 'Christ died for our sins' (1 Cor. 15: 3), but filled out these formulas by including the resurrection: '[Jesus] was put to death for our trespasses and *raised for our justification*' (Rom. 4: 25). The Letter to the Romans moved on to enshrine the Apostle's mature thought on the universal impact of the resurrection. Not only human beings but also created nature will share in the deliverance from bondage to come (Rom. 8: 18–25).

In his own cryptic style Mark catches the way God had acted to transform radically the situation of Jesus' death and burial

---

[27] On all this see R. Bauckham, 'Descent to the Underworld', *ABD* ii. 145–59, at 156–9; A. Kartsonis, *Anastasis: The Making of an Image* (Princeton, NJ: Princeton University Press, 1986); A. E. Lewis, *Between Cross and Resurrection: A Theology of Holy Saturday* (Grand Rapids, Mich.: Eerdmans, 2001).

[28] H. U. von Balthasar, *Mysterium Paschale* (Edinburgh: T. & T. Clark, 1990), 148–88.

(Mark 16: 1–8). While never formally named in the eight verses of Mark's concluding chapter, God has triumphed over the evil and injustice which struck Jesus down. Glorious new life and not death have the final word. Two verbs in the passive voice point to the divine activity which has utterly altered the situation. The link between the crucified Jesus and the risen Jesus is the victorious power of God. The great stone blocking the entrance to the tomb 'has been rolled away', and one understands 'by God'; Jesus himself 'has been raised', and one understands 'by God'. Even before the three women arrive, the divine power has dramatically reversed the situation of death and injustice.

Subsequent chapters of this book will explore at length the victorious, liberating action of God, the reconciliation of sinners, and the redemptive power of love which can already be gleaned from the Easter stories of the Gospels.[29] Here I wanted only to cite Paul and Mark as witnesses for the crucifixion and resurrection being essentially interconnected in the full story of redemption. One might call on many other witnesses and testimonies, such as a ninth-century antiphon for Good Friday: 'We adore your cross, Lord, and we praise your holy resurrection . . . For behold on account of the wood [of the cross] joy has come into the whole world (crucem tuam adoramus, Domine, et sanctam resurrectionem tuam laudamus . . . ecce enim propter lignum venit gaudium in universo mundo).'[30] The wood of the cross is held together with the Easter joy of the holy resurrection which affects the entire world.

In the story-line of the redemption, the NT understands the relationship between Jesus and the Holy Spirit to be transformed by the crucifixion and resurrection, or at least to be disclosed as strikingly different from what seemed to be the case during the earthly life of Jesus. The active role of the Holy Spirit is highlighted by Matthew and Luke at the virginal conception of Jesus, and by all four Gospels at the baptism of Jesus. With his death and resurrection, however, the exalted Jesus was seen to share in God's prerogative of being the Sender or Giver of the divine Spirit. Luke and John, in particular, speak of Christ as co-sending the Spirit. Exalted 'at the right hand of God and having received from the Father the promise

---

[29] See G. O'Collins, *Easter Faith: Believing in the Risen Jesus* (London: Darton, Longman & Todd, 2003), 76–81, 90–102.

[30] See Bennett, *Poetry of the Passion*, 11.

of the Holy Spirit', Christ along with the Father pours out the Spirit with the perceptible effects that follow (Acts 2: 33; see Luke 24: 49; John 16: 7; 20: 22). Christians understood themselves to have been 'inserted' in Christ through faith and baptism (e.g. Rom. 6: 3, 11, 23), and the Holy Spirit to have been 'poured' into their hearts (e.g. Rom. 5: 5; 8: 9, 11, 16). The creative force of the Spirit brings a new way of living, a communion or fellowship in the Spirit (2 Cor. 13: 13), the formation of the Church as a new and enduring family through which the saving impact of past redemption is mediated.

Later chapters (Chapters 10 and 11) will have much more to say about the outpouring of the Holy Spirit and the Spirit's place in the whole plot of redemption. It is through the Spirit that the crucified and risen Jesus becomes 'the cause of eternal salvation' (Heb. 5: 8)— both in the Christian community and beyond. Without the Spirit the redemption achieved by Christ would not have its present impact.

During this final age that stretches from (1) the events of Easter and Pentecost to (2) the end of history, the risen Christ has not gone on a kind of extended sabbatical leave. In a multiplicity of ways he remains powerfully, if mysteriously, present to the community of believers and the whole world. We return to this theme later. Likewise we will need to return later to the climax of the whole story of redemption when the history of the world will end with the 'parousia'. Christ will 'return' in glory to judge the human race and then God will be 'all in all' (1 Cor. 15: 28). This will be the consummation of the whole redemptive story, launched with the birth of Christ, accomplished with the crucifixion, resurrection, and outpouring of the Spirit, and lived during the time when human beings have been waiting, knowingly or unknowingly, for the end of all things. This whole story of growth, development, and consummation reflects an image of God as wonderfully wise and patient and uniquely powerful.

VERBAL IMAGES

The NT yields around 130 titles for Christ: distinctive names that illuminate his identity and point to his redemptive functions. I must say 'around', since there can be a debate about a few of the titles that

I recognize, such as 'Alpha and Omega' (Rev. 1: 8; 21: 6; 22: 13). The titles coincide, by and large, with verbal images which picture Jesus and even vividly describe him (e.g. as 'the Lamb of God'). The titles for Christ relate to the visual images that we see on the walls of catacombs, on the ceilings of churches, along the corridors of some schools, and in many art galleries. Thus early Christians took the title 'Good Shepherd' and translated it visually as a beardless, curly-haired youth who rescues his persecuted flock from the devouring wolves. Such titles and verbal/visual images pull together the *eight stages* of the redemptive story that this chapter has outlined: from the conception and birth of Christ to his coming in glory.

The verbal/visual images, together with their associated stories, *also* achieve two purposes. First, they illustrate the 'character' of God. They complement each other in telling us what God is like, both in himself and in the mission of his Son and that of the Spirit. Second, the images and their stories play their part in actualizing the past in the present and so ensuring that redemptive events in the past have their saving impact on the present situation.

(1) In Matthew's story of the birth of Jesus the Magi arrive in search of the newborn 'King of the Jews'. They bring royal gifts; Christian tradition was to interpret the gift of gold, in particular, as referring to the kingship of the Christ Child. Since the Magi carried three gifts, Christian tradition and art understood them to be three, gave them names, frequently turned them into kings, and often pictured them arriving with rich retinues and then laying down their crowns as they knelt to pay homage to the Christ Child. The whole of the NT was to give Jesus 38 times the title of 'King'. He was born to be just that: 'King of kings and Lord of lords' (Rev. 17: 14). Familiar visual images of the visit of the Magi and verbal images from our Christmas carols join forces with Matthew's story to reinforce a sense of what the newborn Jesus will do in a royal way for the redemption of the world.

(2) The NT occasionally names Jesus as the 'pais' of God (e.g. Acts 3: 13, 26): that is to say, God's 'servant' or 'boy'. The 'youthful' overtones of 'pais' make it appropriate as a title or verbal image to summarize the years of 'advance from infancy to manhood' (Gregory of Nyssa) in the whole narrative of salvation. Those years were, as we saw from Luke's Gospel, characterized by a visible obedience to Mary

and Joseph, which mirrored the more radical obedience of the boy Jesus to his heavenly Father. Painters have been drawn by Luke's story of 'the Finding in the Temple' or 'Christ among the Doctors/ Teachers', as it is also called: a first-rate example is that by Bernardino Luini from around 1520, now held in the National Gallery, London. Sometimes painters highlighted the loss and pain Mary and Joseph felt when Jesus went missing. The state gallery in Dresden has a work by Albrecht Dürer (d. 1528), 'the Seven Sorrows of Mary' in which the third scene/sorrow pictures her at the moment when she and Joseph find Jesus in the Temple. Sir Edward Burne-Jones (1833–98) imagined and painted a scene from the carpenter's shop of Joseph (also found in the National Gallery, London). The boy Jesus has just cut his finger and, with an obvious reference to his future passion and death, Mary and Joseph look with deep concern at his slight wound.

(3) To express the ministry of Jesus and its saving function, one might choose the title 'Christ' or 'Messiah (the Anointed)' and recall his being anointed by the Holy Spirit at his baptism. That anointing empowered him for the proclamation which he was soon to start in the service of God's kingdom. The verbal image of anointing for his redemptive mission finds its visual counterpart in many marvellous paintings of his baptism (e.g. by Giovanni Bellini and Piero della Francesca). Another title which obviously fits the ministry of Jesus is that of 'Teacher' or 'Rabbi', a verbal image which turns up 66 times in the Gospels (and nowhere else in the NT). We recalled above the striking authority in his teaching style, and what he expects from his disciples. They are not simply pupils who can learn his doctrine and move away; they are called to follow Jesus personally and commit themselves to the kingdom of God which his words and deeds make present. Christian painters have shown Jesus acting as Teacher when preaching the sermon on the mount or when calling Peter and other disciples.[31]

(4) For the redemptive story of the passion and death of Jesus, various other titles suggest themselves: for example, the Suffering

---

[31] See G. O'Collins, 'Jesus as Lord and Teacher', in J. C. Cavadini and L. Holt (eds.), *Who Do You Say that I Am? Confessing the Mystery of Christ* (Notre Dame, Ind.: University of Notre Dame Press, 2004), 51–61.

Servant and the Lamb of God. Later we will have to scrutinize questions of sacrifice and the expiation of sins which such titles obviously raise. For the moment I want only to note how these verbal images have passed over into visual images. Everyone cherishes different portrayals of Jesus as the Suffering Servant. My first vote would go to the haunting images left by Rembrandt (d. 1670) of Jesus before Pilate, on the way to Calvary, and then nailed to the cross itself. Sheer vulnerability defines the 'Agnus Dei (Lamb of God)' by Francisco de Zurburán (d. 1664), a work brought from the Prado in Madrid for the 'Seeing Salvation' exhibition which drew so many visitors to London in 2000. The image is utterly simple, a lovely lamb with its feet tied, lying on a butcher's slab, and standing out against a dark background. It conveys a powerful sense of what human sin has done to the Lamb of God in his work of redemption.

(5) One Western artist, Albrecht Dürer (d. 1528), left us a dramatic woodcut of Christ's descent to the underworld, the 'limbo of the fathers (limbus patrum)'. The victorious Christ has already set free Adam and Eve and is busy delivering others. Adam stands holding the cross, while Christ the New Adam delivers others from their long imprisonment in Hades. But the Christ as the New Adam is more wonderfully pictured in icons used for the liturgy of Eastern Christians and in the decoration of their churches. He has descended to the dead, forced open the doors of the underworld, broken the chains with which Adam, Eve, and the assembly of OT saints had been bound by the satanic powers, and is liberating all the just to share with them the glorious happiness of the redeemed life.

(6) John's Gospel tells of Jesus' dramatic encounter with Martha before raising her brother Lazarus from the dead. Jesus declares himself to be in person 'the Resurrection and the Life' (John 11: 25). These Easter titles sum up the saving force of what happened when Jesus rose gloriously from the dead. They belong with many marvellous paintings of the resurrection such as that by Piero della Francesca to be found in San Sepolcro (Italy). The victorious Christ stands majestically alone above the prostrate soldiers. No one else is present. But, as I argued in Chapter 2, Eastern icons of the 'Anastasis (resurrection)'—such as the one in the monastery of Chora (Istanbul)—do much better by introducing Adam, Eve, and their companions to

indicate vividly that the resurrection is not an individual victory for Christ alone but also the saving event for all humanity. These icons are called 'Anastasis'—a way of linking intimately the descent to the dead and the resurrection. Such icons hint at the cosmic impact of what has happened. Huge rocks, which have been shattered to open Christ's passage down into the 'limbo of the Fathers', suggest that the Easter transformation includes the whole world.

(7) St Paul called the crucified and risen Christ 'a Life-giving Spirit' (1 Cor. 15: 45), the One who gives life, above all the life of the Holy Spirit. An Easter scene in John's Gospel shows Christ performing this role when he breathes on his disciples and communicates to them the Spirit (John 20: 22). Even from the cross, however, Jesus has already imparted the Spirit—in his very death 'he gave up his spirit', 'handed over the Spirit' (John 19: 30). Then the flow of blood and water that came from his pierced side (John 19: 33) fulfil what the Fourth Gospel has announced earlier: the gift of the Spirit will take the form of 'streams of living water' coming 'from his heart' (John 7: 37–9). I mention this because very often the Lukan scenario of Pentecost dominates the way Christians imagine the outpouring of the Spirit. The book I wrote with Mario Farrugia, *Catholicism*, used a fourteenth-century image of Pentecost (from John of Berry's *Small Hours*) for the front cover.[32] Yet we can well link the title of 'Life-giving Spirit' with an image of the saving communication of the Holy Spirit that, according to John, began at the very death of Jesus. In Western iconography 'the throne of grace (Gnadenstuhl)' has expressed this gift of the Spirit in a painted or sculptured form. The composition shows the Father holding the dead body of the Son, with the Holy Spirit as a dove hovering between them. Sometimes, as in El Greco's version exhibited in the Prado (Madrid), the dead body of Jesus already hints at the luminosity of Easter. At his death and resurrection, together with the Father he bestowed on us the Holy Spirit.

(8) The NT supplies a title regularly connected with the end when Christ will come in glory: the Saviour (e.g. Phil. 3: 20; Titus 2: 13). My favourite visual counterpart comes from the Basilica of St Cecilia

---

[32] G. O'Collins and M. Farrugia, *Catholicism: The Story of Catholic Christianity* (Oxford: Oxford University Press, 2003).

in Trastevere (Rome). As the strong, majestic Saviour, Christ looks out from a medieval fresco of the Last Judgement.

In conclusion, let me emphasize an advantage in using titles or verbal images to headline the eight stages in the complete story of salvation. They offer a scheme for studying the dramatic sequence of events in what Jesus did as Redeemer. At his birth he was already acknowledged as King; he grew to manhood as Boy or Servant; in his ministry he showed himself to be Messiah and Teacher; he died as the Suffering Servant and the Lamb of God; he descended to the dead as the New Adam; he rose from the dead as the Resurrection and the Life; with the Father he acted as the Life-giving Spirit; he will come in glory as the Saviour. For each of these stages I could have used further titles or *verbal* images. Likewise innumerably many other works of art could have been cited as the *visual* images which correspond to the verbal images. But this sampling can at least establish the value of putting the images into an order which provides shape and movement to the complete story of redemption. (Here and earlier I use 'story' in the sense of a history that is narrated and personally witnessed to, not in the sense of some freely created fiction.) But it is one thing to tell the full story of redemption. It is quite another thing to indicate how that story worked and works. The chapters that follow will take up that challenge.

6

Redemption as Deliverance from Evil

O Death, I will be your death ('O Mors, ero mors tua'; an antiphon for the offices of Holy Saturday in Vulgate translation).

Hosea 13: 14.

No one can enter a strong man's house and plunder his property without first tying up the strong man, and then indeed the house can be plundered.

Mark 3: 27.

The Bible and the Christian tradition are rich with the language of redemption and not least with the language of deliverance from bondage. Chapter 1 clarified in a preliminary way the terms and images for deliverance. We now explore more fully this interpretation of redemption, which features centrally in the modern theologies of liberation that have come from Latin America.

CHRIST THE DELIVERER

Whenever the treatment of Christ's redemptive achievement skips straight from the incarnation to his death and resurrection, we miss the historical mindset of the Redeemer himself—something which can be gleaned from a discerning and critical use of the Gospels. During his ministry Jesus presented his activity in the service of the present and coming kingdom of God as a victorious conflict with satanic powers (e.g. Mark 3: 27). He taught his followers to pray for deliverance 'from the evil one' (Matt. 6: 13; Mark 14: 38; Luke 11: 4). Jesus knew his redemptive work to involve liberation from sin, evil, and a misuse of the law and to bring the gift of life in abundance. The last chapter filled out in detail what Jesus knew this liberation and gift to involve, right through to his climactic coming to the Jerusalem Temple. The 'cleansing' of the Temple and the words about the 'new Temple' to be 'built' let us glimpse Jesus' redeeming intentions. He was dramatically enacting God's promise to come and save his people.[1]

In pursuing the salvific activity and intentions of the historical Jesus, we have relied primarily on the Synoptic Gospels. They reflect a widespread dread of demons, a great sense of helplessness in the force of demonic activity, and an astonished joy at the power of Jesus over Satan and his forces. But how should we understand Satan and demons today? Should we simply translate that NT language in terms of various forms of bondage which afflict human beings and from which they need deliverance: for instance, those obsessions and compulsions that hold people helplessly captive (see the end of Chapter 3)? Two recurrent experiences encourage me to continue thinking in terms of personal powers of evil from which we need deliverance. First, the massively destructive and self-destructive folly of savage conflicts continues to hint at the existence and influence of invisible satanic evil that inspires the visible, human protagonists. In an article published at the start of the recent wars in the Balkans ('Satan laughs at Yugoslavia', *The Times*, 19 September 1991), Bernard Levin remarked: 'we don't believe in the devil. But the trouble is that the devil does believe in us'. The murderous determination to kill other people has, Levin argued, 'nothing to do with recognisable and logical explanations'. There was, he suggested, 'a powerful scent of brimstone that fills the air'. At that point he anticipated 'the imminent death of twenty thousand' people; in fact over 200,000 died in the four cruel years of the death throes of Yugoslavia. A brilliant, secular journalist, Levin made a good case for attributing to a personal power of evil the blatant insanity and mutual destructiveness of so many wars. Second, C. S. Lewis published in

---

[1] See N. T. Wright, 'Jesus' Self-Understanding', in S. T. Davis, D. Kendall and G. O'Collins (eds.), *The Incarnation* (Oxford: Oxford University Press, 2002), 47–61.

1942 *The Screwtape Letters*, supposedly a collection of letters from a senior devil to his nephew, a junior devil, which wittily express what experts on 'the spiritual life' had taught from the time of early Christianity about the activity of evil spirits in tempting human beings. What Lewis and the long tradition behind him had to say about 'good people' being led astray rings true in my own experience. Such people, with the best of intentions, can be mysteriously led astray into doing things that are in fact evil or at least into failing to do the great things that they might or should have done for the good of others. Obviously, there is very much more to be said about interpreting the NT and what it says about satanic powers. But those two experiences boost my sense that we should not rush into removing the personal reference from the NT's talk about demonic powers.

The last chapter also noted how the NT recorded the faith of the first Christians that redemption decisively came through the death and resurrection of Christ (along with the outpouring of the Holy Spirit). They were not content to interpret the crucifixion as a terrible miscarriage of justice, which God set right through the resurrection. For them these events meant that death itself was 'swallowed up in victory': 'the sting of death is sin, and the power of sin is the law. But thanks be to God, who gives us the victory through our Lord Jesus Christ' (1 Cor. 15: 54, 56–7). In the language of the Book of Revelation, 'the Lamb who was slain' brought a universal deliverance from evil (5: 6–13). Of course, it is paradoxical to identify a 'slain Lamb' as the victor over the world's evil. Yet Paul proposed a similar paradox. Powerful deliverance came in and through the appalling vulnerability of Christ crucified: 'he was crucified in weakness but lives by the power of God' (2 Cor. 13: 4). The viciously cruel crucifixion of Jesus, while symbolizing the failure of suffering, has become the powerful means of human redemption. What Jesus went through has broken the curse of death and the power of sin, so that death itself was transformed into a passage from the dominion of sin into an eternal, utterly satisfying life. For the NT Christians, Christ's death and resurrection meant a triumph over sin, death, and the demonic powers that menace, enslave, and terrify human beings. From Paul's vision of Christ 'reigning until he has put all his enemies under his feet' (1 Cor. 15: 25) to John's 'fear not, I have overcome the world' (John 16: 33), and from Paul's gospel of liberation from the curse of the law (Galatians) to the conflict and victory imagery which pervades the Book of Revelation, we find the NT pressing the language of deliverance into service to express salvation. Central in all this language was the theme that by overcoming sin, evil, and their tragic consequences, Jesus has effected a new exodus from bondage.

No extraordinary theological imagination was needed to make the connection with the exodus from the slavery of Egypt. When he was executed, Jesus had come to Jerusalem for the Passover, the Jewish family feast celebrated in spring at the time of the full moon and commemorating the original exodus (Exod. 12: 1–28; Deut. 16: 1–8). On the afternoon of the 14th of the Jewish first month, Nisan, which overlaps with March–April, the paschal lambs were sacrificed; that evening at the Passover meal itself unleavened bread was eaten with roast lamb. Whether it was a Passover meal (the Synoptic Gospels) or not (John's Gospel), the Last Supper, followed by Jesus' crucifixion and resurrection, coincided with the Passover and its associated week-long Feast of the Unleavened Bread (Mark 14: 1–2, 12–16). Christians quickly came to understand how Jesus' dying and rising had fulfilled the original exodus and its commemoration in the Passover festival. He was seen as the paschal lamb whose sacrifice of deliverance had taken away the sin of the world (John 1: 29, 36). Paul presumed that the Corinthian Christians would easily catch what he meant when he referred to the Feast of Unleavened Bread and the Passover, now reinterpreted in the light of Christ, 'our paschal lamb' who 'has been sacrificed' (1 Cor. 5: 6–8).

Christian liturgies were to take over songs with which Moses and Miriam were understood to have led the people in praising God for their victorious liberation from slavery (Exod. 15: 1–21). The Easter Vigil would include this classic hymn with which the Israelites praised God for their deliverance from Egypt: 'I will sing to the Lord, glorious his triumph! Horse and rider he has thrown into the sea! . . . The Lord is a warrior! The Lord is his name. The chariots of Pharaoh he hurled into the sea . . . Your right hand, Lord, glorious in its power, your right hand, Lord, has shattered the enemy' (Exod. 15: 1, 3–4, 6). While the story of the exodus from Egypt has always remained the prototype *par excellence* of such redemptive deliverance and the new life of freedom, from the earliest times Christian writers and artists found other precedents in such stories as Noah and his family being delivered from the great flood (Gen. 6: 5–8: 22), Daniel from the lions' den (Dan. 6: 1–28), the three youths from the fiery furnace (Dan. 3: 1–30), Jonah from the large fish (Jonah 1: 17–2: 10),[2] and Susannah from the two wicked elders (Sus. 1: 5–59; LXX).

The language of redemption flourishes right from the first Christian writer, St Paul. He tells of the human race being, along with the whole creation, 'in bondage to decay' and 'groaning' for 'redemption' (Rom. 8: 18–23), of Jews being slaves to the law (Gal. 4: 1–7; 5: 1), and of Gentiles being enslaved to 'gods' and 'elemental spirits' (Gal. 4: 8–9). Christ has 'redeemed' or 'bought' us (Gal. 3: 13; 4: 4), delivering us from all those forms of bondage. At times the NT authors speak of Christ 'buying' us at 'a price' (1 Cor. 6: 20; 7: 23), 'ransoming' us with his 'precious blood' (1 Pet. 1: 18–19), 'giving himself to ransom/free us' (Tit. 2: 14), and giving 'his life as a ransom ('lutron' or 'antilutron') for many' (Mark 10: 45; 1 Tim. 2: 6). It is important to note here that the NT nowhere speaks of this 'price' or 'ransom' being paid to someone (e.g. God) or to something (e.g. the law).

In the first millennium and later, some Christians expanded the content of this metaphor,[3] taking 'ransom' as if it described literally some transaction, even a specific price paid to someone. They correctly recognized the hopelessly enslaved condition of sinful human beings, who were set free only by Christ's atrocious death. But in treating the metaphor literally and thus failing to observe its limits, they even spoke of human beings as finding themselves in the possession of the devil, whose 'rights' of ownership were 'respected' by the price of Jesus' blood being paid to release them from bond-

---

[2] This application of 'the sign of Jonah' to Christ's deliverance from death began with Matt. 12: 40.

[3] Along with the primary language of 'redemption' Paul used, as we shall see later, other such metaphors as expiation and self-sacrificing love to express the saving effects of the Christ-event: for a full list of Paul's version of these effects, see J. A. Fitzmyer, *Romans*, The Anchor Bible 33 (New York: Doubleday, 1993), 116–24; and G. D. Fee, 'Paul and the Metaphors for Salvation: Some Reflections on Pauline Soteriology', in *Redemption*, 43–67. The use of metaphorical language suggests how problematic it is to express redemption in literal speech; the use of a plurality of metaphors indicates how no metaphor by itself is even minimally adequate. The role of paradoxes in Paul's letters reveals the difficulty the Apostle felt in stating God's redemptive activity in any speech: see J.-N. Aletti, ' "God Made Christ to be Sin" (2 Corinthians 5: 21): Reflections on a Pauline Paradox', in *Redemption*, 101–20.

age.[4] For the NT, however, the act of redemption was 'costly', in the sense that it cost Christ his life. The beneficiaries of this redeeming action became 'free' (e.g. Gal. 5: 1) or, by coming under Christ's sovereignty, 'slaves' to him (e.g. Rom. 1: 1; 1 Cor. 7: 22). Nowhere does the NT accept or even imply that Satan has any rights over human beings. The metaphor of 'redemption' represents Christ as effecting a deliverance but not as literally paying a price to anyone. In developing his logically structured theory or fully worked out under- standing of redemption, St Anselm of Canterbury (d. 1109) was to vigorously oppose any talk of the devil's 'rights' and, for all intents and purposes, put an end to this idea. However, the notion of a price paid by Christ to his Father developed, flourished at the time of the Reformation, and in some circles has continued more or less down to the present. The next chapter will discuss (and reject) such an idea.

SOME DEVELOPMENTS

Christian liturgy and personal prayer kept thoroughly alive the notion of redemption as a victorious liberation from various evils. The Psalms remained the prayer-book for Christians. Very often the Psalms pray for deliverance from enemies (personal or national) and for healing from serious illness. They also express thanksgiving for the mighty deeds of God, including victory over enemies, healing from sickness, and deliverance from various troubles. The Psalms celebrated as well the powerful kingship of God who prevails over any wicked forces. Deliverance from the evil one was also enshrined in such NT prayers as the Lord's Prayer; the final petition is 'deliver us from the evil one'. The 'Benedictus' (its name coming from the first word in the Latin translation) encapsulates classically the ideas of being 'saved from' and 'saved for'. It prays that we might 'be saved from our enemies and the hand of all who hate us', so we might serve God 'without fear, in holiness and righteousness all our days'. We

---

[4] In the fourth century St Gregory of Nazianzus vigorously protested against the whole idea of divine redemption as a ransom paid to the devil (*Oratio* 45. 22), but for a long time his protests failed to carry the day.

may 'sit in darkness and the shadow of death', but our Saviour will 'guide our feet into the way of peace' (Luke 1: 68–79). These biblical prayers ask for a deliverance that *also* has its impact here and now and is not merely postponed into a more or less distant future.

One of the finest prayers of the Latin liturgy, the 'Exultet' or Easter Proclamation, sung on the vigil of Easter Sunday, can be traced back at least to the seventh century. In its rich account of redemption, it also evokes key symbolic details from the story of the original exodus from Egypt: 'This is the night when first you saved our ancestors: you freed the people of Israel from their slavery and led them dry-shod through the sea. This is the night when the pillar of fire destroyed the darkness of sin.' The 'Exultet' praises Christ for the victory which he has won: 'Rejoice, O earth, in shining splendour, radiant in the brightness of your King! Christ has conquered! Glory fills you! Darkness vanishes for ever!' Then, using phrases which echo some traditional language of the descent to the dead or 'the harrowing of hell', the 'Exultet' proclaims: 'This is the night when Jesus Christ broke the chains of death and rose triumphant from the grave.' By repeating 'this is the night', the 'Exultet' intensifies a central conviction of faith: the redeeming events of Israel's history and of Christ's resurrection from the dead have lost nothing of their saving impact in the present.

By the time the 'Exultet' took its familiar shape, other voices in the Christian tradition had picked up and built on the biblical language about deliverance coming through victorious conflict over evil. An outstanding Latin poet and bishop of Poitiers, Venantius Fortunatus (d. around 610), celebrated the victory Christ won on the cross, by composing two hymns which became an integral part of the Holy Week liturgies in the Western Church: the 'Vexilla Regis prodeunt (the banners of the King go forward)' and 'Pange, lingua, gloriosi proelium certaminis (sing, [my] tongue, of the battle of the glorious struggle)'.[5] Along the same theological lines is the equally famous Easter sequence, or chant sung just before the singing or reading of

---

[5] Over six centuries later, St Thomas Aquinas (d. 1274) echoed this hymn in the opening words of his eucharistic hymn composed for the newly established feast of 'Corpus Christi': 'Pange, lingua, gloriosi Corporis mysterium (sing, [my] tongue of the mystery of the glorious Body)'.

the Gospel at Mass, composed by Wipo (d. after 1046), 'Victimae Paschali Laudes (praises to the Easter Victim)'. This short and dramatic hymn acclaims the redemptive victory Christ has won through his death: 'Agnus redemit oves (the Lamb has redeemed the sheep)'. 'Death and life fought in an extraordinary conflict; the Leader of life [was] dead [but now] is alive and rules (mors et vita duello conflixere mirando; dux vitae, mortuus, regnat vivus)'.

By the time of Wipo, a significant shift of imagery had taken place: from Christ as 'king' to Christ as 'warrior'. The Gospel of John calls him 'King' fifteen times; the Book of Revelation names him 'King of kings' (Rev. 17: 14; see also 1 Tim. 6: 15). The theme of 'Christ the King (Christus rex)' gave way to that of 'Christ the Warrior (Christus miles)', usually the young and heroic Warrior whose endurance wins the victory, despite the apparent defeat of the crucifixion. The hymns of Venantius Fortunatus reflected and encouraged this shift. So too did the feast of the Exaltation of the Cross, which commemorated the recovery in 629 of the cross of Christ that had fallen into the hands of the Persians. This feast seems to have been instituted in the Western Church by Pope Sergius around 689. Christian art had played its part in this development. In the apse of Santa Pudenziana, one of the oldest churches in Rome, there is a mosaic which dates from around 390. A towering, jewelled cross with five red stones (which symbolize the five wounds of the crucified One) illuminates the whole sky above an enthroned figure of Christ.

An OT image played its part as well, that of a warrior with garments stained red who comes to save: 'Who is this who comes from Edom, from Bozrah in garments stained crimson? Who is this so splendidly robed, marching in his great might?' A prophet or a watchman challenges the one who approaches: 'Why are your robes red, and your garments like theirs who tread the wine press?' The mysterious figure responds: 'I have trodden the wine press alone, and from the peoples no one was with me; I trod them down in my anger and trampled them in my wrath; their juice spattered on my garments, and stained all my robes' (Isa. 63: 1–3). Anger and violence characterize this picture of the divine victory over Edom, a hated group who symbolize all the enemies of God's plans for Israel. For sheer ferocity, few OT images outdo this picture of God's garments splashed with enemy blood. Bozrah, with its Hebrew meaning of vintage time, strengthens the image of wine pressing. Single-handed God defeats the enemy. But what was originally a poem about the divine vengeance was strikingly reinterpreted by Christians when they read of Jesus being scourged and clothed in a purple cloak during his passion (Mark 15: 15–20 parr.). They turned the verses from Isaiah into a picture of Christ the young warrior who suffered alone when he came to save humanity. It was his own red blood, not that of his enemies, which stained his garments and body, and turned the cross into a tree of triumph and glory.

The early eighth-century 'The Dream of the Rood', the full text of which is found in a collection of Anglo-Saxon homilies and verse preserved in Vercelli (North Italy),[6] describes a vision of the cross of Christ in which the cross itself speaks: 'Far off I saw the King of all mankind coming in great haste, with courage keen, eager to climb me.' The cross goes on to say: 'Then the young Hero—it was God Almighty—strong and steadfast, stripped himself for battle. He climbed up on the high gallows, constant in his purpose, mounted it in the sight of many, mankind to ransom.' The cross pictures Christ stretched out in pain, pierced by nails, and drenched with blood. 'The Dream of the Rood' gives Christ various titles: such as 'the World's Ruler', 'my Saviour', and 'the High King of Heaven'. But the chief image is that of 'the young Hero' who died 'wet with teeming blood' but became the 'Conqueror, Mighty and Victorious'.[7]

The picture of Christ as the young Warrior or 'Christus miles' became associated with jousting or combat between knights on horseback with lances. His love led to his death on the battlefield, yet paradoxically meant that in the fight he had won humankind.[8] In his *Piers Plowman* William Langland (d. around 1400) portrays Jesus as a young knight who came to a tournament and engaged in combat with the Devil and Death. Seemingly defeated, he was in fact triumphant: 'for Jesus [had] jousted well'. In radiant light he then descends to the underworld, binds Satan with chains, and liberates Adam, Eve, and all the others waiting to be brought up from the depths

---

[6] A long extract in runic form is carved on a cross which still stands at Ruthwell in Dumfriesshire (Scotland).

[7] The translation is taken from H. Gardner, *The Faber Book of Religious Verse* (London: Faber & Faber, 1972), 25–9.

[8] See the anonymous medieval poem, 'Christ's Love-Song', ibid., 38.

to heaven.[9] In medieval (and sometimes later) art and plays, as well as in Eastern icons, Christ often tramples underfoot the soldiers who had been guarding his tomb and descends to the underworld, where he makes his cross the weapon with which he 'harrows hell'—that is to say, defeats the powers of evil and releases its victims. At times it is a lance which he carries, but a lance with a pennant showing a red cross.

In a further twist to the image of Christ as the young Warrior, he was pictured as the Knight-Lover. In a late fourteenth-century poem, 'Quia Amore Langueo (For I am faint with love)', we overhear a love-complaint, coming from Christ himself. The poem echoes a little the 'Improperia' or reproaches of the Crucified Christ to his ungrateful people, which go back at least to the ninth century and have been chanted on Good Friday in the Latin Church.[10] But, as its title indicates (Song 2: 5), much of the imagery is taken from the Song of Songs. A 'gracious' knightly figure, bleeding under a tree and wounded from head to foot, tells the story of all that he has suffered in pursuit of the lady ('my sister, man's soul') whom he loved so dearly. Calling her 'my fair love and my spouse bright', he complains how 'I saved her fro[m] beating and she hath me bet (beaten)'; 'I clothed her with bliss, and she me with thorn[s]; I led her to chamber, and she me to die.' The white gloves of a knight which he wore 'when I her sought', are now red, 'embroidered with blood'. The 'wide' wound in the side of Christ the Knight-Lover is the bridal chamber where 'my spouse' shall 'rest'.[11]

Another (anonymous) medieval love-vision, 'Corpus Christi Carol', also portrays the suffering and death of Christ the heroic Warrior. But it does so from a different point of view, that of a maiden who weeps and prays as she contemplates a dead knight: 'And in that bed there lieth a knight,/ His woundes bleeding day and night./ By that bed's side there standeth a may [maiden],/ And she weepeth both night and day.'[12] This remarkable carol exemplifies wonderfully Caroline Walker Bynum's vision of redemption theology

---

[9] Helen Gardner provides the relevant section from Langland's long visionary poem: ibid., 39–48.

[10] The anonymous medieval poem 'Woefully arrayed' (ibid., 64–5) makes the direct appeal: 'My blood, man, for thee ran . . . Thus naked am I nailed, O man, for thy sake. I love thee, then love me.'

[11] Ibid., 56–60.   [12] Ibid., 67.

in the late Middle Ages. This theology emphasizes blood and suffering and expresses a 'piety of blood', even where the shedding of
Christ's blood is not seen as making satisfaction for human sin.[13]
The maiden in the 'Corpus Christi Carol' who weeps as she contemplates the bleeding wounds of Christ blends easily with the Virgin
Mary keeping her lonely vigil at the foot of the cross or holding in her
arms the blood-soaked body of her Son. The maiden also links
readily with Mary Magdalene and with another figure pictured at
times by medieval artists: the Church as a lovely and noble lady
standing beside the cross.

Back in Chapter 1, we saw how the Scottish poet William Dunbar
(d. around 1520) used interchangeably the language of salvation and
redemption. In an Easter hymn ('The Lord is Risen') he celebrated
Christ as our heroic 'Champion', who did 'battle on the dragon black'
and broke the gates of hell 'with a crack'. Souls are liberated and 'to
the bliss can go'. The poem ends by proclaiming: 'The field is
won, overcome is the foe,/ Despoiled of the treasure that he kept.'[14]
The language of Christ the Warrior (or Champion) and the victory
he won emerged from the NT and lasted for centuries. But does
this language still communicate, and does it truly say something
about the way in which redemption has worked and continues
to work?

DELIVERANCE FROM EVIL

(1) Every now and then someone dismisses images of redemptive
deliverance as 'mythological' and 'medieval': they belong to the
ancient biblical world and to the mythology espoused by Venantius
Fortunatus, Wipo, William Langland, and the anonymous poets
whose works we have just recalled. Who is moved any more by
pictures of Christ the heroic Warrior doing battle with the forces of
evil and descending to the underworld where he liberates the dead?

---

[13] C. W. Bynum, 'The Power in the Blood: Sacrifice, Satisfaction, and Substitution
in Late Medieval Soteriology', in *Redemption*, 177–204.

[14] Gardner, *The Faber Book of Religious Verse*, 70–1.

Yet the huge success of such books and films as *The Lord of the Rings* and the 'Harry Potter' series would suggest otherwise: even (or especially?) in advanced industrial societies, stories of cosmic struggles and victories continue to fascinate and communicate well to readers and viewers. Many critics spurned Mel Gibson's *The Passion of Christ*, but around the world it proved a box-office triumph. Evidently the general public had little difficulty over Christ's victorious combat with Satan, pictured as a loathsome, androgynous figure and as a threatening serpent.

J. R. R. Tolkien (d. 1973), C. S. Lewis (d. 1963), and their friends never doubted the powerful impact on 'modern' people enjoyed by epic fantasies of combat between good and evil, even those written primarily for children like Lewis's *The Chronicles of Narnia*. During Holy Week and at Easter, Christians around the world keep on singing cheerfully versions of texts from Venantius Fortunatus ('Sing, my tongue, the glorious battle' and 'The royal banners forward go'), Wipo ('Christ the Lord is risen today', and 'Bring, all ye dear-bought nations, bring,/ your richest praises to your king'), and other such hymns as 'Battle is o'er, hell's armies flee' and 'Ye choirs of new Jerusalem'. Experience of Christians at worship shows how accounts of redemption as conflict with and victory over the demonic and other evil forces continue to flourish. Eastern Christians have not stopped drawing insight and inspiration from their icons of the triumphant Christ descending into the underworld to rescue the dead from the power of Satan and his minions.

Finally, those tempted to dismiss redemptive deliverance as quaintly 'medieval' language, which had its last hurrah with Gustaf Aulén's 1931 book, *Christus Victor* (Christ the Victor), need to be reminded of the way Latin American 'liberation' theologies have galvanized widespread action. This form of deliverance language has energized people in the struggle against sinful structures of power. Add too the way some European and North American biblical scholars and theologians have perceptively translated the NT language of 'principalities and powers' in terms of state ideologies and controls that become oppressive and even 'demonic'. What the NT says about 'disarming' anti-God forces has been rightly pressed into service in the cause of activating opposition to such latter-day idols.

(2)   A more telling objection finds the language of victory *unrealistic*. Faced with the massive and pervasive presence of sin and evil in our world, how can believers proclaim: 'Christ conquers, Christ reigns (Christus vincit, Christus regnat)'? When we recall the injustice, violence, cruelty, and apparently senseless suffering which millions of human beings endure, how can we justify calling Christ 'the conqueror of sin and death' (Preface of the Ascension 1)? Would honesty suggest picking out and defending that telling remark at the end of 1 John: 'The whole world is in the power of the evil one' (5: 19)? An answer can come by retrieving a distinction drawn years ago by Oscar Cullmann:[15] that between the 'already' and the 'not yet'.

It is important to hit some kind of balance between the fullness of redemption which is obviously *not yet* here and the liberation *already* achieved. The NT is properly realistic. On the one hand, it speaks of deliverance as something which has in principle already happened. Christ has 'disarmed the cosmic powers and authorities' and made 'a public spectacle of them' (Col. 2: 15). Here the image is taken from the treatment of captive soldiers who were stripped of their armour and led in a triumphal procession to display some victory. Christ has already achieved his purpose of 'destroying the works of the devil' (1 John 3: 8). In John's Gospel, Christ even before his death and resurrection assures his followers: 'Take heart; I have overcome the world' (John 16: 33). The Letter to the Ephesians describes Christ's redemptive work as 'all things being put under his feet' (Eph. 1: 22). The First Letter of Peter chimes in: 'Jesus Christ has gone into heaven and is at the right hand of God, with angels, authorities, and powers made subject to him' (1 Pet. 3: 22). On the other hand, the NT recognizes that sin is still active and evil powers can here and now still operate against Christ's followers. Satan remains a powerful force for evil (1 Cor. 5: 5; 2 Cor. 2: 11); like 'a roaring lion he prowls around looking for someone to devour' (1 Pet. 5: 8–9). In a particularly vivid way Paul's Second Letter to the Thessalonians pictures the dire struggle with the mystery of iniquity (or lawlessness) which is now

---

[15] O. Cullmann, *Christ and Time: The Primitive Christian Conception of Time and History* (London: SCM Press, rev. edn., 1962). J. D. G. Dunn remarks on the way this helpful distinction has been ignored by many in recent decades: *The Theology of Paul the Apostle* (Grand Rapids, Mich.: Eerdmans, 1998), 466–72.

taking place before the final return of Christ (2 Thess. 2: 3–10). While insisting on what has already taken place through Christ's death and resurrection, Paul acknowledges that the full working out of this liberating redemption has yet to take place: Christ 'must reign until he has put all his enemies under his feet. The last enemy to be destroyed will be death' (1 Cor. 15: 25–6).

Paul strikes the right kind of balance. Victories of redemption and grace are *already* present and experienced by Christians. They know that through faith and baptism they are enabled to 'walk in newness of life' (Rom. 6: 4). They have experienced the liberating and life-giving impact of the Holy Spirit (Rom. 8: 1–27) and the way in which the former religious, social, and gender barriers have been transcended through being incorporated into Christ. Paul reminds the Galatians: 'In Christ Jesus you are all children of God through faith. As many of you as were baptized into Christ have clothed yourselves with Christ. There is no longer Jew or Greek, there is no longer slave or free, there is no longer male and female; for you are all one in Christ Jesus' (Gal. 3: 26–8). At the same time, the Apostle insists on hoping for the full adoption into the divine life and the full redemption of ourselves which is still to come: 'All creation has been groaning in labour pains until now, and not only the creation, but we ourselves, who enjoy the first fruits of the Spirit, groan inwardly while we wait for adoption, the redemption of our bodies. For in hope we are saved' (Rom. 8: 22–4). Final redemption will complete the being made 'in the image and likeness of God' (Gen. 1: 26–7).

(3) A further challenge to the interpretation of redemption as deliverance through Christ claims that such a view turns believers into *mere spectators*. They watch and applaud as their Champion wins the victory for them, but remain uninvolved themselves. Beyond question, over the centuries some Christians have strayed into this false way of interpreting salvation. But they have done so and do so by missing the clear teaching of the NT and of the mainstream Christian tradition. The recipients of the blessings of redemption must in their turn, through the power of Christ and the Holy Spirit, take part in an ongoing battle against the powers of evil and become for others subordinate agents of redemption. The NT sometimes presents the continuing challenge of evil through the figure of the 'Antichrist' (1 John 2: 18, 22; 2 John 7) or 'man of lawlessness'

(2 Thess. 2: 1–12). In his *Passion of Christ* Mel Gibson seemingly had this figure in mind when he pictured the devil carrying in his arms during Christ's scourging a deformed child, the 'son of evil' who will be in conflict with Christ and his followers until the end of time.

In the NT the beneficiaries of Christ's redemptive liberation are called to take up their spiritual weapons. Paul in his earliest letter cautions against 'falling asleep' through sin or carelessness, and urges the members of a church that he founded to wear constantly their Christian armour: 'Let us not fall asleep as others do, but let us keep awake...and put on the breastplate of faith and love, and for a helmet the hope of salvation' (1 Thess. 5: 6, 8). A decade or so later, the Apostle uses similar imagery when encouraging Roman Christians to live honourably—that is to say, to live up to the demands of the new existence God has created for them through Christ: 'Let us lay aside the works of darkness and put on the *armour of light*' (Rom. 13: 12). When presenting his ministry of reconciliation, the Apostle emphasized how his own 'truthful speech' under 'the power of God' was exercised 'with the *weapons* of righteousness for the right hand and for the left' (2 Cor. 6: 7). In the OT there is a rich source for this language, where it is applied primarily to God. The Book of Isaiah, for instance, echoes Exodus 15: 1–8 and praises God the victorious warrior: 'The Lord goes forth like a soldier, like a warrior he stirs up his fury; he cries out, he shouts aloud, he shows himself mighty against his foes' (Isa. 42:13). Some chapters later, the same book even pictures God as putting on armour before dealing with oppression and injustice and bringing victory: 'He put on righteousness like a breastplate, and a helmet of salvation on his head' (Isa. 59: 17). The classic passage about God's armour and Christian warfare comes from the Letter to the Ephesians. But here it is a question of the armour which God supplies for the continuing combat with the forces of evil: 'Put on the whole armour of God, so that you may be able to stand against the wiles of the devil.' Christians struggle, not so much against 'flesh and blood' or mere mortal enemies, as against the 'cosmic powers of present darkness', 'spiritual forces of evil'. The passage spells out the armour and weapons needed for the ongoing battle against evil: 'Fasten the belt of truth around

your waist, and put on the breastplate of righteousness... take
the shield of faith, with which you will be able to quench all the
flaming arrows of the evil one. Take the helmet of salvation and the
sword of the Spirit, which is the word of God' (Eph. 6: 11–17). The
armour is defensive; the only offensive weapon listed in the entire
passage is the sword, the word which God speaks through his
servants (Matt. 10: 19–20; Heb. 4: 12).

The experience of believers verifies the paradoxical principle
of divine power showing itself in and through human weakness
(2 Cor. 12: 9–10) and of life coming through the struggle with
death. In his Letter to the Galatians Paul moves from the once-
and-for-all, historical event of Calvary, when Christ 'gave himself to
deliver us from the present evil age' (Gal. 1: 4), to note a continuing
counterpart in the life of Christians. In their case the combat of the
passion still goes on. The Apostle declares: 'I have been crucified with
Christ' (Gal. 2: 20; see 6: 14). Hence he can also say: 'I bear on my
body the marks of Jesus' (Gal. 6: 17). To believe, receive baptism, and
suffer in the ministry is to identify with Jesus in his dying. Paul's
apostolic sufferings amount to a continuing experience of death
(2 Cor. 4: 10–11). Yet to share in the crucifixion is to share in that
unique, victorious death which led to resurrection. The consequence
of dying with Christ is a state of life in him (Gal. 2: 19–20). Identi-
fying with the crucified Christ entails suffering evil, finding it transformed into good, and experiencing even now something of the
victory of his life through death.

The Easter liturgy expresses the same conviction: those who have
been delivered through Christ's victory over evil must themselves
become participants in the struggle. The Sequence 'Victimae Paschali
Laudes' speaks, as we saw above, in the past tense: 'Death and life
fought in an extraordinary conflict; the Leader of life was dead but
now is alive and rules.' So too does a modern version of Wipo's
original text, 'Christ the Lord is risen today!': 'when in strange and
awful strife/ met together death and life ... Christ the Lord is ris'n on
high;/ now he lives, no more to die.' But for the followers of Jesus,
death remains a potent force. The combat goes on. The alternative
reading which precedes the Sequence calls on Christians to continue
to celebrate the Easter festival with 'sincerity and truth' by driving
out 'malice and evil' (1 Cor. 5: 8). In short, while Christ has won his

victory over death and evil, his followers are called to continue the
battle and become under him and through his Spirit subordinate
mediators of salvation. Such a call is central to the thrust of various
theologies of liberation. Those whom Christ has liberated must join
in the battle against evil.

Here too the question with which our preface began finds part of
its answer. By being summoned and empowered to join in the
struggle against evil, those set free by Christ *already* experience the
victory he has achieved. The causality at work in redemption also
works that way.

We recalled above one redemptive theme from Mel Gibson's *The
Passion of Christ*, the victory that Christ won over the devil and
death. By opening with a quotation from the fourth Servant Song
(Isa. 52: 13–53: 12), the film also endorsed another interpretation of
Christ's redemptive accomplishment. In and through his atrocious
suffering he dealt with the sins of the world, expiated them, and so
reconciled all people to God. More than four centuries ago Edmund
Spenser (1552–99) also aligned the theme of 'triumph over death and
sin' with that of Christ's blood having 'clean washed from sin' those
for whom he died.[16] This washing clean from sin will be the issue for
our next two chapters.

---

[16] In his poem 'Easter', Spenser wrote: 'Most glorious Lord of life, that on this day/
Didst make thy triumph over death and sin;/ And having harrowed hell didst bring
away/ Captivity thence captive, us to win:/ This joyous day, dear Lord, with joy
begin,/ And grant that we for whom thou didest die/ Being with thy dear blood clean
washed from sin,/ May live forever in felicity.'

7

Penal Substitution Theories

> Who is Jesus except the Saviour?
>
> St Anselm of Canterbury, *Meditatio I ad concitandum timorem.*

> If we have any concern for the clarity of the Gospel and its intelligibility to the present generation, theological responsibility compels us to abandon the ecclesiastical and biblical tradition which interprets Jesus' death as sacrificial.
>
> Ernst Käsemann, *Jesus Means Freedom.*

Some of the troublesome issues about redemption as purification from guilt and sin have already been briefly raised above, when Chapter 1 introduced the language of 'expiation' and its scriptural roots. From the start of Christianity, this dimension of redemption was expressed in terms of Christ the great high priest and victim offering a unique sacrifice that once and for all expiated sins (Heb. 2: 17–18) and brought a new and final covenant relationship between God and human beings. From the Middle Ages, through the sixteenth-century Reformation, and into modern times various aspects of this approach to redemption have emerged for debate. By his theory of 'satisfaction', St Anselm of Canterbury (d. 1109) established an enduringly standard expression for Christ's redemptive work when understood as expiation. During the lifetime of Anselm, Christians, or at least Christians in Europe, were already moving beyond the image of Christ as the heroic, young warrior ('Christus miles') to imagine him as 'the man of sorrows (vir dolorum)' and lamb slain on the altar of the cross. On the eve of the Reformation we find William Dunbar (d. around 1520) mixing the language of 'our Champion Christ' who breaks the power of the devil and death with the language of the lamb prepared for a bloody sacrifice.[1] By that time Anselm's theology of satisfaction was long established but had undergone some fateful modifications. That story can serve to open up this chapter and prepare the way for the next chapter.

ANSELM AND HIS AFTERMATH

When reflecting on pervasive, human sinfulness and the need to make reparation for sin,[2] Anselm argued: 'Every sin must be followed either by satisfaction or by punishment' (*Cur Deus Homo*, 1. 15). Anselm ruled out the latter solution as a way of undoing the past and preparing for a new future. God does not wish to punish but to see the good project of creation 'completed' (ibid., 2. 5). Now satisfaction, Anselm insisted, requires from human beings not only that they should stop sinning and seek pardon but also that they do something over and above existing obligations towards God: namely, a work of supererogation that will satisfy for the offence. However, since all sin offends against the divine honour of the infinite God, the reparation must likewise have infinite value—something of which finite human beings are incapable.[3] Moreover, they have nothing

[1] See H. Gardner (ed.), *The Faber Book of Religious Verse* (London: Faber & Faber, 1972), 70–1. For rich detail on the shift from 'Christus miles' to the 'vir dolorum', see J. A.W. Bennett, *Poetry of the Passion* (Oxford: Clarendon Press, 1982).

[2] From the time of St Augustine of Hippo (*Enarrationes in Psalmos*, 68. 1. 9), Western theologians were encouraged to think of Christ vicariously ransoming human beings by paying the penalty for their sins. The Vulgate translation of Psalm 69: 4 was interpreted as Christ himself speaking: 'I paid back what I never took (quae non rapui, tunc exsolvebam)'. As Augustine put it: 'I had not stolen, yet I paid the price. I did not sin, and I paid the penalty [for sin] (non rapui, et exsolvebam; non peccavi, et poenas dabam)'. This psalm provides a key text for Thomas Aquinas on Christ's passion causing our salvation by way of satisfaction (*Summa Theologiae*, 3a. 48. 2).

[3] Anselm did not argue, as P. F. Carnley states, that 'the sheer amount of human sin demanded an infinite offering' (*Reflections in Glass* (Sydney: HarperCollins, 2004), 140). That would have laid Anselm open to the objection that Carnley correctly makes at once: 'the sin of humanity, though of enormous proportions, is not really an infinite amount'. For Anselm it is rather the infinity of God, who is sinned against, that underpins the requirement of an infinite satisfaction.

extra to offer God, since they already owe God everything (ibid., 1. 19–20, 23). Thus Anselm concluded to the 'necessity' of the incarnation. Only the *God*-man can offer something of infinite value; the hypostatic union or personal union with the Word of God confers such value on the human acts of Christ. Only the God-*man* has something to offer; being without sin, Christ is exempt from the need to undergo death, and hence can freely offer the gift of his life as a work of reparation for the whole human race (ibid., 2. 6–7, 11, 14, 18–19).

Anselm laid fresh stress on the humanity and human freedom of Christ, who spontaneously acts as our representative and in no way is to be construed as a penal substitute who passively endured sufferings to appease the anger of a 'vindictive' God.[4] Anselm's theology of satisfaction had its cultural roots in monasticism and the feudal society of northern Europe. The 'honourable' service owed by monks to their abbots and vassals to their lords was a religious and social factor that guaranteed order, peace, and freedom. Denying the honour due to superiors meant chaos. Anselm's thoroughly logical version of redemption looks vulnerable on some grounds: for instance, his non-biblical version of justice and sin—something obviously linked to the audience he envisaged. He aimed to present a rational case for the coherence and even 'necessity' of the incarnation to readers who were not Christians or Christians with doubts. Apropos of justice, the commutative sense of justice Anselm adopted for his argument seems to picture God as so bound to a fair and balanced order of compensation that it would be 'unthinkable' simply to grant forgiveness without requiring reparation. Likewise, instead of interpreting sin very clearly as infidelity and disobedience which brings a break in a personal relationship with an all-loving God, Anselm pictured sin as an infinite dishonour that upset the just order of things. Although elsewhere Anselm richly recognized the merciful love of God, *Cur Deus Homo* contains only a brief closing

---

[4] We return below to issues raised by this language of 'representation' and 'substitution'. Caroline Walker Bynum has persuasively argued that Christian theology might be better served by abandoning debates over representation versus substitution and retrieving medieval notions of communion with or incorporation in Christ's suffering and death; see her 'The Power in the Blood: Sacrifice, Satisfaction, and Substitution in Late Medieval Soteriology', in *Redemption*, 177–204.

reference to the divine mercy. Given its scope, intended audience, and focus on reparation and not on the sinner's new relationship with God, the book omits some very notable items: (1) the resurrection (with the gift of the Holy Spirit and that major patristic theme, the divinization of the redeemed), and (2) the full significance of Jesus' life and public ministry. For the scheme of satisfaction it was enough that the incarnation occurred and that Christ freely gave his life to make reparation for human sin. *Cur Deus Homo* turned Christ's life into a mere prelude to death. Along with its limits, Anselm's theology of satisfaction still retains its grandeur and fascination.[5] It continues to be wrongly presented as the first articulation of 'the penal substitutionary theory'.[6] But, as we saw above, Anselm explicitly rejected the notion of God exacting retribution by *punishing* his Son in the place of sinful human beings. Such penal ideas crept in later. We can spot the early stages of this change in the third part of the *Summa Theologiae* by Thomas Aquinas (d. 1274).

Before he reaches the passion and death of Jesus, Aquinas has already taken up the Anselmian notion of satisfaction (1. 2). But he does not endorse its 'absolute' necessity. In detailing reasons for the 'fittingness' of the incarnation, Aquinas highlights the destructiveness of sin and the 'repairing' of human beings themselves more than the 'repairing' of sinful offences against God (1. 2, 4). He mitigates Anselm's position by maintaining that God could pardon sin even though adequate satisfaction was not made and by stressing the way love makes satisfaction valid: 'In satisfaction one attends more to the affection of the one who offers it than to the quantity of the offering' (79. 5).[7] Christ's passion is expounded as a meritorious sacrifice, undergone by Christ and truly accepted by God as being inspired by love (48. 3 resp.).

Unfortunately Aquinas went on to interpret the specific purpose of sacrifice to be that of 'placating' God: 'In the proper meaning of the

[5] See D. Deme, *The Christology of Anselm of Canterbury* (Aldershot: Ashgate, 2003); P. Gilbert, H. Kohlenberger, and E. Salmann (eds.), *Cur Deus Homo*, Studia Anselmiana 128 (Rome: S. Anselmo, 1999); B. Sesboüé, *Jésus-Christ l'unique médiateur: Essai sur la rédemption et le salut*, i (Paris: Desclée, 1988), 328–45.

[6] See Carnley, *Reflections in Glass*, 4; see also 75, 76, 84, 132.

[7] In his *Summa contra gentiles* Aquinas stated in an unqualified way: 'the offence is cancelled only by love' (3. 157). It was the quality of Christ's love (rather than the quantity of his suffering or of the blood he shed) that counted with Aquinas.

term one calls sacrifice that which is done to render God due honour with a view to placating him' (48. 3 resp.; 49. 4 resp.). In general, Aquinas dealt with Christ's passion and sacrifice in the light of satisfaction which he saw as the act of a particular form of justice: namely, penance that involves a penal or punitive element (47. 3), an element expressly excluded by Anselm. This helped to prepare the way, sadly, for the idea of Christ being punished and so propitiating an angry God by paying a redemptive ransom. Aquinas himself held that by offering his blood, Christ paid this price to God (48. 4 ad 3um). But he denied that Christ's work of reconciliation meant that God began to love us again only after the punishment was effected and the ransom paid. God's love for us, he insisted, is everlasting; it is we who are changed by the washing away of sin and the offering of a suitable compensation (49. 4 ad 2). Yet, despite some improvements (e.g. the stress on Christ's *loving* acceptance of his passion), the way Aquinas adjusted Anselm's theory of satisfaction helped open the door to a sad version of redemption: Christ as a penal substitute who was personally burdened with the sins of humanity, judged, condemned, and deservedly punished in our place. Thus through his death he satisfied the divine justice, paid the required price, and propitiated an angry God. Thus Anselm's theory about Jesus offering satisfaction to meet the requirements of commutative justice and set right a moral order damaged by sin acquired, quite contrary to Anselm's explicit statements, elements of punishment and vindictive (or retributive) justice.

At the heart of the Reformation initiated by Martin Luther (1483–1546) was the question of grace ('Where/how do I find a gracious God?'), which amounted to the question of the sinner's justification. Two years after it finally opened in 1545, the Council of Trent took up the question of justification, which—as in the case of Luther's teaching—necessarily involved some interpretation of Christ's work as redeemer. In its 1547 decree on justification the Council, when explaining the various causes of human justification, repeated the medieval doctrine of Christ's merit and satisfaction: 'The meritorious cause [of justification] is the beloved, only-begotten Son of God, our Lord Jesus Christ who, "while we were sinners" (Rom. 5: 10), "out of the great love with which he loved us" (Eph. 2: 4), merited for us justification by his most holy passion on the wood of the cross and made satisfaction for us to God the Father' (DzH 1520; see 1523, 1690; ND 1631, 1932). Without offering any definition of 'merit' and 'satisfaction' and without introducing the term 'sacrifice', Trent here interpreted the saving impact of Christ's passion (but not his resurrection) with language that reached back, as we have seen, through Aquinas to Anselm.

The Reformation disputes about the nature of the Eucharist also required taking some stand on the salvific meaning and efficacy of Christ's death (and resurrection). The Council of Trent dedicated its twenty-second session (1562) to the sacrifice of the Mass. It repeated traditional Catholic teaching: the bloody sacrifice Christ offered once and for all on 'the altar of the cross' (DzH 1740; ND 1546) is re-presented 'in an unbloody manner' (DzH 1743; ND 1548), but not repeated, 'under visible signs' to celebrate 'the memory' of Christ's 'passage from this world' (DzH 1741; ND 1546) and to apply 'the salutary power' of his sacrifice 'for the forgiveness of sins' (DzH 1740; ND 1546). The Council could not recognize the Mass as sacrificial and salvific without linking it to the once-and-for-all, historical sacrifice of Christ on Calvary. Trent did not, properly speaking, define the term 'sacrifice', but it did have some things to say about its characteristics. Christ's 'clean oblation' was 'prefigured by various types of sacrifices under the regime of nature and of the law'; as 'their fulfilment and perfection', it included 'all the good that was signified by those former sacrifices' (DzH 1742; ND 1547). This was to place Christ's sacrifice in the context of OT sacrifices and of those offered by other religions. Here the Council relied on a classic passage from Malachi: 'from the rising of the sun to its setting my name is great among the nations, and in every place incense is offered to my name, and a pure offering' (Mal. 1: 11). This generously open teaching from Trent was followed by statements which gave a penal description (not definition). As 'truly propitiatory', the eucharistic sacrifice serves to 'appease (placare)' God, who 'grants grace', the 'gift of repentance', and 'pardon'. Hence the sacrifice of the Mass is rightly offered 'for the sins, punishments, satisfaction, and other necessities' of the faithful, both living and dead (DzH 1743; see 1753; ND 1548, 1557).

By aligning 'satisfaction' with 'punishments' and speaking of God being 'appeased', the Council of Trent accepted penal elements which

Aquinas and others had introduced into Anselm's theory. Satisfaction was now officially depicted as involving punishment. The Council of Trent went that far, but did not go further to speak (in its decree on the Mass) of the divine anger being discharged against Christ as the one who literally carried the guilt of the world's sins. Others talked that way. In place of Anselm's commutative version, God's justice was being interpreted as vindictive—with the divine anger venting itself on Christ, the penal substitute for sinners, whose suffering on the cross was the rightful punishment imposed on human sin.

Protestant reformers did not accept Trent's teaching on the sacrificial character of the Mass, but they had no difficulty in using (and expanding) the language of punishment and propitiation for Christ's sacrificial death on the cross. Luther and John Calvin (1509–64) wrote of a war between God (the Father) and God (the Son). They understood Christ to have literally taken upon himself the guilt of human sin, just as if he had personally committed all these sins himself. He suffered as our substitute on the cross, and his atrociously painful death placated the anger of God and so made justification available for us. This view of redemption as penal substitution was regularly 'supported' by various texts from Paul (e.g. Gal. 3: 13 and 2 Cor. 5: 21) and from elsewhere in the Bible (e.g. Ps. 22; Isa. 53; Lev. 16).

The changes made in Anselm's theory did not remain a Protestant monopoly. Catholic preachers like J. B. Bossuet (1627–1704) and L. Bourdaloue (1632–1704) spoke of God's vengeance and anger being appeased at the expense of his Son. As victim of the divine justice, Christ even suffered the pains of the damned. French religious eloquence, both in the seventeenth century and later, turned God into a murderer who carried out a cruel vendetta before being appeased and then exercising the divine mercy. The merciful initiative of God as the key to human redemption, proposed by John (e.g. 3: 16; 1 John 4: 10) and Paul (e.g. Rom. 5: 6; 8: 6–11, 31–2), had slipped right out of the picture.[8]

---

[8] On the Council of Trent, as well as on Calvin, Luther, and others who developed a soteriology of penal substitution, see Sesboüé, *Jésus-Christ l'unique médiateur*, i. 67–83, 238–47, 280–7, 360–5.

One must insist that the NT never speaks of redemption altering God's attitudes towards human beings and reconciling God to the world.[9] The sending or coming of God's Son and the Spirit presupposes God's loving forgiveness. Through Christ and the Spirit, God brings about redemptive reconciliation by renewing us; it is our resistance to God that needs to be changed. Both John and Paul bear eloquent witness to the loving initiative of God the Father in the whole story of redemptive reconciliation of human beings and their world. Years before Paul and John wrote, Jesus summed up his vision of God in the parable of the prodigal son, better called the parable of the merciful father (Luke 15: 11–32). Any talk of placating the anger of God through the suffering of a penal substitute seems incompatible with the central message of that parable.

PSALM 22

Yet what should we make of the scriptural texts that have been repeatedly cited in support of the thesis of penal substitution? Let us examine first Psalm 22 and its opening 'cry of abandonment' to which some theologians, preachers, and exegetes have appealed in support of their view that God carried on a 'war' against his Son on the cross. Since he cried out the opening words of the psalm ('My God, my God, why have you forsaken me?'), the crucified Jesus was understood to be the object of the divine anger, a substitute for sinful human beings, treated by God as the worst sinner of all times, and even punished with the pains undergone by those condemned to the eternal sufferings of hell. To take one example, Ernest Best appeals to the cry of dereliction to argue for the 'terrible' conclusion that the crucified Jesus was 'himself the object of the wrath of God'.[10]

For Christian believers the NT has made Psalm 22 one of the key OT texts for understanding and interpreting the history of Jesus,

---

[9] See the remarks on reconciliation in Chapter 1 above.

[10] E. Best, *The Temptation and the Passion: The Markan Soteriology* (Cambridge: Cambridge University Press, 1965), 153.

above all his passion and death. Around twelve times the NT authors seem to echo or make allusions to this psalm (e.g. Luke 18: 7; Heb. 5: 17). The NT includes eight quotations from the psalm, in particular Jesus' cry of abandonment on the cross (Mark 15: 34; Matt. 27: 46). The probability, even high probability, that Jesus, when dying on the cross, quoted the opening words of Psalm 22 gives this verse and the whole psalm a unique importance as his interpretation of what he went through. Even if an early Christian tradition or Mark himself put the cry of abandonment in the mouth of the dying Jesus, it remains a precious biblical key for elucidating his passion and death.[11] What should be said about Psalm 22 first in its OT setting[12] and then in the NT rereading of it?

The protagonists of the psalm are the psalmist, God, and the others (evildoers, brothers, the people, and all the nations). The psalm divides into two major sections: the personal lament which is almost an accusation (vv. 1–21), and then thanksgiving and praise for the dramatic change in the situation (vv. 22–31). An antithetic 'inclusion' holds together the entire psalm: it opens with God not offering help (v. 1) and ends by proclaiming the 'deliverance' which God has effected (v. 31). The psalmist suffers atrociously, even to the point of feeling abandoned by God; yet God vindicates and saves him. Let us look more closely at the two sections or the movement from complaint to praise.

The sufferer feels God to be 'far off' or distant in space (vv. 1, 11, 19), absent by 'day' and 'night' or in time (v. 2), and failing to 'answer' or silent (v. 2). The intensity of the psalmist's prayer, but not precisely of his suffering as such, is indicated by the doubled 'My God, my

---

[11] On the biblical and theological issues, see F. Bigaouette, *Le cri de déréliction de Jésus en croix: Densité existentielle et salvifique* (Paris: Cerf, 2004); R. E. Brown, *The Death of the Messiah*, ii (New York: Doubleday, 1994), 1085–8, 1455–67; C. Focant 'L'ultime prière du pourquoi. Relecture du Ps 22 (21) dans le récit de la Passion de Marc', in J.-M. Auwers and A. Wenin (eds.), *Lectures et relectures de la Bible* (Leuven: Leuven University Press, 1999), 287–305.

[12] On this and related psalms see L. Alonso Schökel and C. Carniti, *Salmos: Traduccion, introduciones y comentario*, 2 vols. (Navarra: Verbo Divino, 1992–3); F.-L. Hossfeld and E. Zenger, *Die Psalmen: Psalm 1–50* (Würzburg: Echter, 1993); H.-J. Kraus, *Psalms 1–150: A Commentary*, 2 vols. (Minneapolis: Augsburg, 1988–9); J. Limburg, *Psalms* (Louisville, Ky.: Westminster John Knox Press, 2000); K. Schaefer, *Psalms* (Collegeville, Minn.: Liturgical Press, 2001); C. Westermann, *Praise and Lament in the Psalms* (Edinburgh: T. & T. Clark, 1981).

God' of v. 1—something 'unique in the Bible'.[13] Everything is concentrated in a cry: 'Why am I suffering? Why is God silent and seemingly inactive?' Unlike other psalms, there is no protestation of innocence (e.g. Ps. 17: 1, 3–5), no confession of personal guilt (e.g. Ps. 38: 18), and no call for vengeance on the enemies (e.g. Pss. 2–3, 5–7, and 9–10). Psalm 22 does not offer any explanation for the suffering being undergone, still less any hint about its expiatory value for the sufferer or others.

The repeated 'my God' (vv. 1, 2, 10), rather than 'our God', supports a very personal note in the first section of the psalm. What is happening in the psalmist's personal experience seems radically different from what God has done in the story of the people. Their 'trust' (repeated three times) called for deliverance and salvation from God: 'In you our ancestors trusted; they trusted and you delivered them. To you they cried, and were saved; in you they trusted, and were not put to shame' (vv. 4–5). The psalmist feels as low as possible, 'a worm' (v. 6) who is utterly inferior to the throne of the holy God (v. 3). Nevertheless, in praying to God, he recalls the tender, divine care shown from the very beginning of his life and closely associated with his own mother's love: 'It was you who took me from the womb; you kept me safe on my mother's breast. On you I was cast from my birth, and since my mother bore me you have been my God' (vv. 9–10).

Views differ about the nature of the suffering the psalmist undergoes. Often it has been understood to be a serious illness. He suffers even more when others mock him because they believe sickness to be a sign of God's displeasure (vv. 6–8). Those who favour this view interpret some verses as vividly describing the psalmist's fever: 'I am poured out like water, and all my bones are out of joint; my heart is like wax; it is melted within my breast; my mouth is dried up like a potsherd, and my tongue sticks to my jaws' (vv. 14–15). His feverish state has left him emaciated and debilitated: 'My hands and my feet are shrivelled; I can count all my bones' (vv. 16–17). An alternative interpretation proposes that the sufferer has been put on trial, within a cultural system which, in the case of conviction, involved his clothes being given to the prosecutor or to the one

---

[13] Limburg, *Psalms*, 69.

who arrested him: 'they divide my clothes among them, and for my clothing they cast lots' (v. 18). The powerful men or 'bulls' who persecute him are led by a 'lion'; the sufferer is about to be executed by the 'sword' (vv. 12–13, 20–1).[14]

Whether we follow the first or the second explanation, the enemies of the sufferer are presented as savage beasts: bulls, wild oxen, dogs and a lion (vv. 12–21). Yet they too (as we shall shortly see) seem to undergo a remarkable change, when God intervenes to transform radically the situation. Dramatically delivered from danger and persecution, the psalmist vows to make a formal thanksgiving to the Lord: 'I will tell of your name to my brothers and sisters; in the midst of the congregation I will praise you' (v. 22). Then follows a hymn (vv. 23–31), sung 'in the great congregation' (v. 25) or, apparently, in the context of worship in the Temple. God has once again proved the defender of the 'afflicted' (v. 24) or the 'poor' (v. 26). Powerful human beings have threatened to kill the sufferer or at least mocked him in his serious illness, but his prayer has been heard by God. He has not died from his illness or been sentenced and put to death. God has rescued him and heard a prayer that is very similar to one that concludes (rather than opens) another psalm: 'Do not forsake me, O Lord; O my God, do not be far from me; make haste to help me, O Lord, my salvation' (Ps. 38: 21–2).

Seemingly, the persecutors themselves undergo a change. At all events, the psalmist abruptly begins to speak of 'my brothers and sisters' (v. 22), the 'offspring of Jacob/Israel' (v. 23), and those who make up 'the great congregation' and can join in praising God (v. 25). The psalmist then looks beyond the Israelites to 'all the families of the nations', who will turn to the Lord and worship before him (v. 27). 'Future generations' will be told about the Lord and serve him (vv. 30–1). The divine rule will also extend to the dead (v. 29). Thus the psalm which begins with the cry of an individual who suffers ends with an eschatological vision of God's universal rule.

We have seen above how some of the language from the opening verse of Psalm 22 recurs in the final verse of Psalm 38: 'Do not forsake

14 See A. Lacoque, 'My God, My God, Why Have You Forsaken Me?', in A. Lacoque and P. Ricoeur, *Thinking Biblically: Exegetical and Hermeneutical Studies* (Chicago: University of Chicago Press, 1998), 187–209, at 201.

me . . . O my God, do not be far from me.' Other psalms pray to God for deliverance from enemies or from illness (e.g. Ps. 17), and with few exceptions (e.g. Ps. 88: 10–18) such deliverance is confidently expected. In general the psalms of lament are also psalms of praise and thanksgiving. Yet some illuminating parallels to Psalm 22 are to be found elsewhere: in the prophetic literature.

In a language of being 'forsaken' that evokes Psalm 22, prophets raise the question of personal or collective suffering: 'Zion said, "The Lord has forsaken me, my God has forgotten me"' (Isa. 49: 14). The servant is 'pierced for our sins' (Isa. 53: 5)—a detail which some compare to the psalmist's 'I can count all my bones' (Ps. 22: 7). Yet Psalm 22 differs from the fourth Servant Song (Isa. 52: 13–53: 12), inasmuch as the servant is said to atone vicariously for the sins of others and is seemingly executed and buried (Isa. 53: 4–9). The communal complaints from Lamentations reproach the Lord and plead for remembrance: 'Why have you forgotten us completely? Why have you forsaken us these many days?' (Lam. 5: 20). The Book of Jeremiah, in particular, shares much terminology with Psalm 22: that of being 'despised' (Ps. 22: 6; Jer. 49: 15), 'mocked' (Ps. 22: 7; Jer. 20: 7), being the object of those 'who shake their heads' (Ps. 22: 7; Jer. 18: 16), and being 'formed in the womb and born' (Ps. 22: 9–10; Jer. 1:5; 15: 10; 20: 14, 17–18). All in all, the phraseology and personal experiences we find in Jeremiah line up with the prayer of the sufferer in Psalm 22.

And then there is the book of Job. Those who search here for parallels to Psalm 22 sometimes overlook the considerable differences. Beyond question, both the psalm and Job present someone who suffers dreadfully and whose faith is tested: an anonymous sufferer in Psalm 22 and Job from the land of Uz in the Book of Job. Both cry out their laments; Job even curses the day he was born (Job 3: 1–26). But the two figures differ: the first is clearly an Israelite, the second a saintly Edomite. Job presents the mysterious fate of someone who is quite innocent being subjected to terrible suffering, whereas neither innocence nor guilt is attributed to the sufferer in Psalm 22. To account for Job's sufferings, his 'friends' consistently presuppose a framework of retributive justice, a theme which does not turn up in Psalm 22. The epilogue to Job (42: 1–17) reports God's verdict in favour of Job and the restoration of his fortunes. But this is not the point of Job's long and dramatic story, which reflects the theological sophistication of ancient schools of wisdom. The public praise and thanksgiving which follow God's intervention in the much shorter Psalm 22 form the essential, second part of what happens.

It is obviously helpful to compare and contrast Psalm 22 with a range of OT texts. Yet the other psalms of lament and praise remain the most useful point of reference. While falling into this category, Psalm 22 has its own particular 'shape': in the movement from personal lament to praise in the context of Temple worship, and on to a vision of God's future rule over all the nations. What then of the NT rereading of this psalm?

Mark and the other evangelists (and presumably traditions on which they drew) borrow language from Psalm 22 when they tell the story of Jesus' passion and death. Some language from Psalms 31 and 69 is also reread in the passion stories found in the Gospels. All the evangelists, for example, echo Psalm 69: 21: 'and for my thirst they gave me vinegar to drink'. Mark writes of Jesus being twice offered wine: once (apparently) as a painkilling drink which he refused to take before being crucified and then a drink on a sponge just before he died (Mark 15: 23, 36). Matthew, who unlike Luke and John keeps the double offer, makes the first drink echo more clearly Psalm 69 (Matt. 27: 34, 48). John adds that Jesus himself by saying 'I am thirsty' (see Ps. 22: 15) 'fulfilled the scriptures', seemingly by provoking the bystanders into offering him a sponge full of vinegar (John 19: 28–9). But it is language from Psalm 22 which bulks large when the evangelists tell the story of Jesus' death on the cross. It is understandable that they (and the traditions behind them) would do so, if the dying Jesus himself was remembered as having invoked the opening line of this psalm.

The psalmist complains: 'They divide my clothes among themselves, and for my clothing they cast lots' (v. 22)—a detail of Mark's passion narrative (15: 24) in which Matthew and Luke follow him (Matt. 27: 15; Luke 22: 34). Once again John explicitly finds a fulfilment of the psalm in what happens to Jesus' clothing (John 19: 23–4). What the psalmist says about those who 'shake their heads' as they mock him and his plea to be saved (vv. 6–8, 12–13, 16–17, 19–21) finds its counterpart when the bystanders at the crucifixion 'shake their heads' as they ridicule Jesus and his inability to save himself (Mark 15: 29–32 with the parallels in Matthew and Luke). When the mockers in Matthew (alone) go on to say, 'he has trusted in God; let God deliver him now, if he wants to' (Matt. 27: 43), the reference to what we read in our psalm becomes even clearer: 'All who see me mock me; they make mouths at me, they shake their heads: "Commit your cause to the Lord; let him deliver—let him rescue the one in whom he delights!"' (vv. 7–8). Finally, the 'loud cry' with which Jesus invokes our psalm and then dies (Mark 15: 4, 17) recalls the cry of our psalm (vv. 2, 5, 24) and also of other psalms (e.g. Ps. 27: 7). With these 'last words' the crucified Jesus, according to Mark 15: 34, speaks for the first and only time during the crucifixion.

Some commentators have argued that many details in the passion narratives (such as the offer of the vinegar, the distribution of Jesus' clothing, the mockery which he suffered, and his repeated loud cry at death) were not historically factual but simply entered the narrative through reflection on Psalms 69 and 22 and further OT texts. In other words, the evangelists (and/or the traditions on which they drew) moved from their inherited biblical texts to create events which never happened (e.g. the offer to the dying Jesus of the sponge soaked in vinegar). Yet one can more plausibly argue that through the earliest traditions these details go back to the history of the crucifixion. To be sure, they were expressed and reshaped in the language of psalms and other scriptural texts, but the details came out of the history underlying the passion narratives.[15] In telling the story of the last hours of Jesus, Psalm 22 provided a key source of language; what was originally a psalm of lament and thanksgiving became *the* passion psalm or, more accurately, 'the crucifixion psalm'.

In particular, there is a dramatic shift from the familial confidence with which Jesus, even in great distress, prays on the eve of the crucifixion to God in a distinctive way as 'Abba, Father' (Mark 14: 35–6). On the cross he speaks to God in words that all suffering human beings can share, 'My God' (Mark 15: 34). Mark, who obviously contrasts the prayer on the cross with that in Gethsemane, makes the difference even more poignant by having Jesus in both cases pray in his mother tongue, Aramaic.

---

[15] See R. E. Brown, *The Death of the Messiah*, i. 14–17.

Psalm 22 provides a vivid example of the interplay between events and words through which the saving self-revelation of God is mediated. The central event, the death of Jesus by crucifixion, is beyond dispute, no matter what one decides about secondary items in the passion narratives. Even if we argue—I would say wrongly—that the dying Jesus did not invoke the opening verse of Psalm 22, that psalm remains a key text in conveying the revelatory and salvific meaning of Jesus' death. The meaning has two faces: on the one hand, the physical and mental suffering of Jesus and, on the other hand, the confidence that God will deliver him. Ironically, those who mock the dying Jesus, without realizing it, make clear what will happen: Jesus has 'committed his cause to the Lord' and God will deliver him. When reread by the evangelists in the new context of Jesus' crucifixion, Psalm 22 gains fresh meanings which attest and illuminate the saving self-revelation of God. The evangelists, along with the authors of the traditions they used for the passion narratives, saw and presented to their audience the potential significance effectively present in the words of that psalm.

To sum up: the cry of dereliction reported first by Mark does not represent Jesus on the cross as bearing the sins of the world nor does it support seeing him as the object of the anger of God. Such ideas do not emerge from a careful exegesis of text. As Raymond Brown observes, 'the issue of Jesus' prayer on the cross is God's failure to act, without any suggestion as to why. Nothing in the Gospel would suggest God's wrath against Jesus as the explanation.'[16]

From Justin Martyr (d. around 165) to Thomas Aquinas (d. 1274) and beyond, Psalm 22 was consistently read as an OT prophecy about the coming Messiah who was to suffer. Certain difficulties arose for this line of rereading. The psalm pictures someone who faces a life-threatening situation but who, unlike the suffering servant in Isaiah 53, does not die. Moreover, the (Greek) Septuagint and the (Latin) Vulgate versions, unlike the Hebrew original, rendered the second part of Psalm 22: 2 as 'far from my salvation are the words (or recounting) of my sins'. Given the NT witness to the total sinlessness of Jesus (e.g. John 8: 46; 2 Cor. 5: 21; Heb. 4: 15), talk of 'my sins' obviously raised difficulties for a Messianic reading of Psalm 22.

---

[16] Ibid., ii. 1051 n. 54; see 1045 n. 38.

Nevertheless, many other features of the text encouraged such a reading: for example, the psalmist does not pray for the punishment of the evildoers, and the reversal of the situation brings the promise that all nations will worship the God of Israel. The lack of vindictiveness and the eschatological setting made it easier to read the psalm in the light of the expected Messiah, now identified as the merciful Jesus who brings final salvation to the world.

Above I drew attention to the fateful modifications which Aquinas and others introduce into Anselm's theory of satisfaction. One should also note the major passages in the third part of the *Summa Theologiae* where the cry of dereliction features in Aquinas's treatment of Christ's passion: question 47 (on 'the cause' of the passion) and question 50 (the death of Christ). Aquinas quotes the cry to support the conclusion that the Father 'delivered' Christ into the hands of his persecutors, but did not do so against his Son's will. The Father had inspired in Christ 'the will to suffer for us' (47. 3 resp. and ad prim.) Such an inspiration to suffer for others, we should note, is absent both from Psalm 22 itself and from the way the evangelists use the psalm in their passion narratives. But one should also note that Aquinas differs here from later writers who were to appeal to the psalm in support of the conclusion that the crucified Jesus suffered the anger of God and even the pains of the damned. So far from being angry with Jesus, the Father (according to Aquinas) inspired him with the love needed to endure the passion.

To rebut views about Jesus as our penal substitute who suffered the divine anger on the cross, I have delved deeply into one biblical passage, the cry of dereliction from Psalm 22. Let me deal more briefly with some other passages to which views of penal substitution frequently appeal.

ISAIAH 53 AND LEVITICUS 16

The fourth 'Servant Song' (Isa. 52: 13–53:12) has been used to prop up the position of those who move beyond claims about Christ's vicarious suffering expiating the sins of others to make claims about God transferring our sins to Christ and then punishing him. After all we read in the song, 'the Lord has laid on him the iniquity of us all', and at even greater length: 'we accounted him one stricken, struck down by God, and afflicted...he was crushed for our iniquities; upon him was the punishment that made us whole' (Isa. 53: 4–6). Beyond question, we read here a dramatically powerful song, which NT and later Christians have rightly treasured and used (at times with creative rereadings) in presenting the redemptive work and destiny of Jesus. The NT contains eleven quotations from and at least thirty-two allusions to the fourth 'Servant Song'. By the end of the first century, when the last books of the NT were being composed, it seems that Isaiah 53 had become *the* key text for interpreting the redemptive value of the crucifixion. St Clement of Rome simply quoted the whole of this text when expounding the meaning of Jesus' death (1 Clement 16). But does this passage support the thesis of penal substitution?[17]

To begin with, the identity of the servant in this and in the earlier three 'Servant Songs' is by no means clear: the nation of Israel, an individual (e.g. Zerubbabel or even the anonymous author of Deutero-Isaiah himself), or both the people and an individual. After the return from Babylon the prophet Zechariah speaks of a messianic figure, Zerubbabel, who will usher in the new age (Zech. 3: 8; 4: 1–14), a leader to whom in all probability another passage originally referred (Zech. 6: 9–15). We have only a little information about Zerubbabel, a civil governor who was considered chosen by God to become the Davidic king after the return from exile and the reconstruction of the temple in Jerusalem (Hag. 2: 20–3). The suffering figure in Isaiah 53 could be such a leader, a innocent person who was killed by the community and whose death brought healing to them. Hence they rationalized his death as determined by God (Isa. 53: 4). But this remains guesswork, since we have no evidence about the death of Zerubbabel, whether violent or natural, still less about the fate of Deutero-Isaiah.

---

[17] As a way into the very extensive literature on Isaiah 53, see W. H. Bellinger and W. R. Farmer (eds.), *Jesus and the Suffering Servant: Isaiah 53 and Christian Origins* (Harrisburg, Pa. : Trinity Press International, 1998); J. Grelot, *Les Poèmes du Serviteur* (Paris: Cerf, 1981); R. Meynet, 'Le quatrième chant du serviteur', *Gregorianum* 80 (1999), 407–40.

Whether the meaning is more individual or collective, the fourth song tells of the servant's innocence of life, total obedience towards God, his cruel suffering, his vindication by God, and the expiatory value for others of what he suffers. The servant has been seized, put on trial, and convicted. But is it clear that he was killed and buried (53: 8–9)? Not necessarily, since the language used here turns up elsewhere in the OT without denoting a death (e.g. Jer. 11: 18–20; Lam. 3: 54).[18] Even if we want to read these verses in terms of a violent death, we should note that they do not mention crucifixion as the manner of his violent death. Messianic allusions in the text of the fourth song are slight at best (possibly Isa. 53: 2). Moreover, Jewish messianic expectations hardly show a hint of envisaging a suffering and martyred Messiah, who would be a/the persecuted and vindicated 'servant of God' and whose suffering would atone for the sins of others and so bring reconciliation with God.[19] A *crucified* (and resurrected) Christ was even more alien to Jewish messianic expectations. It was precisely over this point that the Christian proclamation of a crucified Messiah proved so new and even scandalously offensive (1 Cor. 1: 23). The OT contains very little about anyone who might die willingly 'for others' and so expiate their sins. In fact, a death 'for others' is at times excluded; no persons can be freed in that way from the responsibility for their own (sinful) actions and from the need to repent and make appropriate reparation (Num. 5: 5–10; Deut. 24: 16; 2 Kgs. 14: 6; Ezek. 3: 18–19; 18: 1–32). Finally, one should note that the fourth 'Servant Song' never invokes the anger of God. What God plans is to exalt his cruelly disfigured servant and so astonish the rulers of the world (Isa. 52: 13–15).

Having indicated these limits, let me agree that the fourth 'Servant Song' presents the heroic obedience to the divine will of an innocent person whose sufferings can expiate the sins of others. What then of

[18] See J. A. Soggin, 'Tod und Auferstehung des leidenden Gottesknecht', *Zeitschrift für die alttestamentliche Wissenschaft* 87 (1975), 346–55.

[19] We do not have to modify substantially the judgement of H. H. Rowley, who wrote: 'there is no serious evidence of the bringing together of the concepts of the Suffering Servant and the Davidic Messiah before the Christian era' (*The Servant of the Lord* (London: Lutterworth Press, 1952), 85). See also N. T. Wright: 'It seems very unlikely…that there was a well-known pre-Christian Jewish belief, based on Isaiah 53, in a coming redeemer who would die for the sins of Israel and/or the world' (*The Climax of the Covenant* (Edinburgh: T. & T. Clark, 1991), 60).

the language about God 'laying on him the iniquity of us all' and punishing him (Isa. 53: 4–6)? Since it involves a breakdown in a relationship with God (see Chapter 3 above), surely personal sin cannot be transferred? Language about being 'burdened with' and 'carrying' sins, as well as that about Christ 'taking away' our sins, can too easily bewitch us into presuming that sin is a burdensome 'thing' which can be transferred from one person to another, carried, and taken away. The Greek version of the OT (the LXX) seems to show some sensitivity to this issue and translates the Hebrew ('the Lord has laid on him the iniquity of us all') as 'the Lord has handed him over to our sins' (Isa. 53: 6). The same Greek verb ('paradidômi') is later picked up by Paul: 'he was handed over [by God] for our sins' (Rom. 4: 25); 'God did not spare his only Son but handed him over for us all' (Rom. 8: 31–2). We still have to struggle with the question of the suffering of Christ serving as a sin-offering which can representatively cleanse the stain of all sin. But in the meantime the LXX and Paul should stop us from interpreting the intensely dramatic language of our poem in a way that is theologically, and philosophically (I would add), impossible.

What then of the language of punishment and the talk about 'the will of God to crush him [the servant] with pain' (Isa. 53: 10)? First, Deutero-Isaiah (40–55) at times pictures God as inflicting suffering on a people who have ignored or offended their divine Lord (e.g. Isa. 42: 18–22, 24–5; 43: 24, 27–8). Through the discipline of such 'punishment' they can be turned from their evil ways and healed. This is to privilege the collective impact of the servant's suffering in the fourth 'Servant Song'. Second, if we prefer to highlight an individual meaning which prefigures Christ, one should also remember that in the sixth century BC no distinction had yet been drawn between the 'absolute' will of God and the 'permissive' will of God. This distinction allows us to understand how God may allow even his totally innocent Son to be 'handed over' to suffering and cruel punishment at the hands of human beings. Such suffering, as will be argued in the next chapter, aims at revealing God's extraordinary love towards human beings and being the means for purifying a sinful world.

To sum up: the fourth 'Servant Song' deserves to be treasured as a uniquely brilliant OT statement on the value of expiatory suffering for others, and to be applied to the passion of Christ. Yet this dramatically intense poem should neither be pushed beyond what it actually says nor misread as if it were a later theological treatise.

What then of the scapegoat in Leviticus 16, which has also been pressed into service by those who favour a theology of penal substitution? This use (or rather misuse) of the scapegoat goes back to Theodor Beza (1519–1605), who was followed by various Protestant and Catholic authors down to the twentieth century.[20] The relevant section of Leviticus (11–16) dealt with the avoidance and elimination of impurity. This section introduced Chapters 17–26, normally called 'the Holiness Code', since it stressed that Israel must be holy as God is holy. Chapter 16 described in detail the ritual for Yom Kippur ('the day of expiation'). To expiate Israel's sins, an elaborate rite was performed in the Temple, which included choosing two goats. The one chosen for the Lord was sacrificed as a sin offering; the other goat was chosen for an evil spirit or desert demon called 'Azazel'. The rite ended with a scapegoat being charged with the people's sins and led out into the desert: 'Aaron shall lay both his hands on the head of the live goat, and confess over it all the iniquities of the people of Israel, and all their transgressions, all their sins, putting them on the head of the goat, and sending it away into the wilderness' (Lev. 16: 21). The ceremony was intended to symbolize the transfer of the people's sins to the animal, which carried the sins off into the wilderness without being killed. Transferring sins from human beings to an animal comes across as a spectacular gesture but seems quite incompatible with the nature of sin as a breakdown in a personal relationship with God. Moreover, this goat driven away alive into the desert seems a strange candidate for any prefiguring of Christ. The goat was not in solidarity with human beings in the way Christ was, nor could it freely accept its destiny as Christ did. Far from being an 'escape' goat, Christ suffered and died on the cross. In the NT, the Letter to the Hebrews was to use the imagery of Yom Kippur to express the meaning of redemption, but emphasized that Christ, having died once and for all for our sins, expiated them and so made the whole ceremony of Yom Kippur superfluous (Heb. 9: 1–10: 18).

---

[20] See L. Sabourin, 'Le bouc émissaire, figure du Christ?', *Sciences Ecclésiastiques* 11 (1959), 45–79.

THREE TEXTS FROM PAUL

A favourite text summoned up in support of penal substitution theories is Galatians 3: 13: 'Christ redeemed us from the curse of the law by becoming a curse for us. For it is written: "Cursed is everyone who hangs on a tree." ' This has been frequently understood as if Christ 'suffered the divine curse on behalf of others'.[21] In Deuteronomy 21: 22–3 a curse was originally directed against the corpses of criminals who had been executed and then hung up on a gibbit: 'When someone is convicted of a crime punishable by death and is executed, and you hang him on a tree, his corpse must not remain all night upon the tree; you shall bury him that same day, for anyone hung on a tree is cursed by God (or under God's curse).' Hanging or impaling the corpse of a criminal on a tree was regarded as the worst disgrace, the ultimate dishonour reserved for accursed criminals.

By the time of Jesus this text had come to be applied to those who suffered the penalty of crucifixion and were hung up alive on a cross to die.[22] But in quoting this passage, Paul omits the words 'by God' and so avoids the suggestion of a divine curse. On the cross Jesus was cursed by the law and by those who administered the law, but not by God. By dying on a gibbit, to all appearances like a legally condemned criminal, Jesus delivered us—paradoxically—from the curse entailed by the regime of the law and vain human attempts to be justified through keeping that law.

A further Pauline text often cited to back up penal substitution theories is 2 Corinthians 5: 21: 'For our sake he [God] made him [Christ] to be sin who knew no sin, so that in him we might become the righteousness of God.' This verse is obviously laconic and leaves much unsaid. Paul does not, for instance, state that Christ is now 'no longer sin', since God has raised him from the dead and made him 'righteousness' so that we might become righteous by sharing in his

---

[21] L. W. Hurtado, *Lord Jesus Christ: Devotion to Jesus in Earliest Christianity* (Grand Rapids, Mich.: Eerdmans, 2003), 188.

[22] Before the time of Paul, in at least one place the Qumran scrolls apply the text of Deuteronomy to the fate of someone crucified; see G. O'Collins, 'Crucifixion', *ABD* i. 1207–10, at 1207.

righteousness. The connection between Christ 'being made sin' and our becoming 'the righteousness of God' is left unexplained. Moreover, even though the initiative of God is strongly to the fore, nothing is said about the love of God and Christ, unlike such passages as Romans 5: 8 and Galatians 2: 20. But for the purposes of this chapter, we need to unpack the first half of Paul's dense and paradoxical or seemingly contradictory statement about the One who 'knew no sin' being 'made sin'.

Some commentators still understand the verse to state that Christ really became a sinner. Our transgressions were counted against him, and he was punished in our place. Thus R. H. McLean writes: 'Paul teaches that Christ became the receptacle of the power of sin and its curse... Though innocent and sinless, Christ became a transgressor through an act of substitution... A real transfer of sin and curse to Christ was essential. Christ must truly become polluted.'[23] Such exegesis follows, as we have seen above, in the tradition of Bossuet, Luther, and others. It reads the concrete ('sinner') for the abstract ('sin'). Centuries before the Reformation, St Augustine led the way in understanding the passage differently—in terms of a sin offering. The One who was quite blameless and hence fulfilled the conditions to be sacrificed became the offering for our sins. But there are difficulties with this earlier interpretation: for instance, unlike Romans 3: 25, blood and sacrificial rites are not mentioned by our verse and its context.[24] Should we then follow the line of Bossuet, Luther, and others, and conclude that Christ became a sinner? Against such exegesis, Jean-Noël Aletti notes that in our passage God is 'the only active protagonist' and raises the objection: 'How could God, who hates sin, transform good into evil and an innocent person into a sinner?' Aletti then examines a slightly mitigated view: 'God did not transform Christ into a sinner, but associated him with all sinners and charged him with their sins. Thus, even though he did not sin, Christ would be taken to be guilty.' Aletti rightly comments

[23] B. H. McLean, *The Cursed Christ: Mediterranean Expulsion Rituals and Pauline Soteriology* (Sheffield: Sheffield Academic Press, 1996), 144.

[24] For further such difficulties, see J.-N. Aletti, ' "God made Christ to be Sin" (2 Corinthians 5: 21): Reflections on a Pauline Paradox', in *Redemption*, 101–20, at 111–14. Aletti provides an appropriate bibliography for the recent literature on this verse and its context.

that 'Paul does not use a judicial vocabulary here. God is not said to accuse, charge, judge, or punish.'[25]

If we do not follow either Augustine or Luther, who have represented for many the two major options for interpreters, we can glean from Paul's paradoxical statement at least this. Without being or becoming a sinner, Christ endured the deadly results of sin: he was rejected, condemned, tortured, and died. In these terms, the Apostle's laconic verse sums up what we read at length in the passion narratives. Christ was 'made sin', in that he suffered outrageously at the hands of sinners. In an utterly unexpected way, God turned this brutal outrage into the means for reconciling sinful human beings and transforming their lives so that they become righteous (2 Cor. 5: 18–21).

The last text to be examined is a description of God's saving act in which Paul writes of God sentencing sin to death: 'God has done what the law, weakened by the flesh, could not do: by sending his own Son, in the likeness of sinful flesh and as a sacrificial offering for sin, he condemned sin in the flesh, so that the just requirement of the law might be fulfilled in us, who walk not according to the flesh but according to the Spirit' (Rom. 8: 3–4). Unlike the passage from 2 Corinthians 5, Paul introduces here the incarnation, God 'sending his own Son', which aimed at defeating sin and the transformation of believers. Where the law, despite its holiness, had failed, God succeeded in breaking the power of sin and introducing the new order of the Spirit. Paul is not saying that Christ himself was sin, became a sinner, or was treated as a sinner. 'The *likeness* of sinful flesh' parallels what he says in the Second Letter to the Corinthians about Christ 'not knowing sin' (2 Cor. 5: 21). Being sent in the human condition, Christ suffered the effects of sin and lived in solidarity with sinners, without personally being sinful. As Aletti expresses the paradoxical meaning of Paul, 'God accomplished his work of salvation' by making Christ 'live our [human] condition in all its dimensions—except sin. Far from rendering the salvific plan of God weak or even incapable, the passage of the Son through the fragility of the human condition rendered him, on the contrary, fully

[25] Ibid., 115.

efficacious and effective.'[26] Even though Paul does not explicitly mention here the death of Christ on the cross, the reference to 'a sacrificial offering' encourages some to think in those terms and then even to understand the words 'he condemned sin in the flesh' to mean that God condemned Christ, nailed in his flesh to the cross, as if he were a sinner. N. T. Wright understands Paul to say that God punished sin and did so in the flesh of Jesus, even if Wright adds at once that 'God was punishing sin rather than punishing Jesus'.[27] The language of 'destroying the power' or 'eliminating' through an effective verdict seems closer to the Apostle's meaning than that of 'punishing'. Moreover, what Paul seems to have in mind is the way 'sin prevailed in the flesh of humanity not yet justified by faith in Christ'. 'Carnal humanity' was 'inhabited by sin and delivered to its power'. It was precisely where it had prevailed ('in the flesh') that sin was condemned (by God's verdict against it), defeated, and, in principle, eliminated.[28]

ANGER AND SACRIFICE

This chapter has aimed at rebutting the biblical arguments that have been used to support penal substitution theories and so at clearing the ground for the next chapter (on Christ cleansing the guilt of humanity through his sacrifice). But before closing this chapter we need to reflect on the language of God's just or even vindictive 'anger', which some writers and communities still speak of as being propitiated and appeased through the sacrifice of Christ as our penal substitute. Theologians, preachers, and poets have written and spoken in this way, like John Milton in 'Upon the Circumcision'. He recalls how the Christ Child at his circumcision, because of our sin, 'now bleeds to give us ease'. But 'ere long / Huge pangs and

---

[26] J.-N. Aletti, 'Romans 8: The Incarnation and its Redemptive Aspect', in S. T. Davis, D. Kendall and G. O'Collins (eds.), *The Incarnation* (Oxford: Oxford University Press, 2002), 93–115, at 108.

[27] N. T. Wright, 'Redemption from a New Perspective? Towards a Multi-Layered Pauline Theology of the Cross', in *Redemption*, 69–100, at 89.

[28] Aletti, 'Romans 8', 111–12.

strong/ Will pierce more near his heart'. That happened on the cross when Christ 'the full wrath beside / Of vengeful Justice bore for our excess'.

Various translations introduce the language of God's anger and so reflect a theology of penal substitution. Thus the New International Version, after translating 'hilasterion' in Romans 3: 25 as 'a sacrifice of atonement', adds in a note an alternative translation: 'as the one who would turn aside wrath, taking away sin'. The NIV seems guided here by doctrinal convictions when using thus twelve words (in what looks like a commentary) to translate a single Greek term, which, as we saw in Chapter 1 above, is normally rendered 'means of expiation'. Not surprisingly the NIV study edition takes 'the fuller meaning' of the Greek 'hilasmos' in 1 John 2: 2 to be 'the one who turns aside God's wrath' and adds: 'God's holiness demands punishment for man's sin. God, therefore, out of love (1 John 4: 10; John 3: 16) sent his Son to make substitutionary atonement for the believer's sin. In this way the Father's wrath is propitiated (satisfied, appeased); his wrath against the Christian's sin has been turned away and directed towards Christ'.

Sadly the NIV limits to 'the believer' or 'the Christian' what Christ did in atoning for sin. This seems to forget how 'God so loved the world' (John 3: 16) and 'was in Christ reconciling the world to himself' (2 Cor. 5: 19). It looks as if there is no atonement for sin available 'outside Christian believers'. In the use of 'satisfied', one also detects here the unfortunate modifications (about punishment and anger) which subsequently crept into Anselm's theology of satisfaction. Undoubtedly the NIV and the Christian tradition it represents are right in taking very seriously the terrible evil of human sin. But attributing to the NT the notion of God's anger being 'propitiated' or 'appeased' by that anger being directed against his Son does not correspond to what John (e.g. 1 John 4: 10) and Paul wrote. In Romans 3, it is God who lovingly provides the 'hilasterion' or means of expiating the corruption of sin and destroying its power. Two chapters later Paul writes: 'Christ died for us while we were yet sinners, and is God's proof of his love towards us' (Rom. 5: 8). Paul does not say that Christ's death on the cross is proof of God's anger towards us, an anger redirected against his Son.

When discussing 'hilasterion' or means of atonement, Gordon Fee marshals the difficulties against the view that God's anger against sin is propitiated and places the language of 'wrath' correctly. Those who transgress the law, whether the Mosaic law (in the case of Jews) or the law written in their hearts (in the case of Gentiles; Rom. 2: 15), become guilty, are therefore 'destined for wrath', but are forgiven by God. One difficulty with the view espoused by NIV is that it presents God as propitiating or appeasing himself, since in Romans 3 it is God who provides the 'hilasterion'. A second, double difficulty, emphasized by Fee, is that 'in most of Paul's use of the language' of 'the wrath of God', it 'refers to God's *future* punitive judgement on those who have rejected him. Moreover, not one of the occurrences of this expression in the Pauline corpus is associated with sacrificial language. For example, Jesus 'rescues us from the coming wrath' (1 Thess. 1: 10); 'God did not appoint us to suffer wrath but to receive salvation through our Lord Jesus Christ (5: 9).' Likewise, in Romans 5: 9 it is a question of those who have been justified being saved from the future 'wrath'. Finally, Fee draws attention to the fact that the OT never speaks of 'the sacrificial system as a way of removing God's wrath from his people. Not only is that not said anywhere explicitly in the texts, but for the most part a quite different picture emerges. For example, in the great penitential psalms (32, 51) the appeal is to God's mercy and his willingness to forgive sin'.[29]

Fee, in challenging the language of propitiating the divine wrath, certainly does not want to deny that, among his metaphors for salvation, Paul also uses a sacrificial metaphor: for instance, 'Christ our Passover was sacrificed for us' (1 Cor. 5: 7); 'we have been justified by his blood' (Rom. 5: 9). 'One would neglect' the sacrificial metaphor, he declares, 'at one's own loss.'[30] James Dunn concurs. In *The Theology of Paul the Apostle*, he distances himself from talk of appeasement and propitiation of divine anger, but rightly shows how that does not involve dropping the language of 'sacrifice'.[31] Sacrificial language may be open to abuse, but it should not therefore be abandoned, as Ernst Käsemann demanded. In *Jesus Means Freedom* Käsemann wrote: 'If we have any concern for the clarity of the Gospel

---

[29] G. D. Fee, 'Paul and the Metaphors of Salvation: Some Reflections on Pauline Soteriology', in *Redemption*, 43–67, at 59.

[30] Ibid., 55; see 55–60.

[31] (Grand Rapids, Mich.: Eerdmans, 1998), 212–33.

and its intelligibility to the present generation, theological responsibility compels us to abandon the ecclesiastical and biblical tradition which interprets Jesus' death as sacrificial.'[32] René Girard likewise demands a non-sacrificial interpretation of the death of Jesus: 'the sacrificial interpretation of Jesus' passion must be criticized and exposed as a most enormous and paradoxical misunderstanding'.[33]

In this chapter I have put the case against theories of penal substitution that repeatedly draw (wrongly, I have argued) on certain scriptural passages. Christ did not suffer, in order to placate or satisfy the anger of God. Yet he did participate in the human predicament, a situation in which sinful men and women transgress the law, become guilty, and bring on themselves a condemnation expressed by death (see Rom. 5–7). The judgement of God against them was not something imposed externally but was the natural result of their sinfulness. In this situation, by suffering and dying, Christ participated in our death, in order to conquer sin and enable us to share in his risen life. Here some want to include among the deadly results of sin endured by Christ not only the acts of human sinners against him but also the natural consequences of sin which came from Christ's loving identification with the human condition. This meant that he too was 'judged' by God, but not in the sense of propitiating and appeasing God.

Perhaps one can support this picture of Christ 'coming under divine judgement' but not in order to propitiate and appease an angry God. However, as we saw above, the notion of Christ also being under divine judgement does not seem supported by the key passage from Paul and its language of God 'condemning sin in the flesh' (Rom. 8: 1–4).

Our being cleansed from the stain of sin through Christ's sacrifice will be the theme of the next chapter. But it seems appropriate to end here with some words against dropping the theme of sacrifice in any adequate account of redemption.[34] The language of sacrifice expresses the costly self-giving of Christ who let himself be victimized

[32] (Philadelphia: Fortress Press, 1970), 114.

[33] *Things Hidden Since the Foundation of the World* (Stanford, Calif.: Stanford University Press, 1978), 180.

[34] See The Doctrine Commission of the General Synod of the Church of England, *The Mystery of Salvation* (London: Church House Publishing, 1989), 114–17.

by the powers of this world. Over and over again, the Synoptic Gospels show us how he valued every individual, and not simply the socially advantaged (e.g. Mark 10: 21), as unique and irreplaceable. Through love Christ made himself vulnerable, and his loving self-sacrifice produced life and growth; this sacrifice brought a renewed communion between human beings and the tripersonal God.[35] Through a sacrifice which comprises Christ's death and resurrection, along with the coming of the Holy Spirit, human beings were made fit to enter a new and loving fellowship with the all-holy God. Here the root of the term proves illuminating: by Christ's 'sacri-ficium' or 'holy making', men and women have been made holy. His 'sacri-fice' enables them to join him in entering into the very sanctuary of God (Heb. 9: 11–12, 24) and enjoy the heavenly 'banquet' (e.g. Matt. 8: 11). With this brief support for loving self-sacrifice, we move to the next chapter.

---

[35] In expounding Christ's passion as a 'meritorious sacrifice', Thomas Aquinas stresses how, from beginning to end, it was inspired by love (*Summa Theologiae*, 3a. 48. 3 resp.).

8

Redemption as Cleansing through Christ's Sacrifice

True sacrifice is every work which acts so as to unite us with God in holy fellowship, every work, that is, which is directed to that final good by which we can be truly happy... True sacrifices are works of mercy done to ourselves or our neighbours which are directed to God.

St Augustine, *The City of God*, 10.6

Nothing is so needful for us to build up our hope than for us to be shown how much God loves us.

St Augustine, *On the Trinity*, 13. 10.

Many theologians have written about Christ as high priest and victim atoning for the sins of the world through a unique, once-and-for-all sacrifice in which he acted as our representative and which reached its highpoint with his death and resurrection. Variant terms often slip in here: some write, for instance, of 'expiating' sins instead of 'atoning' for them. Debates swirl around the notions of sacrifice and representative (or, as some prefer, 'mediator'). The literature on these interconnected themes continues to be extensive, not least the literature about sacrifice.[1] Let me begin with sacrifice, for which I mounted a preliminary defence at the close of the last chapter.

---

[1] See (in chronological order) such representative works as: J. Neusner, 'Map without Territory: Mishnah's System of Sacrifice and Sanctuary', *History of Religions* 19 (1979), 103–27; F. Young, *Sacrifice and the Death of Christ* (London: SCM Press, new edn., 1983); R. Girard, *Things Hidden from the Foundation of the World* (Stanford, Calif.: Stanford University Press, 1987); G. Ashby, *Sacrifice: Its Nature and Purpose* (London: SCM Press, 1988); S. W. Sykes (ed.), *Sacrifice and Redemption* (Cambridge: Cambridge University Press, 1991); J. Moses, *The Sacrifice of God:*

SACRIFICE

Religious thought, tradition, and imagination persistently relate two items. 'Sacrifice' naturally suggests 'priest'; sacrifices are offered ritually by priests in some kind of sacred setting. Priests serve the divinity at the altar, and perform cultic, sacrificial acts on behalf of the community. St John Chrysostom (d. 407) expressed concisely this connection in his homilies on the Letter to the Hebrews: Christ 'was a priest. But there is no priest without a sacrifice. It is necessary that he should also have a sacrifice' (24. 2). Nevertheless, even from OT times, the language of sacrifice has been used in a wider sense, as being a matter of inner dispositions and praiseworthy behaviour. Thus Psalm 51 seemed to have originally ended by proposing a 'contrite heart' as 'the sacrifice pleasing to God' (v. 17). A later addition (from the time of the Babylonian exile or shortly thereafter) aimed to modify what seemed an anti-cultic sentiment and to bring the psalm into line with liturgical ritual. It asked God to 'rebuild the walls of Jerusalem. Then you will delight in right sacrifices, in burnt offerings and whole burnt offerings; then bulls will be offered on your altar' (vv. 18–19). But the wider, non-cultic sense of sacrifice would persist.

St Paul used the language of sacrifice in both a cultic (e.g. 1 Cor. 5: 7) and a non-cultic way. Gordon Fee rightly illustrates how the Apostle's use of the imagery of *blood* shows how he understood Christ's death in a cultic, sacrificial way.[2] The non-cultic sense of sacrifice was to the fore when he appealed to the Christians of Rome: 'present your bodies (your selves) as a living sacrifice, holy and acceptable to God, which is your spiritual [or reasonable] worship' (Rom. 12: 1). The Apostle called on believers to live self-sacrificing lives. Sacrifice was not merely something that had happened on their behalf; it was something in which they should be intimately involved, even to the point of self-surrender to a new, demanding form of

---

A Holistic View of Atonement (Norwich: Canterbury Press, 1992); I. Bradley, *The Power of Sacrifice* (London: Darton, Longman & Todd, 1995); R. K. Seasoltz, 'Another Look at Sacrifice', *Worship* 74 (2000), 386–413.

  [2] G. D. Fee, 'Paul and the Metaphors of Salvation', in *Redemption*, 43–67, at 55–60.

existence. St Augustine of Hippo also took up the theme of sacrifice in both ways. On the one hand, he declared: 'he [Christ] is a priest in that he offered himself as a holocaust for expiating and purging away our sins' (*Sermo* 198. 5).[3] On the other hand, Augustine stressed the interior relationship of love, without which the mere external performance of ritual would never bring the desired communion with God: 'all the divine precepts' which 'refer to sacrifices either in the service of the tabernacle or of the temple', are to be understood symbolically 'to refer to the love of God and neighbour. For "on these two commandments depend the whole Law and the Prophets" [Matt. 20: 40]' (*The City of God*, 10. 5). It was the interior disposition that gave value to the exterior, cultic actions: 'every visible sacrifice is a sacrament, that is, a sacred sign of the invisible sacrifice' (ibid.).

In the light of Psalm 51, St Thomas Aquinas endorsed a broad, non-cultic account of sacrifice: 'whatever is offered to God in order to raise the human spirit to him, may be called a sacrifice' (*Summa Theologiae*, 3a. 22. 2). Yet in the very same article Aquinas proposed a more cultic reading of sacrifice, or at least of the sacrifice of Christ, who was 'a perfect victim, being at the same time victim for sin, victim for a peace-offering, and a holocaust'. Like many others before and after him, Aquinas drew here on the Letter to the Hebrews. That extensive treatment of Christ as 'high priest according to the order of Melchizedek' (Heb. 5: 10; 6: 20), on the one hand, lavishly used imagery from sacrificial rituals followed by Moses and the levitical priesthood, with the aim of showing both (1) the superiority of Christ's priesthood to that of Moses and that of the levitical priests and (2) the superiority of the sacrifice Christ offered once and for all (Heb. 9: 12, 26–8). Then, on the other hand, Hebrews recalled that Christ did not die in the sacred setting of an altar in the sanctuary of the Temple but in a profane setting, with his bloody death on a cross taking place 'outside the city gate' (Heb. 13: 11–13). Despite the cultic imagery, Hebrews ended with a non-cultic version of the sacrifice of Christ, priest and victim.

The Letter to the Hebrews encourages four convictions about Christ's priesthood (and the related reality of sacrifice). First, we

---

[3] *Sermons*, III/1: *Newly Discovered Sermons*, trans. E. Hill (Hyde Park, NY: New City Press, 1997), 219.

should not simply apply to his sacrifice and priesthood models that we have drawn from elsewhere. We would miss much of what Christ did and does as priest, if we tried to describe and explain it even along the lines of the levitical priesthood, which had been developed by Moses at the command of God. There is something radically new about the sacrifice and priesthood of Christ. We should evaluate priesthood and sacrifice in the light of Christ, and not vice versa. The author of Hebrews, like other NT authors, approached Christ's death and resurrection in the light of existing notions of sacrifice, but had to reinterpret dramatically his inherited images and views.[4] Both in the ancient world and later, sacrifice was often understood as human beings in a cultic setting surrendering something (or someone) valuable to God (especially a victim who was slain), with a view to bringing about communion with God and changing the participants who took part in a shared feast. Hebrews, however, while presenting Christ as a sacrificial victim in his death, explicitly denied that this death took place in a cultic setting (see above), and at best only hinted at a sacred feast shared by believers (perhaps Heb. 13: 9–10). The most startling difference, however, from any 'conventional' understanding of sacrifice which Hebrews and other NT books illustrate is that it was not human beings who went to God with their gift(s) or victim(s); it was God who provided the means for the sacrifice to take place (e.g. Rom. 3: 25; see Chapter 1 above). As Hebrews put it, 'in these last days' God provided his Son for the priestly work of 'purification for sins' (Heb. 1: 1–3). The normal roles are reversed: in this sacrificial process the primary initiative is with God and not with human beings. In the words of Edward Kilmartin,

---

[4] Apropos of the modern situation Robert Daly criticizes pertinently those who approach the sacrifice of Christ in the light of conventional theories: 'We have usually started from the wrong end. We should have tried to learn from the Christ event what it was that Christians were trying to express when, at first quite hesitantly, in earliest Christianity they began to speak of the Christ-event...as sacrificial; instead, we went to look at the practice of different religions in the world, drawing up a general definition of sacrifice, and then seeing if it were applicable to Christ. The usual definition drawn from the history of religions or cultural anthropology is reasonable enough in itself—but when made to apply to Christ, it is disastrously inadequate': 'Sacrifice Unveiled or Sacrifice Revisited: Trinitarian and Liturgical Perspectives', *Theological Studies* 64 (2003), 24–42, at 25.

Sacrifice is not, in the *first* place, an activity of human beings directed to God and, in the *second* place, something that reaches its goal in the response of divine acceptance and bestowal of divine blessing on the cultic community. Rather, sacrifice in the New Testament understanding . . . is, in the *first* place, the self-offering of the Father in the gift of the Son, and, in the *second* place, the unique response of the Son in his humanity to the Father, and, in the *third* place, the self-offering of believers in union with Christ by which they share in his covenant relation with the Father.[5]

Second, whatever Christ did by way of external sacrifice symbolized and expressed his interior self-giving to the Father. Far from being centred on himself, Christ related in love and obedience to God the Father and was ready for painful self-renunciation; he had come to do God's will (Heb. 10: 7, 9). The interior dispositions of Christ made all the difference. Third, his whole life was a continual free gift of himself (or sacrifice) to God and to others. The compassionate service of others described by the Gospels filled out the obedient self-giving through which the Letter to the Hebrews sums up the human life of Jesus (Heb. 2: 17–18; 5: 1–3). A spirit of sacrifice characterized the entire human existence of the Son of God, from his incarnation through to his completing his work of 'purification for sins' and sitting at the right hand of God (Heb. 1: 1–3). It is a mistake to limit Christ's sacrificial performance to his death and exaltation.

Fourth, the idea that through his 'single sacrifice for sins' (Heb. 10: 12) Christ *placated an angry God* seems quite foreign to Hebrews and its teaching. Hebrews never speaks of placation and only twice of God's 'anger', but never of anger in connection with Christ and his suffering. The divine 'anger' comes up when Hebrews quotes Psalm 95 on the rebellion of Israel in the wilderness, a rebellion which stopped the people from enjoying immediately a peaceful settlement in the promised land of Canaan (Heb. 3: 7–11). Sadly the notion that Christ's sacrifice placated God crept into Christian discourse a long time ago. Commenting on Psalm 95, St Augustine of Hippo told his hearers that Christ is 'a priest' through whom 'you can placate your God' (*Sermo*, 176. 5). At the same time, Augustine questioned the

---

[5] E. Kilmartin, *The Eucharist in the West: History and Theology*, ed. R. J. Daly (Collegeville, Minn.: Liturgical Press, 1998), 381–2; italics mine.

view of those Christians who were misinterpreting atonement as if it meant the Son appeasing the Father's anger and thus winning back the divine love for humanity. So far from this being the truth, right from the outset the Son was sent by the Father to forgive and save fallen human beings. Augustine asked: 'is it necessary to think that being God, the Father was angry with us, saw his Son die for us and thus abated his anger against us? But what then could be the meaning of the words of St Paul? How shall we respond to his question: if God is for us, will he not give us all things? Unless he had already been "appeased", would the Father have given over his only Son for us?' (*De Trinitate*, 13. 11. 15). Wherever we place Augustine on the issue of 'placating' God, Thomas Aquinas, as we saw in the last chapter, argued that 'in the proper meaning of the term, one calls sacrifice that which is done to render God due honour with a view to placating him' (*Summa Theologiae*, 3a. 48. 3 resp.).[6] The way was open to those who waxed eloquent about Christ's sacrifice appeasing an angry God.

Many people in the Western world find the idea of sacrificing an animal and especially that of sacrificing an innocent human being to placate an angry and 'blood-thirsty' God strange and even morally repulsive. It seems horrendous to picture God as punishing and avenging. In any case many Europeans and North Americans are repelled by any version of sacrifice. Nico Schreurs writes: 'sacrifices, in general, and blood sacrifices, in particular, disgust most of our contemporaries'.[7] Years earlier J. S. Whale had recognized how for many people the very idea of such sacrifices is 'revolting' and 'both morally and aesthetically disgusting'.[8] In the Western world and beyond, the language of sacrifice seems irreconcilable with contemporary 'ideals' of self-realization and self-fulfilment, the 'good life' promoted by endless advertisements and TV soap operas. Add too

---

[6] Earlier in the *Summa Theologiae*, Aquinas dedicated an entire question to sacrifice (2a2ae. 85). He stressed the obligation to offer sacrifice and do so to God alone, but he never introduced in this context the purpose of placating God.

[7] N. Schreurs, 'A Non-Sacrificial Interpretation of Christian Redemption', in T. Merrigan and J. Haers (eds.), *The Myriad Christ: Plurality and the Quest for Unity in Contemporary Christology* (Leuven: Leuven University Press, 2000), 551.

[8] J. S. Whale, *Victor and Victim* (Cambridge: Cambridge University Press, 1960), 42.

that political rhetoric about dying for one's country which has been employed for two thousand years or more—not least by unscrupulous twentieth-century leaders. For the sake of power, wealth, and prestige, they have debased the language of sacrifice and self-sacrifice and led millions to their death. Perhaps the sharpest criticism of sacrificial interpretations of Christ's death has come from contemporary feminism. Some feminist theologians point out how some traditional presentations about Christ the innocent victim sacrificially offered to atone for the sins of others have been misused to legitimate the sufferings of innumerable women. They have been encouraged to endure all kinds of violent injustice and victimization by imitating the self-sacrificial love and redemptive death of Christ on the cross.[9] For various reasons, one can understand why Ernst Käsemann and others have wanted to abandon the whole notion of sacrifice.[10]

A DEFENCE OF SACRIFICE

Nevertheless, other writers have been thoroughly concerned to rehabilitate this notion. John Moses, for instance, insists that 'no theory of atonement can stand within the Christian tradition if it does not incorporate the element of sacrifice'.[11] Gordon Fee, without privileging it unilaterally, insists on the sacrificial language which forms part of St Paul's understanding of Christ's death on the cross.[12] The Doctrine Commission of the General Synod of the Church of England has protested against any 'veto on sacrificial imagery'. 'To put

[9] See e.g. M. Grey, *Redeeming the Dream: Feminism, Redemption and Christian Tradition* (London: SPCK, 1989); R. R. Ruether, *Introducing Redemption in Christian Feminism* (Sheffield: Sheffield Academic Press, 1998).

[10] E. Käsemann, *Jesus Means Freedom* (Philadelphia: Fortress Press, 1970), 114. In his *Le Salut par la Croix dans la Théologie Contemporaine (1930–85)* (Paris: Cerf, 1988), Michel Deneken put the case for simply banishing 'sacrifice' from Christian vocabulary. At the end of the last chapter, we noted the anti-sacrificial attitude of René Girard and his followers; for him Christ's death enjoyed a salvific impact precisely by abolishing sacrifice.

[11] J. Moses, *The Sacrifice of God*, 122.

[12] G. D. Fee, 'Paul and the Metaphors for Salvation', in *Redemption*, 55–60.

a moratorium on all sacrificial language', it declared, 'would be to cut ourselves off from one of the primary biblical images of salvation. A vital dimension of biblical revelation would be lost. Sacrifice is one of the most prominent images for the death of Christ in the New Testament.'[13] Undoubtedly the language of sacrifice and self-sacrifice has at times been misused massively, but the NT witness makes it a normative way of characterizing Christ's death and resurrection. Moreover, in ordinary speech and journalism it turns up regularly and helpfully when describing, for instance, how someone has died in rescuing another person in mortal danger. In the case of Christ's death we can and should continue to use this language, provided we hold on to *five positions.*

First, the meaning of Christ's death is not to be reduced to its *simply* being an expiatory sacrifice which cleansed the 'pollution' of sin. The Letter to the Hebrews, our longest NT sacrificial treatment of Christ's death, does not do that. Repeatedly it *also* interprets that death and its aftermath as sealing a new covenantal relationship between God and human beings (e.g. 9: 15; 12: 24). The OT itself understood sacrifices as involving at least overlapping categories: gift-offerings, sin-offerings, and communion-offerings. Thus the sacrificial elements connected with the Jewish Passover, for instance, did not involve a sin-offering, but a gift-offering of praise and thanksgiving for the deliverance from slavery.[14] Second, the OT teaches that external rituals were worthless without the corresponding interior dispositions and compassionate behaviour. One psalm acknowledges that doing God's will counts more than any formal sacrifices of thanksgiving (Ps. 40: 6–8); these verses are quoted and endorsed by Hebrews 10: 5–7. Matthew explains Jesus' practice of forgiveness by having him quote Hosea 6: 6 and so challenge conventional ideas about divine forgiveness and sacrificial sin-offerings: 'I desire mercy, not sacrifice' (Matt. 9: 13; see 12: 7).

---

[13] *The Mystery of Salvation: The Story of God's Gift* (London: Church House Publishing, 1995), 115.

[14] See G. A. Anderson and H. J. Klauck, 'Sacrifice and Sacrificial Offerings', *ABD* v. 871–91; G. B. Grey, *Sacrifice in the Old Testament: Its Theory and Practice* (1st edn., 1925; New York: Ktav, 1971); J. Henninger, 'Sacrifice', in M. Eliade (ed.), *The Encyclopedia of Religion*, xii (London: Collier Macmillan, 1987), 544–57, R. de Vaux, *Studies in Old Testament Sacrifice* (Cardiff: University of Wales Press, 1964).

Most emphatically, a wise scribe reacts to Jesus' teaching on love towards God and one's neighbour by declaring that practising such love 'is much more important than all burnt offerings and sacrifices' (Mark 12: 33). Micah provides the OT background to this statement: rather than all manner of burnt offerings and other sacrifices, what God expects of his people is 'to do justice, and to love kindness, and to walk humbly with your God' (Mic. 6: 6–8). Aquinas, as we saw in the last chapter, stressed Christ's *loving* acceptance of his passion and the way love provides validity for works of satisifaction.

This stress on an inner relationship of love leads on to the third point. Physical pain and other forms of suffering simply as such do not atone for sins and effect human redemption. 'Suffering as such', Aquinas argues, 'is not meritorious'. Only insofar as someone 'suffers willingly' can suffering become 'meritorious' (*Summa Theologiae*, 3a. 48. 1 ad 1). Only because Christ 'suffered out of love' was his death a 'sacrifice' (ibid., 3a. 48. 4 ad 3). This third point ties in closely with a fourth conviction: the sheer quantity of suffering which Jesus endured in his atrocious death is not the central concern. The Letter to the Hebrews invokes his sufferings (Heb. 5: 7–8) but, unlike Mel Gibson in his *The Passion of Christ* and many before him, makes no attempt to highlight or even mention the amount of those sufferings. Gibson concentrates on the physical suffering endured by Christ, in order to bring out the enormity of human sin. But the sheer amount of that suffering is not nearly as important as the identity of the One who suffered to save a world enormously damaged by sin; that identity is underlined by Hebrews right from its opening verses.

Fifth, the death of Jesus came about through a mysterious convergence of human malice and divine love. Back in the fourth century BC, Plato suggested in the introduction to Book II of his *Republic* the kind of fate a perfectly just man could expect: 'The just man, then, as we have pictured him, will be scourged, tortured, and imprisoned. His eyes will be put out, and after enduring every humiliation, he will be crucified.' Christians found this passage to be a remarkable pagan prophecy of what happened to Jesus. Prophecy or not, Plato's words have been fulfilled with depressing frequency. Society continues to make uncompromisingly good individuals suffer both for what they are and for what they try to do. In the case of Jesus we meet someone who was not only perfectly just but also perfectly loving. The wonder is not so much that he was struck down quickly as that he lasted as long as he did. Plato helps us with our answer to the question: did Jesus *have to* suffer and die?

This question comes up when we recall the reproach directed at the two disciples on the road to Emmaus: 'Was it not necessary that the Christ should suffer these things and enter into his glory?' (Luke 24: 26). The passion predictions in the Synoptic Gospels spoke in similar tones: 'The Son of Man *must* suffer many things . . . and be killed and after three days rise again' (Mark 8: 31 parr.). St Paul cited a very early Christian credal statement which also struck the note of necessity: 'Christ died for our sins according to the scriptures' (1 Cor. 15: 3). Those who knew their scriptures could see that the crucifixion *had* to be. The first Christians recognized in the crucifixion much more than human malice which put a violent end to Christ's life. They acknowledged that in the divine plan it needed to be so. What sense can we discern in this 'must' of Jesus' death? If we take up the 'must' of Calvary on the historical level, we can appreciate why it was unavoidable in human terms. At all times in the history of the human race, prophets have been persecuted for refusing to be accommodating and for insisting on faithfully transmitting some message from God. Jesus' fidelity to his mission inevitably brought him into conflict with the ruling classes. In such a conflict he was, humanly speaking, bound to lose. Even a moderately astute analyst of politico-religious affairs in first-century Palestine would have reached that conclusion. Human malice made Jesus' suffering and death inevitable.

Besides such malice, something else fed into the 'must' of Jesus' passion: his own unswerving loyalty to his mission and the service of others. In these terms, Calvary became the inevitable consequence of a commitment which he refused to abandon even at the cost of his life. This loyalty prevented him from escaping, even though his actions placed him at risk and set him on a deadly collision course with those in power. By continuing his ministry, going to Jerusalem for his last Passover, and facing his opponents, Jesus indirectly brought about the fatal situation. In that sense he *willed his death by accepting it* rather than by deliberately and directly courting it. His love, as we shall argue in the next chapter, made him vulnerable, even unto death. He paid the price for his loving project of bringing life to the world. Thus we can see how the self-sacrificing death of Jesus was

not due to his positive and direct will (or to that of his Father) but to
the abuse of human freedom on the part of religious and political
leaders whose vested interests were threatened by the uncompromis-
ing message of Jesus. John's Gospel captures classically the uncon-
scious irony of the way murderous human calculations against a highly
vulnerable individual converged with God's plan of redemption.
Caiaphas, the high priest at the time of Jesus' death, suggested to the
Sanhedrin his solution for the threat Jesus posed to their uneasy
political arrangements with the Roman administration: 'it is better
for you to have one man die for the people than to have the whole
nation destroyed'. The evangelist comments: 'He did not say this on
his own, but being the high priest that year he prophesied that Jesus
was about to die for the nation, and not for the nation only, but to
gather into one the scattered children of God' (John 11: 49–52).

The NT captures this mysterious convergence of divine and human
decisions and actions in Christ's death by applying the same verb to
the human perpetrators and to the divine protagonists: 'hand over
(paradidômi)'. Judas agreed to hand Jesus over at a price (Mark 14:
10–11); the religious authorities handed Jesus over to Pilate the
Roman governor (Mark 15: 1, 10); and then Pilate handed Jesus
over to be crucified (Mark 15: 15). Thus Jesus became a victim of
human sinfulness. Yet Paul writes about the unswerving, faithful love
of Jesus who would not run away: 'he loved me and handed himself
over for me' (Gal. 2: 20). By allowing his only-begotten Son to
become and remain vulnerable to the malicious decisions of human
beings, God too was involved in the 'handing over': 'He did not spare
his own Son but handed him over for us all' (Rom. 8: 32; see 4: 25).
Human malice and divine love astonishingly 'joined forces' in
effecting a 'handing over' to death (and resurrection) which brought
our redemption. Centuries earlier wicked men inflicted dreadful
suffering on the mysterious Servant of the Lord; the acts which belong
to these perpetrators (the secondary causes) are attributed to God
(Isa. 53: 4, 10). No distinction was yet drawn between the decisions
and actions of secondary causes and God, the primary cause.

To sum up: far from dismissing the crucifixion as merely the tragic
result of human sin, we are justified in continuing to apply the
language of sacrifice to the death (and resurrection) of Jesus for at
least four reasons. First, he died because of his self-sacrificing love,

about which the next chapter will have more to say. Second, from the outset of Christianity, his passion, death, and resurrection were linked with the Passover season and its rites of worship (e.g. 1 Cor. 5: 7). Before facing death, the ritual language and actions of the Last Supper signalled a holy fellowship or communion with God, a new covenant relationship offered by God and accepted by Jesus for the benefit of all people.[15] By introducing 'the means of expiation (hilastêrion)', Paul initiated the link between Christ's death and resurrection (and exaltation) and the rituals of the great 'Day of Expiation (Yom Kippur)'—a link then developed massively in the Letter to the Hebrews. The cultic ceremonies of the Passover and Yom Kippur illuminated for NT Christians some of the sacrificial characteristics of what Christ went through. Third, through being drawn into this divine initiative, Christians experienced themselves as undergoing a process of 'sacrum-facere' or being 'made holy' or consecrated by the all-holy God, who alone can make us holy. Fourth, through celebrating this new fellowship in sacred rites (above all through baptism and the Eucharist), they dedicated themselves to the service of God and others in that wider, non-cultic sense of sacrifice we found in Paul (Rom. 12: 1) and others.

Above I argued that the death of Christ is not to be reduced to being an *expiatory* sacrifice which cleansed the pollution of sin. Nevertheless, expiation remains part of the whole story, and we must take up the challenge involved in also maintaining this language.[16]

EXPIATION

To introduce the topic we need to notice that, whereas redemption as victory enjoys a broader sense of overcoming not only sin but also

[15] On Jesus' intentions when faced with death and celebrating the Last Supper, see G. O'Collins, *Christology: A Biblical, Historical, and Systematic Study of Jesus* (Oxford: Oxford University Press, rev. edn., 2004), 67–81.

[16] See H. Hübner, 'Sühne und Versöhnung: Anmerkungen zu einem umstrittenen Kapitel Biblischer Theologie', *Kerygma und Dogma* 29 (1983), 284–305; B. F. Meyer, "The Expiation Motif in the Eucharistic Words: A Key to the History of Jesus?', *Gregorianum* 69 (1988), 461–87; A. Schenker, 'Kôper et Expiation', *Biblica* 63 (1982), 32–46.

Satan, death, and evil in all its forms, expiation concerns sin. It would not make sense to talk of 'expiating death' or 'expiating Satan'. The great day of expiation, Yom Kippur, illustrates classically how sin and expiation are correlative. Any interpretation of expiation depends on what we make of the damage brought by a breakdown in relations with God and our neighbour that constitutes sin (see Chapter 3 above).

Sin, in all its various manifestations, disrupts the life and fabric of the universe. Things become out of place and not as they should be. Wrongdoing damages the sinner and brings evil effects in our social relationships and our basic relationship with God. Flouting the moral order does harm, sometimes great and lasting harm. God is always ready to pardon sinners who allow themselves to be touched by divine grace, acknowledge their guilt, and ask for forgiveness. But God cannot treat an evil past and the lasting damage done by sin as if they were not there. Otherwise, as St Anselm pointed out, 'those who sin and those who do not sin would be in the same position before God' (*Cur Deus Homo*, 1. 12). Anselm rightly argued that 'it is impossible for God to be merciful in this way' (ibid., 1. 24). First, sinners themselves need to be changed, to face (sometimes painful) readjustment, and to be rehabilitated. Second, some things, at times many things, need to be repaired and set right. The moral order, damaged by sin, needs to be reordered. This is where expiation comes into play.

Early Christians felt at home with the OT language of purifying the contamination created by sin. Their symbol-world included cleansing with blood among the ritual ways of dealing with the evil effects of sin. They could appreciate that the sacrificial death of Jesus was the 'means of expiating' these effects through 'his blood' (Rom. 3: 25), and that 'the blood of Jesus' 'purifies us' (1 John 1: 7). When we move beyond the NT world to the first centuries of Christianity, there is much to report in this area. Tullio Veglianti, for instance, has edited fourteen volumes of texts about the blood of Christ drawn from the Greek, Latin, Syriac, and other patristic authors (with a parallel translation in Italian).[17] Many later Christians also felt at ease with

---

[17] T. Veglianti, *Testi Patristici sul Sangue di Cristo*, 14 vols. (Rome: Pia Unione Preziosissimo Sangue, 1992–2003). For the piety and theology of blood in medieval redemption theory, see C. W. Bynum, 'The Power in the Blood: Sacrifice, Satisfaction, and Substitution in Late Medieval Soteriology', in *Redemption*, 177–204.

this language of Christ's self-sacrificing death wiping away the pollution caused by sin. Thomas Aquinas (d. 1274) held that moral wrongdoing of a serious kind leaves a 'stain' on the soul, even though the sinner repents of his evil action. Different kinds of wrongdoing can 'stain' the soul in different ways, and call for various cleansing.[18] Aquinas provided 'much food for verse' and not least in the case of Dante Alighieri (d. 1321). In his *Purgatorio* Dante emphasized the purification of repentant sinners, with the purification corresponding to the kinds of sin which they had committed and of which they had repented. In *Paradiso* Dante was to expound Anselm's theory of satisfaction (Canto 7), but it was the cleansing of the enduring defilement left by wrongdoing that shaped the second part of the *Divine Comedy*. More than two centuries later Shakespeare reached for such images, not least in *Macbeth*. Scotland has been defiled by repeated and horrible crimes and sins; the need to purge away this filth recurs in the closing scenes. When she walks in her sleep, Lady Macbeth rubs her hands together as if to wash them and exclaims: 'Out, damned spot, out'. (Act V, Scene i).

The distaste which many people, including many Christians, in advanced industrial societies show toward the language of 'blood' and any talk of the innocent Christ cleansing guilty sinners from the contamination of their sin shows up in some modern translations.[19] The 1961 NEB (New English Bible) translation of the NT rendered 'hilasmos' in 1 John 2: 2 (and 1 John 4: 10) as 'the remedy for the defilement' ('of our sins'). In the REB (Revised English Bible) of 1989 this became 'a sacrifice to atone' ('for our sins'); any echo of the high priest each year on Yom Kippur smearing blood on the mercy seat (the 'hilasterion') to wipe away the defilement accumulated from the people's sins became fainter. The NEB had already backed away from the blood of Jesus when translating Romans 3: 25 by replacing it with 'sacrificial death': 'God designed him to be the means of expiating sin by his sacrificial death'. The REB saw no reason to restore 'blood' and maintained the identical translation. The concrete image of blood

---

[18] *Summa Theologiae*, 1a2ae. 86. 1–2; 87. 6; 89. 1.

[19] Over 900 years ago in Anselm's dialogue *Cur Deus Homo*, Boso gave voice to this distaste: 'It is surely to be wondered at, if God so derives delight from, or has need of, the blood of the innocent, that he neither wishes nor is able to spare the guilty without the death of the innocent' (1. 10).

used by Paul remains lost. Other modern translations, at least here and there, show a reluctance to mention the blood of Jesus. The most extreme example has to be *Good News for Modern Man*, the NT in *Today's English Version*. It often refuses to translate exactly references to Jesus' blood and introduces a vaguer term, death. Thus it renders Colossians 1: 20: 'Through his Son, then, God decided to bring the whole universe back to himself. God made peace through his Son's death ['blood' in the original Greek] on the cross'.

Nevertheless, as we saw in Chapter 3, Mary Douglas argued in a 1993 study for a universal feeling that sin defiles human beings. Decades earlier she had studied the widespread sense of purity and defilement, pointing out that behind the Code of Holiness in Leviticus and its distinction between clean and unclean lay a common concern for order and completeness. 'Holiness', she wrote, 'means keeping distinct the categories of creation. It therefore involves correct definition, discrimination and order.'[20] The pollution of sin brings dangerous disorder and fragmentation; things must be brought back to harmony and wholeness. Drawing on Douglas, Colin Gunton concluded that 'we shall ... begin to understand the nature of sacrifice when we come to see its function in the removal of uncleanness which pollutes the good creation'.[21]

'Reordering and repairing a world damaged by sin' catches the drift of expiation. But one need not surrender the rich symbolism involved in Paul's language about cleansing sin through the blood of Christ.[22] Israelites remembered how before leaving Egypt they smeared their doorposts with the blood of a lamb (Exod. 12: 7, 13, 22–3). The sign delivered them from the destruction which afflicted the homes of the Egyptians. The blood of the Passover lamb saved the Israelites from losing their firstborn.

[20] Mary Douglas, *Purity and Danger* (London: Penguin, 1970), 53. See also D. P. Wright and H. Hübner, 'Unclean and Clean', *ABD* vi. 729–45.

[21] C. E. Gunton, *The Actuality of Atonement: A Study of Metaphor, Rationality and the Christian Tradition* (Edinburgh: T. & T. Clark, 1988), 119.

[22] See S. D. Sperling, 'Blood', *ABD* i. 761–3; the bibliography does not include several enduringly valuable articles by D. J. McCarthy, 'Blood', *The Interpreter's Dictionary of the Bible*, Supplementary volume (Nashville: Abingdon Press, 1976), 114–17; id., 'The Symbolism of Blood and Sacrifice', *Journal of Biblical Literature* 88 (1969), 166–76; id., 'Further Notes on the Symbolism of Blood and Sacrifice', ibid. 92 (1973), 205–10.

Besides being a sign that brought deliverance from death, blood was closely associated with life. The Israelites understood life to be 'in the blood' (Lev. 17: 11–14; Deut. 12: 23). Since life was sacred, they regarded blood also as sacred. YHWH was the God of life. Hence blood, the seat of life, belonged to God alone. In the ancient Near East and Middle East the Israelites appear to have differed from all their neighbours in linking blood with life and hence with what was sacred and divine. Dennis McCarthy showed how this was a uniquely Hebrew notion—at least in the symbolism dealing with sacrifice. In its own way modern science has more than vindicated the OT conviction that life, the divine and sacred gift *par excellence*, is 'in the blood'. Oxygen, nutrients, hormones, and other items essential for life are carried by our blood. Its complex structure enables us to endure wide variations of temperature and changes of diet. Every day around the world massive transfusions of blood save lives that are slipping away. Medical discoveries and practice have dramatically associated the miracle of life with the miracle of blood.

As well as expressing deliverance and life, blood was believed to cleanse the stains left by human sin. At Yom Kippur, as we have seen, the high priest sprinkled blood as part of a ritual expressing God's willingness to purify the Israelites from the contamination caused by their sins. Today we may not relish the practice of slaughtering bulls and goats to release and use their blood in rituals. But we should still be able to recognize the religious logic of the Israelites. Insofar as it was the element in which life resided, blood enjoyed a peculiarly divine and sacred character. Hence it appropriately served to blot out the effects of sin and the restoration of harmonious relations between YHWH and his people. For millions of Christians nowadays, sprinkling with water exercises a similar role, as sign and symbol of the effects of their sins being washed away.

But we need to go a step further here. One may agree about the need for expiating and 'cleansing the stains' left by evil. But how can this be done *for us by another*? It seems easier to appreciate that Christ won a redemptive victory not merely for himself but also for others. But how could he 'remove the stain' left by the sin of others and repair the results of their evil actions through his death and resurrection? How could his unmerited suffering restore a damaged moral order? In what way can we conceive his relationship as 'Expiator' with the beneficiaries of his expiatory action?

CHRIST AS REPRESENTATIVE?

In the witness of the NT, three prepositions illuminate the role of Christ: 'anti', 'huper', and 'peri'. (1) 'Anti', which can mean 'on behalf of' or 'instead of' ('in place of'), occurs in a classic passage of Mark's Gospel: 'the Son of Man has come not to be served but to serve and give his life as a ransom for many' (10: 45). Jesus speaks here of giving his life and death to gain the release of 'many'. He acts 'on their behalf' (with 'anti' functioning as equivalent to 'huper') and 'to their advantage'. Some writers still read 'anti' as implying substitution: the Son of Man came to give his life as a substitute for many.[23] (2) 'Huper' normally means 'for the sake of' or 'on behalf of', as in 'my body given for you' and 'cup poured out for you' (Luke 22: 19–20). But it can mean 'on account of', as in the early proclamation quoted by Paul: 'Christ died for our sins' (1 Cor. 15: 3). (3) While normally meaning 'concerning' or 'about', 'peri' can also connote 'on account of', 'because of', or 'for', and so can coincide with 'huper'. Thus in Matthew's narrative of the Lord's Supper Jesus speaks of the cup which 'is poured out for many' (26: 28). When used with 'sin (hamartia)', 'peri' carries the sense of 'atoning for sin' (e.g. 1 John 4: 10).

This and related NT language has prompted two pictures of what happened in Christ's sacrifice of expiation. (1) Some, as the last chapter recalled, interpret the biblical data to mean that Jesus as a substitute was personally burdened with the sins of humanity, judged, condemned, and deservedly punished in our place; through his death he thus satisfied the divine justice and propitiated an angry God. This theology of penal substitution directly attributes Christ's passion and death to God's 'vindictiveness' rather than to human violence and cruelty. We have challenged (Chapters 1 and 7)

---

[23] J. McIntyre, *The Shape of Soteriology: Studies in the Doctrine of the Death of Christ* (Edinburgh: T. & T. Clark, 1992), 90.

the interpretation of some biblical passages to which this view appeals. It also forgets that, while sometimes speaking of the divine anger (e.g. Rom. 1: 18; 2: 5, 8; 12: 19; 13: 4–5), the NT never associates that anger with Christ's suffering and death. (2) Others press the picture of representation. Christ acted 'for us' and 'on our behalf' (e.g. the use of 'huper' in Rom. 5: 6; Gal. 1: 4) by representatively carrying through his mission with utter fidelity and freely accepting the horrendous execution that a sinful world thrust upon him. Instead of needing to appease an angry deity who was 'out for blood', Christ was sent by the divine love (e.g. Rom. 8: 3, 32) to reconcile us with God and with one another (e.g. Eph. 2: 12–18). Lovingly accepting for others the undeserved suffering that his sheer goodness faced in a wicked world, Christ removed the defilement of sin and restored a disturbed moral order.

Here and now repentant sinners experience themselves as 'clean washed from sin'—to quote Edmund Spenser's sonnet on Easter. The redemptive act of Christ has removed awful stains from their lives. But did he or does he do this as our representative or our substitute?

Do we have to choose between the 'stories' of Christ the substitute or Christ the representative? Christ acted 'for us' in the sense of acting not only for our benefit and to our advantage, but also, one must add, 'in our place'. St Paul's image of the new or last Adam (see Chapter 2 above) entails accepting that Christ played, in some way or another, a collective role 'in our place'. But by acting for our sake and in our place, was he our substitute or our representative? Without always being mutually exclusive, these two ways of envisaging the relationship reveal major differences. For instance, a substitute may be passively or even violently put in the place of another person or of other persons. One thinks of hostages executed in place of escaped prisoners of war. The escapees do not want this substitution to take place, and in the event they may never even learn about it. Yet such wartime episodes also yield examples of those who actively chose to be substitutes and in a self-sacrificing way took the place of someone condemned to death—as St Maximilian Kolbe did at Auschwitz in 1941. Kolbe suffered the death-penalty when he volunteered to be his fellow-prisoner's substitute. He could not be described as the representative of that other prisoner.

'Substitution', Bishop Tom Wright has argued, should not be played off against 'representation'; they 'belong closely with one another. Substitution (he [Christ] dies, we do not) makes sense within the context of representation (the Member of Parliament *represents* the constituents, and therefore is qualified to act, particularly to speak and vote, *in their place*)'. Hence Wright concludes: 'representation is important not least because it creates the context for substitution'.[24] But do substitution and representation always belong closely with one another? The substitution created by parliamentary elections is both limited in scope and lasts for only a specified term—unlike the case of Kolbe. He was a substitute for a punishment that meant the end of his entire life; he was not representing his fellow prisoner.

What of representation? It is consciously willed by both those represented and the representative, is normally restricted to specific matters, and may well last for only a relatively brief period. In expiating the sins of the world, Christ freely represents human beings to God and before God: on their side they are invited to agree to this redemptive representation.[25] Christ's activity brings deliverance and expiation but does not constitute an 'unlimited' representation: human beings may not, for instance, simply hand over to him their duty to praise and thank God. At the same time, this redemptive representation is no relatively brief affair but lasts forever.

Ultimately, substitution and representation both prove unsatisfactory, 'extrinsic' terms. They imply a certain 'distance'. We can and often should be very grateful to our substitutes or representatives, but we do not identify with them, nor do they necessarily identify very deeply with us. A sense of personal participation is lacking; such persons do not necessarily draw us into the story. In the case of the redemption and the expiatory suffering it involved, everything hinges on the fact that the Son of God wanted to be with us and to share with us our human condition. His devotion to us led to his violent death on a cross, an utter horror transformed by his unconditional

[24] N. T. Wright, 'Redemption from a New Perspective? Towards a Multi-Layered Pauline Theology of the Cross', in *Redemption*, 69–100, at 93.

[25] The First Letter of John expresses the invitation to let Christ plead our cause: 'if anyone sins, we have an advocate with the Father, Jesus Christ the righteous' (1 John 2: 1).

love into a paradoxical beauty that led to his glorious resurrection. It was and is a love that invites human beings to leave behind their violence and malice and allow themselves to be incorporated into the crucified and risen Jesus, personally participate in the drama of redemption, and share a uniquely new communion with God.

Without such personal participation, Christ cannot purify lives or cleanse here and now a stained moral order. But those who are ready to be drawn into the story of Christ's redemptive suffering experience what it is to be 'clean washed from sin' and find their 'polluted' situation somehow set free from defilement.

9

Redemption as Transforming Love

And you, Jesus, are you not also a mother?
Are you not the mother, who, like a hen, gathers her chickens
    under her wings?

> St Anselm of Canterbury, *Prayers and Meditations*.

Love bade me welcome: yet my soul held back,
Guilty of dust and sin.

> George Herbert, 'Love (III)'.

How can we best describe and even define God's saving activity? Those who nominate love as the leading possibility are sometimes told that love is a 'merely moral' influence and that the 'example' of Christ's heroic love can be morally effective only with those who know the story of his passion and death. Even a superb sonnet such as Edmund Spenser's 'Easter' (cited at the end of Chapter 6), falters when it comes to love. He joyfully celebrates the powerful action of Christ both in delivering us from death and sin (Chapter 5), and in washing us 'clean from sin' (Chapters 7 and 8). But when he comes to the third model for redemption, love, it is not pictured as a transforming force but merely as 'the lesson which the Lord us taught'. This is true, but not enough. Like so many others, Spenser overlooks the creative energy which divine love enjoys and exercises in making possible for us a new and lasting mode of existence.

In many theological circles, Peter Abelard (d. 1142/43), who explored love as the key to redemption, is regularly criticized and found wanting for proposing only a 'subjective' view of redemption.[1]

---

[1] In *The Logic of Divine Love* (Oxford: Clarendon Press, 1970), R. C. Weingart convincingly defended Abelard against such critics. No doubt he would have

Those who in this way dismiss such a reading of redemption may need to be reminded of the power and presence of love or the powerful presence of love—something I aim to do in this chapter by drawing together and developing earlier reflections on 'presence'[2] and on 'love'.[3] The powerful presence of love promises not only to provide the most distinctive and encompassing account of redemption, but also, through the themes of the victorious and cleansing power of love, to incorporate the essential insights from Chapters 6[4] and 8 (above). The supreme advantage in approaching redemption through love is that this view shows how salvation is not primarily a 'process', and even less a 'formula', but a person, or rather three divine persons acting with boundless love. Here *personal causality* is highlighted even more than when we interpret redemption as deliverance from evil and as sacrificial, expiating the results of our sins. The tri-personal God exercises causality on human beings and their world, and does so in an utterly personal and loving way. Beyond question, redemption, as the mystery which grasps us (Phil. 3: 12), always resists easy analysis, and this is especially true when we look at it in terms of love. We may see only dim and puzzling 'reflections in a mirror' (1 Cor. 13: 12). But all the same, supported by divine grace, let us try to look.

THE POWER AND AIM OF DIVINE LOVE

The first and probably the greatest of Christian biblical theologians, St Irenaeus (d. around 200), drew together, as we saw in Chapter 2,

---

published further articles and even books to champion Abelard, but Weingart's life and academic career were cut short by a tragic accident.

[2] See my *Christology: A Biblical, Historical, and Systematic Study of Jesus* (Oxford: Oxford University Press, rev. edn., 2004), 306–23.

[3] G. O'Collins and D. Kendall, *The Bible for Theology: Ten Principles for the Theological Use of Scripture* (Mahwah, NJ: Paulist Press, 1997), 53–73.

[4] A saying cherished by the medievals, 'love conquers all (amor vincit omnia)', suggests the way in which Christ as Love in person conquered all the forces opposed to him.

the divine activity of creation and of redemption. He wrote of God creating Adam and Eve, in order to have those 'on whom to shower the divine gifts' (*Adversus Haereses*, 4. 14. 1). If this was true of creation, it remains all the more true of redemption, which aims finally at the divinization of humanity—that is to say, at humanity being effectively drawn into the inner life of God and so drawn to share an existence of eternal love (John 17: 26). From the second century the fathers of the Church wrote of men and women being deified in a 'wonderful exchange (admirabile commercium)'. Many took up the theme of Irenaeus: God became human in order that we humans might become divine (*Adversus Haereses*, 3. 19. 1; 4. 20. 4).

A spontaneous self-giving characterizes this redeeming love of God. Let us begin with two elements of this love: initiative and self-giving. (1) In taking an active *initiative*, God revealed the gratuitous, unsolicited nature of the divine love. That love did not wait to be called upon, but moved spontaneously to help those whom sin and wider evil had left in terrible need. We highlighted earlier (Chapter 1) the remarkable quality of the divine activity in reconciliation: it was God, the offended party, who initiated and carried through the work of reconciling with himself sinful humanity. God did not love us because we were already lovable. But while we were still sinful and estranged (Rom. 5: 8), the divine love was at work to make us beautiful and lovable. When thinking about sin, Augustine of Hippo elaborated not only the three descriptions we saw in Chapter 3, but also the notion of sin being ugly. He depicted his own situation before his conversion to the divine Beauty, 'so ancient and so new', as 'ugliness' (*Confessions*, 10. 27). He interpreted Paul's statement that 'all have sinned and fallen short of the glory of God' (Rom. 3: 23) as all having fallen short of 'the beauty of God'[5] and remaining ugly (*Enarrationes in Psalmos*, 44. 3). But, without being asked, God freely acted to remedy this situation.

(2) *Self-giving* also marked this redemptive initiative of God. Sometimes it is said that 'when we love, we give the best of ourselves'. Certainly the three divine persons gave the best of themselves, first

---

[5] In the OT and the NT the 'glory' and the 'beauty' of God overlap. When Paul writes of seeing 'the glory of God on the face of Christ' (2 Cor. 4: 6), this is tantamount to seeing the beauty of God on the face of the crucified and risen Christ.

through the sign and presence of the Son of God among us. Martin Luther[6] spoke of John 3: 16 as 'golden words' which 'alone make a person a Christian': 'God so loved the world that he gave his only Son'. The human life of Christ was the sign and reality of the gift of the divine self. This free self-giving entailed a new presence that effected a communion of life and love. Visibly sharing his presence, Christ brought about results that were and remain life-giving and life-enhancing—in a word, salvific. One might adapt John 10: 10 to read: 'I came that they might have my presence and have it abundantly'. To enjoy the Lord's bountiful presence means receiving life in abundance.

(3)   The *speech* (and presence) of Jesus prove highly relevant in the context of redemption through love. Since the time of René Descartes (d. 1650), Western philosophy was characterized and even dominated by the theme of consciousness and self-consciousness. Because of Ludwig Wittgenstein (d. 1951), John Austin (d. 1960) and others, however, a philosophy of language has often replaced the philosophy of consciousness as the central interest which grips attention. This shift bears fruit for those interested in exploring the life and mission of Christ and matches the interests of the Gospels, especially those by Matthew, Mark, and Luke. These (Synoptic) Gospels are, in particular, concerned with the language (and presence) of Jesus rather than with reporting and exploring his consciousness. There are, of course, indispensable hints of his self-consciousness to be gleaned from the Gospel texts.[7] But the Gospels are much more interested in the salvific language deployed in his mission, when he went out to be with and to offer himself to people. Over and over again, his speech did redemptive things, by making powerfully present the saving realities of which he spoke. His words proved to be deeds that transformed those who allowed things to happen. Let us see some characteristic examples from his preaching: the language and presence of a doctor with sick patients, a teacher with students, a husband with his wife, and parents with their offspring.

---

⁶ J. Pelikan (ed.), *Luther's Works*, xxii (St Louis: Concordia, 1957), 360.

⁷ See O'Collins, *Christology*, 59–62, 66–7, 121–5, 133–4.

Jesus defended his loving concern for sinners by nominating himself as a doctor totally dedicated to sick patients: 'Those who are well have no need of a physician, but those who are sick do. I have come to call not the righteous but sinners' (Mark 2: 17). The Gospels show how effective was this language (backed up by Jesus' practice of associating with sinners) in attracting to the person of Jesus men and women ashamed of their sins and looking for forgiveness through him (e.g. Mark 2: 15; Luke 7: 36–50). The merciful Doctor put his words into action by joining at table the sinful sick; his language and presence transformed them (e.g. Luke 19: 1–10). St Augustine of Hippo treasured this image of Christ as the humble and loving Physician, and knew how well it worked in his own pastoral ministry. There are over fifty extant texts from Augustine which either allude to or elaborate on the healing and saving activity of Christ the Physician.[8]

The Synoptic Gospels give Jesus the title of 'Teacher' or 'Rabbi' 66 times. Jesus' ministry provided a clear historical foundation for this title. He taught in the synagogues, gave his judgement on disputed points in Jewish law, and gathered around him a body of students or pupils. His method of teaching differed markedly from the scribes, those highly trained religious and legal experts many of whom were Pharisees. He had not received any scribal education. His audience saw how Jesus' teaching diverged from that of the scribes (Mark 1: 22, 27; Matt. 7: 29). The people of his home village of Nazareth were astonished by his wise teaching (Mark 6: 2–3). The scribes themselves challenged the basis of his authority to teach and act as he did (Mark 11: 27–8). According to John, some highlighted Jesus' lack of formal training (John 7: 15). They refused to acknowledge in him one who was a trained and officially authorized interpreter of the law.

It is the striking authority and loving demands of Jesus' teaching style that concern us here. He did not, for instance, appeal to previous 'authorities' when he pronounced upon central matters of the Mosaic law (Matt. 5: 31–42). He spoke with his own authority, prefacing his teaching with 'I say to you' and not with such prophetic rubrics as 'thus says the Lord' or 'an oracle of the Lord'. Through

---

[8] See R. Arbesmann, 'The Concept of "Christus Medicus" in St. Augustine', *Traditio* 10 (1954), 1–28.

such parables as that of the prodigal son (Luke 15: 11–32) and the workers in the vineyard (Matt. 20: 1–15), he firmly and lovingly challenged the world of conventional wisdom. The voices of the prodigal's older brother and that of the workers who had toiled all day in the vineyard express the conventional wisdom of the world. Jesus' subversive wisdom contrasted the normal ordering of life on the basis of rewards and punishments with the astonishing graciousness of the prodigal's father and the vineyard's owner. Cosmic generosity characterized the teaching of Jesus and his vision of God. He invited his hearers to trust him and share his perspective on life.

The decisive authority and love of Jesus the Teacher illuminate the correlative of this title: disciples. They are those who have responded to his utterances, who follow or accompany him on his mission (e.g. Mark 15: 40–1), and who have made a radical break with their previous lifestyle to do so. He has invited them to become involved imaginatively and affectively with him. For them he is much more than an ordinary teacher or rabbi. We are meant to think rather of someone like Elisha abruptly called by the prophet Elijah (1 Kgs. 19: 19–21). That story serves as a model for scenes in which Jesus rebukes those who wish to meet regular family obligations before joining him (Matt. 8: 21–2; Luke 9: 59–60). Those who find in Jesus their 'Teacher' are not simply pupils who can learn his doctrine and move away. They are lovingly and powerfully called to abandon home and family, so as to devote themselves to the task of proclaiming the kingdom of God. In finding salvation in Jesus and committing themselves to him, they share his wandering life and follow him on his mission, to become leaders in the new and final family of God he wishes to create (Mark 3: 35). Their new relationship with Jesus, triggered by his words, entails constructing a new community of followers.

The title for Jesus of 'Teacher' or 'Rabbi' is confined to the Gospels. This is not so with the next redemptive image: that of 'Spouse' or 'Husband', with his followers collectively in the role of the bride. It turns up not only in the preaching of Jesus but also elsewhere in the NT, as well as in the OT. Covenanted love is at least a major line for articulating redemption in the whole story of God's people. Liberating and transforming love found prophetic expression as

God's spousal love for Jerusalem.[9] When challenged about his disciples' failure to practise fasting, Jesus defended them on the grounds that he had come as their Bridegroom (Mark 2: 18–20). Not all biblical scholars agree that this language derives from Jesus himself.[10] Yet they have to reckon with another passage in which Jesus seems to imply that he, albeit mysteriously, is the Bridegroom who has come from God and calls on everyone to wait vigilantly for his final, marriage feast (Matt. 25: 1–14). A NT letter celebrates the Church as the bride of Christ (Eph. 5: 21–32), and the Bible ends with the vision of the New Jerusalem adorned as a bride for her loving Redeemer (Rev. 21: 1–22: 21). Even if Jesus historically never presented himself in terms of the husband/wife image and the intense personal relationship involved, this language clearly 'did redemptive things' for the first Christians and continues to do so as a transforming key to the story of salvation.

Finally, the loving relationship of parents to children provides the language for the longest and most beautiful parable from Jesus. This story of a father dealing so compassionately with the painful difficulties created by his two sons never mentions love explicitly, but transparently points to the divine love at work through Jesus (Luke 15: 11–32). Rembrandt Harmensz van Rijn (d. 1669) and Bartolomé Murillo (d. 1682) have left us major paintings which show how the parable of the prodigal son focused their faith in the Redeemer. Add too the tender picture of Jesus as the mother hen gathering her chickens (Matt. 23: 37 par.), an image much beloved by Anselm of Canterbury, Julian of Norwich, Bernard of Clairvaux, and other medieval Christians. The parable of the prodigal son and this self-image of the mother hen belong among the most touching offers made by Jesus when he invited others to open themselves to the merciful love of God.

Reading what is now numbered as Psalm 102, Augustine of Hippo recalls Christ's picture of himself as a mother hen and draws on an ancient legend of the pelican who sheds her blood on her dead offspring and so dies by bringing them back to life (*Enarrationes in*

---

[9] See K. D. Sakenfeld and W. Klassen, 'Love', *ABD* iv. 375–96.

[10] Joel Marcus, however, argues that the passage 'is rooted in Jesus' ministry': *Mark 1–8*, The Anchor Bible 27 (New York: Doubleday, 2000), 233, see 235.

Psalmos, 101. 1. 7–8). Augustine encouraged later writers to pick up
the image of Christ as 'the loving pelican'. This image features, for
example, in a hymn ('Adoro te devote, I adore you devotedly') which
is normally attributed to Thomas Aquinas and which calls on Christ:
'Pie pellicane Jesu Domine, / me immundum munda tuo sanguine
(loving pelican, Jesus Lord, with your blood cleanse me [for I am]
unclean)'. Along with many (but not all) others, Aquinas recognized in maternal love the great paradigm of unconditional love:
'Mothers—and of all loves theirs is the most intense—are more
concerned to love than to be loved (matres, quae maxime amant,
plus quaerunt amare quam amari)' (*Summa Theologiae*, 2a2ae. 27. 1).
Christ is to be seen as an unconditionally loving mother, as well as the
unconditionally loving father of the parable of the prodigal son.[11]

From the words of Jesus I have picked out four examples (the
doctor, the teacher, the spouse, and the parent) that illuminate the
divine love revealed and at work in Christ and his speech. His language and presence made the redemptive process happen and
continues to do so. One could add further examples, such as that of
the dedicated shepherd who knows his sheep by name, seeks
out the lost ones, and is ready to die for them (Luke 15: 3–7;
John 10: 1–16). Early Christians pictured Christ as a beardless, curly-
haired youth, the Good Shepherd who rescues his persecuted flock
from the devouring wolves. They experienced the powerful impact
of this image.

COSTLY LOVE

Any accounting of the redemptive love deployed by Jesus must
include the costliness of his self-sacrificing love. God is no celestial
sadist, who delights in pain, nor a hard judge who demands the
suffering and cruel death of his Son as the price of redemption.

---

[11] In his first encyclical, *Deus Caritas Est* (published 25 January 2006), Pope
Benedict XVI, while recalling 'love between parents and children', highlights one
love that 'stands out: love between man and woman'. He calls this love 'the very
epitome of love; all other kinds of love seem to fade in comparison' (no. 2).

But his Son entered a world of immense suffering, violence, and hatred. Both Christ and his heavenly Father willed the crucifixion indirectly—by accepting it (see Chapters 7 and 8 above).

Ordinary logic alone can never come even close to explaining and justifying what happened to Christ in his passion and death. Love, above all divine love, has its own logic, which sustains all that it has created and longs to be reconciled with alienated sinners—regardless of the cost. In all that happens, God remains sovereignly free. Nevertheless, God cannot not love, and love always puts those who love at risk. Generous, self-sacrificing, and unconditional love—and that is what we find exemplified supremely in Christ—risks being exploited, rejected, and even murderously crushed. Loving service to those in terrible need can turn people into targets. The last few decades have witnessed thousands of Good Samaritans in Africa, Asia, and Latin America paying with their lives because they stopped for wounded travellers. In less sensational but very real ways those who love constantly make themselves vulnerable by reaching out in their concern for others. No parable from the Gospels evokes more poignantly the risk of love than the story of the merciful father. His love leads him to face and endure the insulting behaviour of his elder son (Luke 15: 29–30), as well as the deep pain caused by the moral and spiritual death of his younger son (Luke 15: 24, 32). Few novelists have pictured the vulnerability of love more brilliantly and disturbingly than Graham Greene in *The Human Factor*; the central character, Maurice Castle, both describes love as 'a total risk' and pays the price for his devoted love to his wife and her son.[12]

Love cost Jesus himself much (2 Cor. 8: 9) and put him at mortal risk, as Paul (e.g. 1 Cor. 1: 13; Gal. 2: 20), the Deuteropauline Letters (e.g. Eph. 5: 2, 25), and John (e.g. John 13: 1; 15: 13) vividly recognized. In the midst of pagan selfishness, cruelty, and despair, Jesus' self-sacrificing love shone from his cross. In various languages a wise choice calls Jesus' suffering and death his 'passion', a term that combines intense love with the mortal suffering it brought the lover. Second to none in its dramatic intensity, Mark's passion story tracks the steadfastness of Jesus' commitment which made him vulnerable right to the end, while one of his male disciples betrayed him,

---

[12] G. Greene, *The Human Factor* (Harmondsworth: Penguin, 1978), 20.

another denied him, and the rest fled in fear.[13] Readers sense that they can count on the unconditional steadfastness and 'folly' of his self-forgetful love in a way that they cannot count on their own. It is his self-sacrificing love that figures in the moving appeal for love made by the First Letter of John (e.g. 1 John 3: 16).

Chapter 6 sketched the picture of Christ as the young Warrior ('Christus Miles') whose love led to his death on the battlefield, which paradoxically meant that in the fight he had won and liberated humankind. For medieval England the archetypal hero was the warrior, a chivalrous figure on horseback, a solitary lover-knight, attached by heroic love to his sweetheart and ready to die for her. A 'Guide for Anchoresses' from the early thirteenth century pictures Jesus as coming to fight without weapons; his shield is his human body stretched out on the cross. The crucifix, set high up on the rood-screen, reminds his sweetheart ('lemman') that his shield had been pierced and his side opened to show her his heart and inward love.[14] Sometimes the sweetheart represented the individual human soul and sometimes the community of believers. We find a late echo of this theme in the nineteenth-century hymn by Samuel John Stone (d. 1900), 'The Church's one foundation': 'From heaven he came and sought her / To be his holy bride; / With his own blood he bought her, / And for her life he died.'

From the time of St Anselm, St Bernard, St Francis, St Clare, and St Bonaventura, a new feeling for the passion of Jesus affected Christian art, devotion, literature, and life. Previously the utter shamefulness of Calvary had generally inhibited Christians from creating realistic images of the Crucified One. On a door of the Basilica of Santa Sabina in Rome, for example, one finds a fifth-century image of Christ's crucifixion. Yet the anonymous artist depicts Jesus as untouched by pain, bypassing death, and already reigning in triumph from the cross. It took a thousand years before Christian artists began portraying Jesus going through a genuine 'passion' and truly dying on the cross in agony.

---

[13] For details, see R. E. Brown, *The Death of the Messiah: A Commentary on the Passion Narratives in the Four Gospels*, 2 vols. (New York: Doubleday, 1993).

[14] *The Ancrene Riwle*, trans. into modern English M. B. Salu (London: Burns & Oates, 1955), part vii, 'Love', 170–81, at 173.

Now no longer represented with a royal crown or dressed like an emperor, the crucified Jesus wore a crown of thorns; often his head was fallen, his eyes closed, his hands and feet gruesomely nailed to the cross, and his body streaming with blood. Through works of art and written accounts of the passion, his sufferings were now graphically described in harrowing detail. Many felt a deep emotional identification with Mary standing at the foot of the cross and ravaged by grief. The 'Stabat Mater (The Mother was standing [at the cross])', a dramatic medieval hymn, described the suffering of the Virgin Mary during her Son's passion and crucifixion; it became widely used at Mass and for the Stations of the Cross (a devotional practice in which the participants prayerfully move around various (normally fourteen) scenes from the suffering and death of Christ). An anonymous poem from medieval England catches this new sensibility towards Mary's sharing in her Son's suffering: 'Now goeth sun under wood—Me rueth, Mary thy faire rode.[15] Now goeth sun under tree—Me rueth, Mary, thy son and thee.' From the end of the twelfth century, Christian drama, as distinct from liturgical drama, was born and spread across Europe; this drama often took the form of elaborately presented passion plays. Books of piety presented the five wounds of Christ and his pierced heart. Such devotion to the five wounds emerged in the twelfth century and reached its height in the fifteenth century. The 'instruments of the passion' or tools of torture used by the Roman soldiers became a popular theme in art. Caroline Walker Bynum has illustrated how 'medieval redemption theory was a piety and theology of blood'—something which often arouses modern antipathy. But she cautions against any facile analyses.[16] Mathis Gothardt Neithardt, known as Grünewald (d. 1528) and acknowledged as the last and most important Gothic painter in Germany, left a compelling vision of the medieval vision of the crucifixion. His Isenheimer altar-piece (now in the Colmar Museum) shows Jesus crowned with horrendous thorns, his body flayed with wounds, and his livid mouth opened in a gasp of pain.

[15] 'I grieve, Mary, for thy fair face.' See H. Gardner (ed.), *The Faber Book of Religious Verse* (London: Faber & Faber, 1972), 30.

[16] See e.g. C. W. Bynum, 'The Power in the Blood: Sacrifice, Substitution in Late Medieval Soteriology', in *Redemption*, 177–204, at 203.

The medievals cherished the love which inspired Christ to accept such suffering. His cry on the cross 'I thirst' (John 19: 28) was transformed into a cry of love.[17] In his meditations on the passion the hermit Richard Rolle of Hampole (d. 1349) stressed the love which made Christ hasten to embrace the cross. A prayer by St Richard of Chichester (d. 1253) captures the best of the new tenderness towards the suffering Christ: 'Thanks be to thee, my Lord Jesus Christ, for all the benefits which thou has given me—for all the pains and insults thou hast borne for me. O most merciful Redeemer, Friend and Brother, may I know thee more clearly, love thee more dearly, and follow thee more nearly.'

LOVE UNITES IN NEW LIFE

Simply by itself the suffering which Jesus endured out of love did not bring about redemption. To be sure, many people have found comfort through seeing the crucified Jesus as their fellow-sufferer. He did not suffer on his cross alone but between two others who underwent the same death by slow torture (all four Gospels) and with his mother standing near to him (the Gospel of John). That scene has been applied and appreciated down through the centuries. Like many other soldiers who fought in France and Belgium during the First World War, my own father found himself in a terrain of wayside shrines, representations of Christ on the cross with the Virgin Mary keeping lonely vigil at the feet of her crucified Son. Often scarred and badly damaged by shells and bullets, those shrines gave soldiers on both sides the feeling of Jesus as their brother in the terrible pain and suffering they faced. Jesus had drawn close to them and they knew his presence in their terrifying situation.

That presence was not of One who wanted to follow the frequent human path of an aggression that struggles to secure and exercise

---

[17] See Ludolf of Saxony (d. 1378), *Vita Christi*, 66. 2; William Langland (d. around 1400), *Piers Plowman*, B. 18. 363–4; Julian of Norwich (d. after 1416), *Showings*, 17 (on the physical thirst of Christ on the cross), 20 and 22 (on his spiritual thirst for love).

power. The deepest paradox of Calvary is that it was through the utter weakness and total humiliation of the crucifixion that God's power worked new life. As St Paul put it, Christ 'died on the cross in weakness but lives through the power of God' (2 Cor. 13: 4). Such self-sacrificing love ends not in death but in the power of new life. John's Gospel has Jesus saying something gentler but very similar: 'unless a grain of wheat falls in the ground and dies, it remains alone, but if it dies, it bears a rich harvest' (John 12: 24). In other words, new life depends on limitation and death. The Gospel stories tell us of a new life growing and blossoming in those gathered by the death of Jesus and the resurrection which follows.[18]

The spare, almost laconic, narrative of the passion and resurrection provided by Mark shows us how Jesus dies seemingly abandoned by everyone. Then suddenly we hear the reaction of the Roman officer in charge of the crucifixion. Seeing the way Jesus died, he confesses: 'Truly this man was Son of God.' At once we also learn of three women who had been present at the crucifixion and of 'many others who had come up to Jerusalem' with Jesus. When Joseph of Arimathea ensures that the body of Jesus is wrapped in a shroud and laid in a tomb, Mary Magdalene and two other women attend the burial (Mark 15: 39–47). They visit the tomb two days later. They find it empty and receive the astonishing news that Jesus 'has been raised'. They are instructed to tell Peter and the other disciples that the risen Jesus will keep a rendezvous with them in Galilee (Mark 16: 1–8). The crucifixion and resurrection are beginning to do something: namely, bring people together into the presence of Jesus or, as John's Gospel puts it, 'gather the children of God who have been scattered' (John 11: 52). Mark does not use the word 'love', but his story requires it.

Love involves freely giving and receiving in the union of reciprocal relationships. During his lifetime Jesus has called people to the relationship of committed discipleship. With his crucifixion and resurrection from the dead, his call finds a definitive response. By being joined together in loving fellowship with him, Mary Magdalene, Peter, and the others find their lasting, redeemed identity bestowed upon

---

[18] On the resurrection, see G. O'Collins, *Easter Faith: Believing in the Risen Jesus* (London: Darton, Longman & Todd, 2003) and its bibliography, 118–20.

them. Matthew signals this enduring reciprocity and presence of redeeming love through the closing promise of the risen Christ: 'I will be with you all days even to the end of time' (Matt. 28: 20). Through much of the OT, the Temple and the ark of the covenant figured forth God's faithful and loving presence with the people—a theme continued by Matthew's sense of Christ as 'God with us' both at his birth and through his permanent presence (Matt. 1: 23; 28: 20). In its closing chapter John's Gospel associates love and an intense mutual relationship with the repeated call from Jesus to 'follow me' (John 21: 15–22).

The uniting power of Christ's redemptive love breaks down barriers and goes beyond the boundaries that so often isolate individuals and entire groups. This love unites, but without a smothering absorption, fusion, and loss of identity. Paul's letters repeatedly testify to such an impact of divine love in the new community that Christ's dying and rising have created: 'Baptized into union with him, you have all put on Christ like a garment. Now there is no longer Jew or Greek, slave or free person, male or female; for you are all one in Christ' (Gal. 3: 27–8; see 1 Cor. 12: 13). This new redeemed fellowship transcends all the old religious, social, cultural divisions. Now united with one another through the saving love of Christ, believers are summoned to conform their existence to this new life of love they have received (1 Cor. 12: 31–14: 1). The greetings with which Paul closes his Letter to the Romans express the way in which the gift of unity enhances and does not detract from the personal identity of believers. He sends personal greetings to 29 people, their families, and the communities that meet in their houses. Beginning with Phoebe, a wonderfully hospitable deacon who 'has been a good friend to many', the Apostle provides vivid sketches of who these early Christians are and what they have been doing (Rom. 16: 1–16).

The Apostle reaches for the image of marriage when expounding the community's graced and loving union with Christ (1 Cor. 11: 2). The Letter to the Ephesians then develops this image to present the Church as the bride of Christ (Eph. 5: 25–32). The Book of Revelation closes the NT by picturing the final stage of redemption as the lasting union between Christ and his beautiful bride (Rev. 19: 7–9; 20: 2; 21: 17). Both here and, even more, hereafter, redemption involves such a radiantly happy union in love, but one that does not entail any dissolving of human beings in God. Such an outcome could never be dignified with the name of love. Genuine love unites without being destructive. The greater the loving union, the more our true selfhood is enhanced. In a striking way Eberhard Jüngel describes the union of love that brings us to ourselves and does not destroy us: 'the beloved Thou comes closer to me than I have ever been able to be to myself, and brings me to myself in a completely new way'.[19] Such a loving union of the redeemed with Christ reflects the way the three persons of the Trinity give themselves to each other in selfless, living communion but do not lose themselves in one another. They live together for each other and with each other, without disappearing into each other. The communion of love between the divine persons is supremely perfect. Yet in no way does this union lessen the distinction of the three persons within the one godhead. I return below to the life of the tripersonal God in which the redeemed are called to share.

In his *City of God* (14. 7) St Augustine of Hippo joins others in highlighting how intense joy inevitably accompanies true love. Jesus himself, in his parable of the merciful father, ends with those lovely words to the elder son to justify the big party celebrating the return of the prodigal son: 'it was fitting to make merry and be glad, for this your brother was dead, and is alive; he was lost and is found' (Luke 15: 32). There is no more obvious spin-off from love than joy.

The boundless joy that God's love holds out to/for us in redemption's consummation at the end is expressed by the NT through two characteristic images: a marriage or a banquet. Sometimes the images merge into a marriage banquet. Jesus pictures the coming kingdom as a final feast: 'many will come from east and west and sit at table with Abraham, Isaac, and Jacob in the kingdom of heaven' (Matt. 8: 11). His parable of the watchful slaves contains the amazing reversal of roles: when he returns, the master himself will serve them at a late-night feast (Luke 12: 35–8). The Book of Revelation portrays our heavenly home, the new Jerusalem, as a beautiful bride coming to meet her spouse, the glorified Christ who is the Lamb of God (Rev. 21: 2, 9–10). Those who

---

[19] E. Jüngel, *God in the Mystery of the World* (Grand Rapids, Mich.: Eerdmans, 1983), 324. For further philosophical and theological reflections on love, see J. Cowburn, *Love* (Milwaukee: Marquette University Press, 2003).

'are invited to the marriage feast of the Lamb' can only rejoice and be glad (Rev. 19: 9). Both now and even more at the end, God's redemptive love brings with it deep and lasting joy.

To express the utterly joyful change which Christ and his love have brought and will bring, the NT uses the language not only of spousal relationship but also of friendship (e.g. John 15: 15) and filiation (e.g. Rom. 8: 29; Gal. 3: 26; 4: 5–7). Love and the joy of love run like a golden thread through all three kinds of relationships: the loving joy of spouses, of friends among themselves, and of children with their parents. At the heart of the poem by George Herbert quoted at the start of this chapter is, one might say, the joy of being loved by Love itself.

ETERNITY, DIVINIZATION AND DISCLOSURE

As Gabriel Marcel classically said, 'To love a being is to say, "Thou shalt not die." '[20] He saw love as maintaining that not even death itself can take away the beloved. In the case of Christ his redemptive love is not short-lived but eternally faithful in what it brings about. Bernard of Clairvaux and other earlier and later mystics drew on the magically fresh and vivid language of the Song of Songs to express the loving relationship between Christ the Bridegroom and his Bride, those he has redeemed. This OT book ends by claiming that the strongest forces of nature cannot quench love (8: 6–7). Paul recognizes how Christ's love, manifested supremely on the cross, continues forever in his heavenly intercession for humanity (e.g. Rom. 8: 34–5, 37). John's Gospel highlights how the loving union through which Christ became 'the bread of God' will bring nothing less than 'eternal life'; whoever is open to this union 'will live forever' (John 6: 26–58). Here and elsewhere the NT promises that God's redemptive love will effect what authentic human love yearns for: an eternal fidelity and permanent union.

---

[20] G. Marcel, *The Mystery of Being*, ii, trans. R. Hague (London: Harvill Press, 1951), 171. See id., *Homo Viator*, trans. E. Craufurd (London: Victor Gollancz, 1951), 57–63.

Marcel appreciated that to love someone is in effect to say to that person: 'you must not die, but live forever'. Love's profound approval cannot tolerate the idea of the beloved no longer being there. The loving approval of God dramatized in the whole story of Christ brings with it something that human love alone can never achieve: the fullness of life forever. The divine love, deployed in creation and even more in redemption, is more powerful than death. It not only delivers from death but also holds out a new, transformed, and definitive life to come. We return to this in Chapter 12.

Sharing in eternal life amounts to what Eastern Christians have called 'divinization' or 'deification'. Eastern Christianity understood this to be a sharing, not in the divine substance, but in the divine life or loving relationship of the Son to the Father in the Holy Spirit. St Athanasius (d. 373) and other ancient writers interpreted in this way the bold language of the Second Letter of Peter about 'becoming partakers of the divine nature'. That letter states that God's 'divine power has given us everything needed for life and piety' and called us 'to his own glory and goodness'. These gifts constitute God's 'promises' to humankind: a divine call to 'escape from the corruption that is in the world through lust' and to become 'participants in the divine nature' (2 Pet. 1: 3–4). This striking picture of grace as sharing in the very being or nature of God appears in what is arguably the last NT work to be written. This text helped encourage the notion of the ultimate happiness of the redeemed as seeing God 'face to face'. This final redemption will complete the being made in the image and likeness of God (Gen. 1: 26–7). It became a key text for the master theme of Eastern theology, divinization.[21]

In lovingly bestowing a share in eternal life, God comes with the gift. All divine giving is self-giving. The 'agapeic' activity that flows in spontaneous abundance from the divine goodness communicates nothing less than the divine reality. Dionysius the Pseudo-Areopagite disseminated the theme of 'bonum diffusivum sui': the good—above all, the divine Good—shares itself (*Divine Names*, 4). Often called

---

[21] See G. O'Collins and M. Farrugua, *Catholicism: The History of Catholic Christianity* (Oxford: Oxford University Press, 2003), 202–5.

'gift-love', this divine 'agape' would be more accurately styled as the 'self-gift of love'.

The 'face to face' vision of God that will be the glorious climax of the life of grace points to a further characteristic of love: its revelatory power. Sometimes Eastern Christians speak of 'Christ the Illuminator'—a happy reminder that his redemptive love entails self-revelation and that self-revelation is an act of love. In John's Gospel, Jesus says: 'those who love me will be loved by my Father, and I will love them and manifest myself to them' (John 14: 21). A little later in the same final discourse, Jesus adds: 'I have called you friends, for all that I have heard from my Father I have made known to you' (John 15: 15). Love means self-manifestation; it breaks out of itself to reveal itself in a self-sharing way that is oriented towards others. Through his loving self-disclosure, Jesus changed and changes those who are open to this self-revelation. His self-manifestation is redemptive. The Letter to Titus puts it this way: 'when the goodness and loving kindness of God our Saviour appeared, he saved us' (3: 4–5). Love prompted the divine self-manifestation, a self-manifestation in Christ that has saved human beings.

Like other books of the NT, the Letter to Titus associates this loving revelation even more with the future, with what it calls 'the appearing of the glory of our great God and Saviour, Jesus Christ' (2: 13). At the end no one will have to look hard to find God. Through the divine love we have already been made the children of God. When Christ comes again, through the divine love both redemption and revelation will reach their definitive consummation. As the First Letter of John states, 'it does not yet appear what we shall be. But we know that when he appears, we shall be like him, for we shall see him as he is' (3: 2). The divine love which has already initiated the process of salvific self-disclosure will definitively complete its work at the end.

Yet we should also insist that the self-giving love which characterized the redemptive activity of Jesus in the past *already* works effectively in the here and now. He *is* love in person, as George Herbert (1593–1633) movingly depicts him in 'Love (III)': 'Love bade me welcome.' This redeeming love works through the personal operation of the Holy Spirit and the initiative of the Father. In the words of Richard Littledale (1833–90), we can sing to the Spirit:

'Come down, O Love divine,/ Seek thou this soul of mine,/ And visit it with thine own ardour glowing.' The loving causality of all three divine persons remains incessantly at work. Hence St Paul can close his Second Letter to the Corinthians with the blessing: 'The grace of the Lord Jesus Christ and the love of God [the Father] and the communion of the Holy Spirit be with all of you.'

10

The Holy Spirit, the Risen Christ
and the Church

The grace of the Lord Jesus Christ and the love of God and the
communion of the Holy Spirit be with all of you.

St Paul, 2 Corinthians 13: 13.

Every authentic prayer is prompted by the Holy Spirit, who is
mysteriously present in every human heart.

Pope John Paul II, an address to the cardinals, December 1986.

The preface to this book raised the issue of the past event or events of
redemption continuing to work for the salvation of human beings
and their world. How can the life, death, and resurrection of Christ
continue to effect our salvation today? What forms the living bridge
between those past events and the present experience of redemption?
We may happily interpret those events in terms of Christ delivering
us from evil, expiating sin, and exercising the power of love. But we
are still left with the hard question: how can these events continue to
be effective? Earlier chapters have drawn attention to the functions of
liturgy, art, and literature in mediating between redemptive events of
the past and present experience of salvation. No answers will prove
fully adequate here, unless they recognize the personal causality of
the tri-personal God and, in particular, the profoundly connected
roles of the incarnate and risen Christ and of the Holy Spirit in their
self-communication to human beings that provides the conditions
for the possibility of appropriating salvation.

The conditions for the possibility of these redemptive roles are
related but not identical. Paul uses the same verb ('exapostellô') for

the Father's sending of the Son and of the Spirit (Gal. 4: 4–6); yet the missions differ. The Son's mission involves assuming the human condition by being 'born of a woman' and born a Jew 'under the law'. In other words, this mission entails an incarnation and assuming a human nature with its human powers and operations. Henceforth, the Son will operate not only through his divine nature and with divine powers but also through created human powers. The Holy Spirit does not become incarnate and assume a human nature. Sent by the Father into 'our hearts', the Spirit operates only with divine power. Irenaeus called the Son and the Spirit 'the two hands of God' (*Adversus Haereses*, 4. 20. 1). But the powers of these two hands vary dramatically: the one hand (that of the Spirit) works with divine power, the other hand (that of the Son after the incarnation) also works with human power.

Add too another difference and distinction. The first Easter brought a dramatic change in the human operations of the risen Jesus: their liberation from the normal, earthly limitations of time and space. During his earthly ministry his loving service of others through his humanity had been limited by the ordinary conditions of human life and its endowments. The radical transformation of the resurrection did not suppress his being human, but rather glorified and freed his human condition to be actively present everywhere, so as both to affect lovingly (and mysteriously) the lives of all men and women and to fashion a new, visible community of love which the NT presents through the figure of the groom/bride relationship (e.g. Eph. 5: 25–32). With his earthly body Jesus had reached out to touch lepers, embrace children, forgive sinners, break bread for the hungry, and communicate the saving growth of God. Through his risen body that service continues in a new and enhanced fashion. He ministers really, if under signs, in the whole sacramental system of the Church and beyond.

What Christian faith has to say about the increase and elevation of Christ's human powers through the resurrection does not apply as such to the Holy Spirit. Faith recognizes rather a transition in the deployment of the (divine) power of the Holy Spirit. At the death and resurrection of Christ, that power became fully and intensely operative in the new community of believers and in the whole world.

In the way it presents the relationship between Christ and the Spirit, the Gospel of John prepares the way for this new development.

Although the other Gospels report the descent of the Holy Spirit at the baptism of Jesus, it is only John who writes of the Spirit descending 'and remaining' on Jesus (John 1: 32–3). Jesus will then speak 'the words of God, for he [God] gives the Spirit without measure' (John 3: 34). God gives the measureless gift of the Spirit, first to Jesus and through him to others. Jesus is uniquely endowed with the Spirit, and will be *the* source of the Spirit, the fountain from whom will flow 'rivers of living water' (John 7: 37–9). John's Gospel understands Jesus' dispensing of the Spirit to be without parallel. At the end this Gospel will offer the most sustained treatment of the relationship between Jesus and the Spirit in any of the NT books (John 14–16). During his ministry Jesus has been the spokesman and agent of the Father; at the death and resurrection of Jesus the Spirit will prove not only the advocate, spokesman and agent of Jesus but also the One who empowers the new 'fellowship' cherished by the First Letter of John.

'KOINÔNIA'

In the last decades of the twentieth century many Christians, and not just scholars among them, went back to some Greek terms in the NT and found a special power in them. One of these terms that exercised a fresh fascination was 'koinônia', often translated as 'communion', 'fellowship', or 'participation'. This term has significant things to say about human beings participating in the redemption effected by Christ and being assimilated to him through the powerful presence of the Holy Spirit.[1] Let me take four examples of this use of 'koinônia', which illustrate with increasing clarity the role of the Spirit in actualizing redemption.

---

[1] On the activity of the Holy Spirit, see Y. Congar, *I Believe in the Holy Spirit*, 3 vols. (London: Geoffrey Chapman, 1981); J. D. G. Dunn, *The Theology of Paul the Apostle* (Grand Rapids, Mich.: Eerdmans, 1998); G. D. Fee, *God's Empowering Presence: The Holy Spirit in the Letters of Paul* (Carlisle: Paternoster Press, 1995).

The introduction to the First Letter of John announces the purpose of writing: 'we proclaim to you what we have seen and heard, so that you too may have fellowship (koinônia) with us. Our fellowship is with the Father and his Son, Jesus Christ' (1 John 1: 3). This witness does not explicitly mention here the Holy Spirit, but this oneness with the Father through Christ takes place through the Spirit. As we learn later, the teachers and preachers ('we') are empowered to witness through the Spirit who is truth itself (1 John 5: 6).

This witness creates and nourishes the emerging Christian communities of the baptized for whom the central act of worship is the Eucharist. Not surprisingly St Paul expounds the Eucharist in terms of fellowship or participation: 'the cup of blessing that we bless, is it not a sharing (koinônia) in the blood of Christ? The bread that we break, is it not a sharing (koinônia) in the body of Christ?' (1 Cor. 10: 16). As well as touching in this context on the theme of sacrifice,[2] Paul appeals also to what the Eucharist means as a sacred meal. He may have this in mind when he recalls the 'spiritual' food and drink provided by the manna and the water from the rock in the desert (1 Cor. 10: 3–4), a hint of what the divine Spirit provided during the exodus and would bring to completion in the bread and wine consecrated and consumed at the Eucharist. Around the end of the first century the *Didache* was to refer to the eucharistic elements as 'spiritual food and drink' (10. 3); that connection may already have been intended by Paul.[3] At all events, the way was open for the development in eucharistic prayers or anaphoras of the 'epiclesis', the prayer asking the Holy Spirit to descend upon the gifts and change them into the body and blood of Christ for the spiritual profit of those who receive them. In the reform of the Roman Catholic liturgy for the Latin rite that followed the Second Vatican Council (1962–5), the new eucharistic prayers contain an 'epiclesis' before the words of institution (praying that the gifts be changed) and after the words of institution (praying that the community be

    [2] See G. O'Collins and M. Farrugia, *Catholicism: The Story of Catholic Christianity* (Oxford: Oxford University Press, 2003), 251.

    [3] See A. C. Thiselton, *The First Epistle to the Corinthians* (Carlisle: Paternoster Press, 2000), 726; on Paul's theology of the Eucharist, see ibid., 848–99 and J. D. G. Dunn, *The Theology of Paul the Apostle* (Grand Rapids, Mich.: Eerdmans, 1998), 599–623.

changed). The Eucharist entails a 'koinônia' made possible by the Holy Spirit.

The Acts of the Apostles pictures the impact of Pentecost and the early life of believers. Those who responded to Peter's initial sermon repented of their sins, were baptized 'in the name of Jesus Christ', and received 'the gift of the Holy Spirit'. Four elements characterize their new life: 'they devoted themselves to the *teaching of the apostles* and *fellowship* (koinônia), to the *breaking of bread* and *prayers*' (Acts 2: 37–42). The two highlights of the new fellowship empowered by the Holy Spirit were assimilation to Christ and communion with one another, both centring on 'the breaking of bread' or a common meal which included the Eucharist or Lord's Supper (see 1 Cor. 11: 17–34).

My fourth example of the redeeming 'koinônia' effected by the Holy Spirit comes at the very end of the Second Letter to the Corinthians: 'the grace of the Lord Jesus Christ and the love of God and the communion (koinônia) of the Holy Spirit be with all of you' (2 Cor. 13: 13).[4] The order of this 'trinitarian' formula is significant in the way it emphasizes the saving function of the Trinity. This closing benediction speaks of 'grace', 'love', and 'communion' or fellowship—associated, respectively, with the first, second, and third figures. Placing the Lord Jesus Christ ahead of 'God [the Father]' highlights the historical mediation of revelation and salvation through Christ. Ending with 'communion' underlines the new communion which the Holy Spirit has created and toward which the gracious activity of the Lord Jesus Christ and the loving concern of God the Father aim. This closing benediction summarizes salvation history in a way that associates Christ with God [the Father] and with the Holy Spirit in bestowing spiritual blessings. One may put it all this way. The grace of Christ is the means by which the love of God reaches human beings and lets them participate in true life and form the community of the final age. Through faith and baptism, they can participate in the fellowship or 'koinônia' engendered and empowered by the Holy Spirit.

One should be properly cautious when expounding this and other 'triadic' formulas in Paul's letters. We do not find here (or even in

---

[4] See M. J. Harris, *The Second Epistle to the Corinthians* (Grand Rapids, Mich.: Eerdmans, 2005), 937–42.

later books of the NT) the doctrine of God as three persons in one nature that would be developed in the fourth-century councils. Nevertheless, the Pauline teaching about the Trinity (along with that from Luke and John) provides a foundation and starting point for that doctrinal development. In particular, the benediction which closes the Second Letter to the Corinthians allows us to appreciate that the new life, initiated by the Father's love and brought through Christ's redeeming work, is radically 'trinitarian' in nature. This redeemed life replicates, through the power of the Holy Spirit, the relationship of the Son to the Father (see Rom. 8: 15–16; Gal. 4: 6).[5]

These then are four NT references to 'koinônia', the new commu- nion or fellowship of redeemed life. With increasing clarity and intensity, they suggest an essential feature in the whole drama of redemption. It is through the Holy Spirit, sent by the Father, that human beings experience here and now the impact of the salvation brought about through the life, death, and resurrection of Christ.

BEAUTY AND LIFE

A further way of expressing the redemptive function of the Spirit is offered by the themes of 'beauty' and 'life'. When commenting on Psalm 45 and expounding the theme of the Church as the beloved spouse of Christ, Augustine refers to Romans 3: 23: 'all have sinned and are deprived of the glory of God'. Since the biblical theme of 'glory' frequently suggests 'beauty', one might also render the verse: 'all have sinned and are deprived of the beauty of God'. Sin means a loss of beauty and a fall into ugliness. This allows Augustine to say of the Church: 'she who is ugly is loved, in order that she no longer remain ugly. [Christ] has eliminated her ugliness and created her beauty' (*Enarrationes in Psalmos*, 44. 3). This allows us to gloss the

---

[5] In his 'How Wonderful the Three-in-One' Brian Wren pictures and praises the Trinity: 'How wonderful the Three-in-One, / Whose energies of dancing light/ Are undivided, pure and good, / Communing love in shared delight.' 'With greening pow'r and loving care', the Spirit 'calls us born again by grace', 'In Love's communing life to share'. Even here and now we can participate in the inner life of love through which the three divine persons relate.

words of Paul in describing what happens when sinners repent of their wrongdoing, turn to Christ, and are baptized: 'you have been washed clean, you have been made holy, you have been justified by the name of the Lord Jesus and by the Spirit of our God' (1 Cor. 6: 11). One might say: 'you have been washed clean of your ugliness and you have been *made beautiful* through Christ and the Holy Spirit'.

St Cyril of Alexandria (d. 444) understood the Spirit to work such a change. Commenting on the words of the risen Christ 'receive the Holy Spirit' (John 20: 22), Cyril wrote of the Spirit restoring the loveliness which human beings had lost through sin. When creating Adam, 'God gave him the most perfect beauty—making him share in his spirit'. After the resurrection, 'Christ breathed on us, renewing the former beauty' (*In Matthaeum*, 24. c–d). Thus it is in terms of beauty that the Holy Spirit defines the appropriation of the redemption achieved by the death and resurrection of Christ. A new beauty is created in all those who share in the Spirit.

In his sonnet 'God's Grandeur' Gerard Manley Hopkins (1844–89) does not start, like Cyril of Alexandria, from the NT story of the risen Jesus appearing to his disciples and sharing with them the Holy Spirit. He begins rather with created nature, the world 'which is charged with the grandeur of God' but which has been smudged, darkened, and tarnished by human beings. Yet, 'for all this, nature is never spent;/ There lives the dearest freshness deep down things'. The poet names the source of this unquenchable vitality and light: 'the Holy Ghost over the bent/ World broods with warm breast and with ah! bright wings'. The 'warm breast' of the Spirit gives life and beauty to a world tarnished by human beings who do not pay heed to God's rule (do 'not reck his rod'). From a different perspective, Hopkins joins Cyril of Alexandria in extolling the Holy Spirit as the source of beauty and life.

St Paul provides what is arguably the classic NT passage about the life-giving Spirit, who determines and shapes the existence of believers. The Spirit is the divine principle or 'law' of the new order created by God through Christ, or the enabling power by which to live (Rom. 8: 1–27). Nine times in this passage the Apostle uses the verb 'live' or the noun 'life'. The Holy Spirit is an ever fruitful life-force. For Paul, redeemed life begins for his converts when they receive the Holy Spirit and experience the Spirit's powerful effects

(Gal. 3: 1–15). The Spirit guides the adopted sons and daughters of God (Rom. 8: 14), blesses them richly with a variety of gifts (1 Cor. 12: 12–31), and brings wonderful fruits in their lives (Gal. 5: 22–5).

The OT prophets sometimes pictured the coming age of the Spirit as the fruitful transformation that occurs when rain pours down on parched land (e.g. Isa. 32: 15; 44: 3–4). Joel's language about this outpouring from on high (Joel 2: 28–9; in Hebrew 3: 1) was to be picked up by Luke when he described the day of Pentecost (Acts 2: 16–21). The outpouring of the Spirit, an essential fruit of Christ's resurrection, far from being a single event, was and remains a transforming power that initiates and continues to support a process. In every way human beings, both together in communities of various kinds and individually, are always in process. As projects, they are on the way towards, and in the state of 'becoming', what they are to be. The Holy Spirit works through ongoing human lives to transform them.

THE PERSON OF THE SPIRIT

Over the years various writers have remarked on the self-effacing quality of the Holy Spirit, who 'makes room for others'—above all, for the risen and glorified Christ. It is this 'letting others come to the fore' that allows some to think and speak of the Spirit as a kind of vague graciousness or, as someone once put it to me, as 'a kind of warm, fuzzy feeling'. But, while being a mysterious power, the Holy Spirit is not an anonymous power. The Spirit's going beyond himself/herself towards Christ and others does not mean a loss of personal identity.

Paul, the earliest Christian writer, is an eloquent witness to the distinct, personal existence of the Holy Spirit. For the Apostle, the resurrection of Jesus reveals a personal power (rather than an unspecified power) to be at work (Rom. 8. 11). This resurrection, the life-giving action *par excellence*, is accomplished by the Spirit who is the Giver of life. For repentant sinners, the life-giving Spirit offers deliverance from the state of death (Rom. 7: 24) and entry into life and peace (Rom. 8: 6). It requires a personal agent to open human hearts to hear this message. The Spirit makes it possible to acclaim Jesus as divine Lord (1 Cor. 12: 3), writes Christ's image on human hearts (2 Cor. 3: 2–3), and thus constitutes interiorly the believer as believer—sanctifying operations that are manifestly the work of a personal agent. In the life of the Church, the personal Spirit imparts a whole range of gifts for the building up of the body of Christ (1 Cor. 12: 4–13). In empowering the baptized to join Jesus in prayer to the Father and in bringing suffering human beings and all creation to their final liberation and transformation (Rom. 8: 14–30), the Holy Spirit has already begun an eschatological work of global proportions that obviously implies a personal (divine) agent. By fashioning relationships between Jesus and human beings, among human beings, and between the whole created world and God, the Spirit achieves effects that imply the presence of a personal power.

To the testimony of Paul, one could add that of Luke, John, and other NT authors to illustrate further a faith in the Spirit as personal agent. Of course, we do not yet have the fully deployed belief that we find in the third article of the Nicene-Constantinopolitan Creed of 381. Yet the NT language about the Holy Spirit allows us to recognize what we would call a 'personal agent' who exercises a personal causality that brings such effects as true spiritual freedom: 'where the Spirit of the Lord is, there is freedom' (2 Cor. 3: 17). Human persons can have a deep and enriching impact on us, above all through the various ways in which they are present to us: for instance, by living with us, working with us, or inviting us to visit them. But the presence of the Holy Spirit, which is no mere gift 'from the outside', goes beyond the possibilities of any such merely human presence.

THE PRESENCE OF THE SPIRIT

According to the way Paul understands the workings of redemption, the Holy Spirit not only brings us into contact with the crucified and risen Christ but also becomes more present to us than any other person. The Apostle writes of the Spirit 'given to us' (Rom. 5: 5), 'sent into our hearts' (Gal. 4: 6), 'pleading' within us (Rom. 8: 26–7), 'bearing witness' within us that we are children of God and joint heirs with Christ (Rom. 8: 15–16), and imparting a uniquely deep wisdom (1 Cor. 2: 6–16). The indwelling of the Spirit (Rom. 8: 9–11) and the believers' incorporation into Christ come across as two inseparable dimensions of the one experience. The indwelling Spirit has been sent to unite believers to Christ and make them live in him. The Spirit mediates and manifests the presence of the risen Christ, awakes faith in him, and prepares hearts to receive him and appropriately respond to him. The thrust of Paul's message in Romans 8 is this: by drawing human beings into union with the Son, the Spirit empowers them to love the Father and return to the Father. Thus the personal missions of the Son and the Spirit converge in effecting human salvation and sanctification.

These inseparable roles (for redemption) of Christ and the Spirit emerge most clearly in the resurrection and the Eucharist. Jesus instituted the Eucharist at the Last Supper, in anticipation of the death and resurrection which would form the climax of his redemptive 'work' for the world. He gave himself totally in obedient love to his mission, and the Father responded by granting the life-giving Spirit and the gloriously immortal life of resurrection (Rom. 8: 11–12). Any reflection on the death and resurrection of Jesus which fails to attend to the Father and the Holy Spirit remains theologically impoverished and cannot claim to hear fully what the evangelists and other NT writers have to say. To remove the crucifixion and resurrection from the context of trinitarian relationships will hide that deep meaning suggested by the mysterious statement in the Letter to the Hebrews: 'the blood of Christ, who through the eternal Spirit offered himself without blemish to God, will purify our conscience from dead works to worship the living God' (Heb. 9: 15). The redemptive self-revelation of the tripersonal God reached its highpoint with the resurrection of the crucified Jesus.[6] Luke expresses this highpoint in a blatantly trinitarian way through the words of Peter in explaining the supernatural phenomena witnessed in Jerusalem on the day of Pentecost: 'This Jesus God raised up, and of that we all are witnesses. Being therefore exalted at the right hand of God [the Father] and

    [6] See G. O'Collins, *Easter Faith* (London: Darton, Longman & Todd, 2003), 71–102.

having received from the Father the promise of the Holy Spirit, he has poured out this which you see and hear' (Acts 2: 32–3). The Father and the Spirit were actively present in the salvific offering, death, resurrection, and exaltation of the Son, and so too are they present with the risen Christ in the Eucharist which communicates the Easter mystery to the believers assembled for worship.

The liturgical celebrations of the Eastern and Western Churches bear witness to and prompt an experience of the tripersonal God. In eucharistic worship, both the 'anamnesis' of the Son and the 'epiclesis' of the Spirit have their inseparable but distinct place in leading up to the doxology or giving glory to God the Father.[7] As an act of remembering, the 'anamnesis' involves bringing to mind God's saving actions in history (especially the saving deeds of Christ's passion, death, resurrection, and glorification) for the assembly that wants to share in the salvation which the Son of God has effected once and for all. As an act of 'anticipation', the 'anamnesis' means looking forward to the end time of final fulfilment and doing so with an expectation that already receives and perceives something of that ultimate future. In the eucharistic prayers the first 'epiclesis' asks that the Holy Spirit descend upon the gifts of bread and wine to change them into the body and blood of Christ for the spiritual profit of those who receive them. The 'epiclesis' after the words of institution prays that the assembled communicants themselves be changed. The Holy Spirit descends to actualize within the assembly Christ's own attitude of self-offering and responsive love towards God and neighbour. Thus in the 'anamnesis' Christ is remembered and anticipated, whereas in the 'epiclesis' the Spirit is invoked to actualize the presence of Christ both in the elements and in the communicants. Then the 'doxology' completes the eucharistic prayer, by directing 'all glory and honour' to God the Father 'through, with, and in' Christ 'in the unity' effected by the Holy Spirit. Thus the eucharistic worship of Christians involves a trinitarian 'anamnesis', 'epiclesis', and

---

[7] *Baptism, Eucharist, and Ministry* (BEM), Faith and Order Paper 111 (Geneva: World Council of Churches, 1982), summarizes very well the Eucharist as 'Thanksgiving to the Father', as 'Anamnesis or Memorial of Christ', and as 'Invocation of the Spirit' (10–13).

'doxology'. A document coming from the Roman Catholic-Orthodox dialogue expresses firmly this trinitarian perspective.[8]

For the purposes of this chapter, what matters essentially is that in the Eucharist the words of institution and the 'epiclesis' or invocation of the Holy Spirit (upon the elements and upon the gathered assembly) belong inseparably together. The second 'epiclesis' prays that the Father might bestow the Holy Spirit upon the community assembled for worship, so that through receiving the eucharistic food and drink they will be transformed and fully incorporated as members of Christ's body into his filial relationship with the Father. In the Eucharist, the Spirit makes Christ present and brings the worshippers into a constantly deeper contact with the redemptive mystery of Easter: that is to say, with the crucified, risen, and glorified Christ. The transforming energy of the Spirit leads people into a new 'embodiment', a communion with the living body of the Son of God: first, through baptism, and then through the ever deepening 'koinônia' of the Eucharist.

The image of Christ's *ascension* offers another way of expressing the dynamic presence of the Spirit in communicating a new life in Christ. This image reveals the destiny of all human beings: a blessed and eternal existence through sharing in the life of the Trinity. The ascension of Christ reveals the movement of all humanity towards and into the life of God, made possible by the death and resurrection of Christ and the outpouring of the Holy Spirit. This movement will be completed when all members of the body of Christ are drawn up to the Father and share in trinitarian life. Through the energy of the Spirit, those who constitute the body of Christ will be finally liberated from sin and death and joyfully return to the Father.

[8] The Joint International Commission for Theological Dialogue Between the Roman Catholic Church and the Orthodox Church, 'The Mystery of the Church and of the Eucharist in the Light of the Mystery of the Holy Trinity', *Origins* 12 (1982), 157–60, at 158: 'By the Eucharist the paschal event opens itself up into the church ... By the communion in the body and blood of Christ, the faithful grow in that mystical divinization, which makes them dwell in the Son and the Father, through the Spirit. Thus ... the Eucharist builds up the church in the sense that through it the Spirit of the risen Christ fashions the church into the body of Christ. Thus the Eucharist is truly the sacrament of the church, at once as sacrament of the total gift the Lord makes of himself to his own and as manifestation and growth of the body of Christ, the church ... Taken as a whole, the eucharistic celebration makes present the trinitarian mystery of the church.'

THE RISEN CHRIST AND THE SACRAMENTS

From early times Christians were aware that the risen Christ exercises his saving mission as primary minister of all the sacraments. Whenever they are administered, he is personally and effectively, albeit invisibly, present. Commenting on John's Gospel, Augustine classically summed up this sacramental ministry of the risen Lord: 'When Peter baptizes, it is Christ who baptizes. When Paul baptizes, it is Christ who baptizes' (*Tract.*, 6. 7). With its talk about sacraments as personal encounters with Christ, modern theology has reinstated the Augustinian principle in a new form. Right from the start of Christianity, the new life of faith and baptism was understood to mean existing 'in' the risen Christ, the inclusive figure whom believers experience and into whom they knew themselves to be incorporated (e.g. Rom. 8: 1; 1 Cor. 15: 22).

By being spiritually washed from sin and made alive to God at baptism, individual Christians knew themselves to form with the risen Christ (1 Cor. 12: 12–13) a single body vivified by the Spirit, and to be engrafted into the very life of the glorified Son of God (John 15: 5). Both these images, the head with its members and the vine with its branches, implied that by means of baptism the unifying force of divine life and love, the Holy Spirit, flowed not only through the risen Lord but also through those who entered into the ecclesial community. Furthermore, since Christ and his Father were understood to be 'one' (John 14: 9–10), those who were rejuvenated with water and anointed with the Spirit experienced themselves as sharing in the being and life of the Father.

But what of later generations of Christians and the mediation to them (through sacraments and in other ways) of the redemption achieved by Christ? Through baptism and the Eucharist, they want to keep continuity with the past and to 're-immerse' themselves in that past. They want to follow Paul's command to 'announce the death of the [risen] Lord until he comes' (1 Cor. 11: 26). But how might we understand the 'bridge' between past and present, between the redemptive deeds of Christ completed once and for all and present experiences of that redemption being mediated through the Church and her acts of worship? What causality is at work here to 'bridge the gap' between the first and the twenty-first centuries? Any thoughtful answer must take its shape around the *personal causality*, not only that of the Holy Spirit but also that of the risen Christ. This personal causality is to be understood as the causality exercised by the three divine persons acting together with boundless love (Chapter 9).

The portrait of Jesus and his interaction with others furnished by St John's Gospel proves illuminating here. Like the sacraments, the language and narrative of John are richly symbolic. In those formulae of self-presentation, such as 'I am the vine', 'I am the light of the world', and 'I am the bread of life', Jesus (who is very much the risen Lord of the here and now) uses simple but vivid symbols to reveal himself. He draws on things we perceive in our world to express something of his saving function and divine identity. The liturgical dimension of John fits in closely with the Gospel's symbolic character. In the past some commentators may have gone overboard in finding a fully sacramental intention in its composition. All the same, the liturgical overtones of such sections as chapter 6 (the Eucharist) and chapter 9 (baptism) are unmistakable. These and other passages in John show a 'deep Christian understanding of the purpose of Baptism and the Eucharist'.[9]

This symbolic and liturgical character of John's Gospel goes hand in hand with its experiential quality. It calls on its readers here and now to experience the living Jesus in deeper and richer ways. Over and over again it shows us representative individuals who allow him to change and transform their lives. They come to 'know' Jesus or, as we would say, 'experience' him. Generally the mainstream translations have been coy about rendering the Greek verb 'oida (know)' as 'experience'. At best they discreetly indicated this in a footnote, as the New Oxford Annotated Bible does in a footnote when it comes to the Samaritans' reaction to what they have heard from the woman who met Jesus at the well (John 4: 39–42): 'Faith based on the testimony of another (the woman) is vindicated in personal experience.'[10] It might have been simpler and better to have translated John 4: 42 as

[9] R. E. Brown, *The Gospel According to John (i–xii)* (Garden City, NY: Doubleday, 1966), cxiv.

[10] *The New Oxford Annotated Bible*, ed. Bruce M. Metzger and Roland E. Murphy (New York: Oxford University Press, 1991).

follows: 'They said to the woman, "It is no longer because of your words that we believe, for we have heard for ourselves, and *experienced* that this is indeed the Saviour of the world."' So often in the Fourth Gospel 'experience' catches the full sense of John's 'know'. Let me give one further example, Jesus' question to Philip: 'Have I been with you so long, and yet you do not know me (= have not really experienced me)?' (John 14: 9).

John's Gospel conveys who Jesus is and what he continues to do in the lives of representative individuals who encounter him. From the meeting with Andrew in Chapter 1 through to that with Simon Peter in Chapter 21, the Fourth Gospel offers individual encounters with Jesus which symbolize astonishingly well the persistent spiritual needs of human beings. This account of Jesus and his interaction with others, nearly two thousand years after the composition of the Gospel, continues to communicate splendidly and constantly elicits the 'I-have-been-there' feeling. The communicative presence of the crucified and risen Jesus is by no means limited to public worship; it is mediated through the reading of scriptures, homilies and sermons, living with other human beings, experiences of suffering, and in other ways. Nevertheless, forms of worship, together with preaching, music, and visual art, remain paramount in mediating the powerful presence of the risen Lord.

If John's Gospel serves splendidly to yield a sense of the living and redemptive presence of Christ, Paul's letters can do the same for the Holy Spirit. Like the OT, which can name the divine Spirit in an impersonal way (as breath or wind), the Apostle at times speaks of the Spirit impersonally: for example, as being 'poured' (Rom. 5: 5), as 'seal' (2 Cor. 1: 22; see Eph. 1: 13; 4: 30), as 'first fruits' (Rom. 8: 23), or as 'down payment' (2 Cor. 1: 22; 5: 5; see Eph. 1: 14). Nevertheless, as we have seen above, he also writes of the Spirit in clearly personal language as 'leading' (Rom. 8: 14), 'witnessing' (Rom. 8: 16), 'interceding' (Rom. 8: 26–7), having aims or 'aspirations' (Rom. 8: 27), 'searching' and 'knowing' (1 Cor. 2: 10–11), 'distributing' gifts (1 Cor. 12: 11), and 'crying out' in the human heart (Gal. 4: 6). Talk of 'choosing' (1 Cor. 12: 11) and 'freedom' (2 Cor. 3: 17) also seems incompatible with the Spirit being impersonal. In summary, the language of Paul's letters implies that the Spirit is a personal subject who continues to engage in personal activities. Those who sense this

ongoing activity of the Holy Spirit can appreciate some of the dimensions of the Spirit's personal agency at work today in mediating
redemption.

THE INTERPLAY BETWEEN THE SPIRIT AND CHRIST

In Christians' experience of redemption here and now there is an
intense interplay between the Holy Spirit and the risen Christ, a
contemporary interplay that reflects what we can glean from Paul's
letters about the experience of believers from the very beginning. For
the Apostle, the Spirit 'in us' (e.g. Rom. 5: 5; 8: 16) is nearly
synonymous with talk about our being 'in Christ' (e.g. Rom. 6: 3,
11, 23; 1 Cor. 1: 30; 3: 1). Paul appreciates that coming to Christ
involves the Spirit (Gal. 3: 1–5), who makes preaching effective
and empowers conversion (1 Thess. 1: 4–6). Hence the Christians'
experience of the Spirit merges with their experience of the risen
Christ (1 Cor. 6: 11). The divine Spirit dwelling 'in you' seems, for all
intents and purposes, equivalent to 'having the Spirit of Christ' or to
Christ being 'in you' (Rom. 8: 9–11). This near-functional identity
has allowed James Dunn to claim not only that for Paul 'the Spirit is
the medium for Christ in his relation' to human beings but even that
'no distinction can be detected in the believer's experience' between
the exalted Christ and the Spirit of God.[11]

Nevertheless, neither Paul's thinking nor continuing Christian
experience identify Christ with the Spirit, despite their intense
links. At the feasts of the Annunciation and Christmas, Christians
continue to profess that Jesus was conceived through the power of
the Holy Spirit (Matt. 1: 20; Luke 1: 35)—a statement that cannot be
reversed. It is the Son and not the Spirit who is experienced as sent 'in
the likeness of sinful flesh' to deal with sin and 'given up for us all'
(Rom. 8: 3, 32). Christians do think of the Spirit as having been
'handed over to death for our sins and raised again for our justification' (Rom. 4: 25). The Father is believed to have raised Jesus and not

---

[11] J. D. G. Dunn, *Christology in the Making* (London: SCM Press, 2nd edn., 1989),
146.

the Spirit from the dead (e.g. Gal. 1: 1). Through his resurrection Christ and not the Spirit has become 'the firstborn' of a new and final family of God (Rom. 8: 29) and the beginning of the general resurrection to come (1 Cor. 15: 20).

'Exalted above the heavens' to the 'right hand' of God, Christ maintains now and forever his mediatorial priesthood and 'lives always' to 'intercede' for those 'who approach God through him' (Heb. 7: 24–6). This intercession 'from heaven' differs from that of the Spirit who 'intercedes' within us (Rom. 8: 26–7). The Christian tradition, so far as I know, has never credited the Holy Spirit with exercising priesthood. To do that would require an incarnation. As Hebrews expounds the high priesthood of Christ, it entails, among other things, sharing in the human condition (Heb. 4: 14–5: 10). The Christian tradition has likewise experienced Christ as the primary minister of the sacraments. It has not attributed this ministerial role to the Spirit, even while invoking the power of the Spirit when the sacraments are administered. The NT's story of Christ's mission, conception, ministry, death, resurrection, and its aftermath in Christian experience today distinguish him from the Holy Spirit. A series of events and actions are attributed either to Jesus or to the Holy Spirit but are not interchangeable. Much of what is attributed to Jesus cannot be attributed to the Holy Spirit, and vice versa. Both the Son and the Spirit are revealed, active, and personally communicated, but in their particularity and differentiated diversity.[12]

Yet the operations of the risen Christ and the Holy Spirit parallel, complement, and mutually condition each other, and not least in the way they universalize the redemption accomplished once and for all. Matthew's Gospel ends with 'eleven disciples' on a mountain in Galilee keeping a rendezvous with the risen Christ. A sense of totality comes through his words: 'all power is given to me in heaven and on earth'; that is to say, he enjoys full authority everywhere in the whole created world. He continues to speak in a universalizing fashion: 'go and teach *all* nations', baptizing them, 'making them my disciples',

---

[12] Significantly the Church is not called the body of the Holy Spirit but the body of Christ (e.g. 1 Cor. 12: 27–8). The Church is the temple or sanctuary of the Spirit (1 Cor. 3: 16–17), whose vivifying 'interiority' led later Christians to call the Spirit 'the soul' of the Church.

and 'teaching them to observe *all* that I have commanded you'. Not surprisingly the scene ends with the promise of an enduring presence: 'I will be with you *all* days, even to the end of time' (Matt. 28: 16–20). The final scene of Matthew's Gospel expresses vividly how the impact of the entire saving mission of Christ (in particular, his teaching ministry, death, and resurrection) is lastingly and universally deployed.

This chapter has reflected on the impact of Christ's redemption on Christian believers, and especially on the impact vividly deployed and revealed through baptism and the Eucharist. The chapter has highlighted, in particular, the communion (the 'koinônia') effected by the Holy Spirit through baptism and the invocation ('epiclesis') of the Spirit on those assembled for the Eucharist. Yet the outward signs of baptism and Eucharist do not circumscribe and limit the operations of the Holy Spirit.

NT authors help us to reflect also on the ways in which the Holy Spirit puts into a universal setting the whole saving event of Christ. The Spirit of love communicates life to all and illuminates the entire pilgrimage of humanity towards God, a pilgrimage in which human beings are to make up the one body of Christ. Thus Luke gathers together into his scene of the first Pentecost representatives from 'every nation under heaven' to witness and experience the outpouring of the Spirit which calls all people into the community of Christ (Acts 2: 5–11). Paul goes even further: the Spirit imparts life and the hope of fulfilment not only to human beings but also to the whole created world (Rom. 8: 1–30). Through the action of the Spirit, Christ remains lovingly and powerfully present in the Church, humanity, and the whole of creation.

11

The Salvation of Non-Christians

I dwelt in the highest heavens, and my throne was in a pillar of cloud... Over waves of the sea, over all the earth, and over every people and nation I have held sway.

Sirach 24: 4, 6.

Jesus Christ is to be praised not only for what he is in himself; he is to be exalted and loved for what he is for us, for each one of us, for every people and for every culture. Christ is our Saviour. Christ is our greatest benefactor. Christ is our liberator.

Pope Paul VI, Manila, 29 November 1970.

From its earliest to its latest books, the NT does not waver in acknowledging Christ as the one Saviour for all men and women of all times and places. As the First Letter of John puts matters, he is 'the expiation for our sins and not for ours only but also for the sins of the whole world' (1 John 2: 2). The first Christians acknowledged his redemptive role to be universal (for all without exception), unique (without parallel), complete (as One who conveys the fullness of salvation), and definitive (beyond any possibility of being equalled, let alone surpassed, in his salvific function). His universal role means that through him the deadly forces of evil are overcome, sins are forgiven and their contamination purified, and a new existence as God's beloved, adopted children has been made available. This NT sense of Christ's indispensable and necessary role for human salvation could be summarized in a new axiom: 'extra Christum nulla salus (outside Christ no salvation)'. This sense of his all-determining role in the whole redemptive drama is suggested by the fact that, unlike the OT where various human beings could be called 'saviour' (e.g. Judg. 3: 9, 15, 31), the NT gives the title of 'Saviour' only to God (eight times) and to Christ (sixteen times).

This chapter will take up three questions. (1) What did the scriptures hold about the universal impact of Christ as Saviour and about the situation of those who were not (or were not yet) aware of his saving function? (2) Why did the first Christians hold what they did about Christ as universal mediator of salvation? (3) What should be said, in the light of two millennia of Christianity, about the salvation of the non-evangelized? Is Christ and how is Christ involved redemptively in all human history? Should we recognize the positive role of non-Christian religions and their founders in the salvation of their adherents (as does Jacques Dupuis[1])? Does such recognition automatically mean recognizing a multiplicity of saviours, who differ only in degree and not in kind (as does John Hick)? The Congregation for the Doctrine of the Faith (in an enquiry that ran from 1998 until 2001) questioned the views of Dupuis.[2] Christian theologians of various denominations have challenged the views of Hick.[3]

(1) UNIVERSAL REDEEMER

Paul insists that Christ died 'for all' without introducing any exception (2 Cor. 5: 14–15). Hence he can say that 'God was in Christ reconciling the world to himself' (2 Cor. 5: 19). In sharp contrast with the collective figure of Adam who brought sin and spiritual death to all human beings, the obedient Christ has led all to justification and life (Rom. 5: 12–21). In fact, this redemption is cosmic in its scope; it will liberate and transform the whole of creation (Rom. 8: 18–23). An early

---

[1] See his *Toward a Christian Theology of Religious Pluralism* (Maryknoll, NY: Orbis Books, 1997).

[2] See G. O'Collins, 'Jacques Dupuis: His Person and Work', in D. Kendall and G. O'Collins (eds.), *In Many and Diverse Ways* (Maryknoll, NY: Orbis Books, 2003), 18–29.

[3]. See S. T. Davis, 'John Hick on Incarnation and Trinity', in S. T. Davis, D. Kendall, and G. O'Collins (eds.), *The Trinity* (Oxford: Oxford University Press, 1999), 251–72; P. R. Eddy, 'John Hick and the Historical Jesus', in D. Kendall and S. T. Davis (eds.), *The Convergence of Theology* (Mahwah, NJ: Paulist Press, 2001), 304–19; G. O'Collins, 'The Incarnation Under Fire', *Gregorianum* 76 (1995), 263–80.

christological hymn quoted by a Deutero-Pauline letter emphatically expresses Christ's universal role in both creation and redemption, through its repeated refrain of his impact on *all* things (Col. 1: 15–20). When it describes the rendezvous 'the eleven disciples' kept with the risen Christ on a mountain in Galilee, the concluding verses of Matthew's Gospel attribute to him the same all-embracing impact for human salvation: 'Jesus came and said to them, *"All* authority has been given to me in heaven and on earth [= everywhere]. Go therefore and make disciples of *all* nations"' (Matt. 28: 18–19). Perhaps the classic NT verse in this regard comes from Peter's reiterated and exclusive claim about Jesus: 'there is salvation in no one else, for there is no other name under heaven given among human beings by which we must be saved' (Acts 4: 12). A later book in the NT highlights Jesus' unique mediatorship for all: 'there is one God, and there is one mediator between God and human beings, the man Christ Jesus who gave himself as a ransom for all' (1 Tim. 2: 5–6; see Mark 10: 45).

The Johannine literature uses its characteristic terms to affirm the universal significance of Christ for revelation ('light', 'way', and 'truth') and salvation ('life'). He is 'the true light that enlightens every human being' (John 1: 9); he is 'the light of the world' (John 9: 5). In his last discourse Jesus declares: 'I am the way, and the truth, and the life; no one comes to the Father, except through me' (John 14: 6). First John endorses the unqualified nature of this claim (*'the* way, *the* truth, and *the* life . . . *no one*) in terms of Christ being the sole source of eternal life: 'God gave us eternal life and this life is in the Son. He who has the Son has life; he who does not have the Son of God does not have life' (1 John 3: 11–12).

Unquestionably, the NT assertions about Christ's universal and unique function for salvation may seem arrogant and even outrageous. How can a particular, Jewish figure of the first century prove eternally determinative as the way of salvation for all people of all times and places? How is Jesus of Nazareth *the* Word of God, *the* new/final Adam, and *the* Mediator of creation and redemption for everyone? Yet without any embarrassment writers in the early centuries of Christianity maintained and elaborated these universal claims. Developing a Pauline theme, Irenaeus of Lyons expounded Christ as the second Adam who 'recapitulates' human history in its entirety. Two centuries later in his *Oratio catechetica magna*, Gregory of Nyssa interpreted our 'deification' as rooted in the fact that through his individual human nature Christ entered into a kind of physical contact with the whole of the human race. This was to acknowledge an ontological unity of all humanity in Christ.

Both in the NT and subsequently, this vision of Christ's universal significance left room, however, for a genuine appreciation of the religious situation of those who did not or could not consciously accept him as their Saviour. A list of heroes and heroines of faith, which reached its perfect climax with Christ (Heb. 11: 1–12: 2) did not simply begin with Abraham and Sarah (who set going the covenanted history of the Jewish people), but reached back to Abel, Enoch, and Noah (Heb. 11: 4–7) and included one non-Jewish woman, Rahab, a prostitute from Jericho (Heb. 11: 31). Thus this cloud of witnesses who were to inspire Christian faith included some who did not share in the special history of promise that Christ brought to its completion and consummation.

We recalled above some words attributed to Peter about Jesus being the exclusive source of salvation (Acts 4: 12). A little later in the Book of Acts, the same Peter continues to preach Jesus as 'Lord of all', but also endorses a broadly inclusive statement about the religious situation of God-fearing people anywhere: 'in every nation anyone who fears him [God] and does what is right is acceptable to him' (Acts 10: 34–6). These two statements, which must be read together, fit into a consistent Lukan pattern of writing: they are 'doublets' or two sections that match each other and clarify each other. Over and over again in Luke's two books we come across such doublets: passage A which says something important and then passage B which adds something important to fill out and modify what we have already read in passage A.[4] In this case salvation

---

[4] In his Gospel, Luke alerts us to an example of such doublets when, for instance, he introduces two distinct stories with the very same question: 'What shall I do to inherit eternal life?' In the first story a lawyer hears the parable of the good Samaritan and is told to '*go* and do likewise' (Luke 10: 37). In the second a ruler is invited to give all he possesses to the poor and then '*come*, follow me' (Luke 10: 37). The identical question produces two seemingly different answers. But on closer scrutiny the two invitations can be seen to complement and support each other rather than proving mutually exclusive. Those who live in loving familiarity with Jesus will have the strength to imitate the selfless compassion of the good Samaritan. On doublets in

coming from no one other than Jesus should not be taken to claim that those who 'fear' God and do what is right will be, nevertheless, unacceptable to God, even if they have not or not yet heard of the name of Jesus.

A little later in Acts, Luke inserts a speech by Paul on the Areopagus, which is a further classic example of esteem for religious traditions 'before' and 'outside', or at least visibly 'outside', Christ and the Christian message (Acts 17: 22–31). The Apostle announced that, while the end of 'the times of ignorance' had come with the message of Christ's resurrection, this did not invalidate the Athenians' prior quest for and experience of 'the unknown God'. In upholding the fact of Christ's universal impact as Saviour without denigrating those who were not (or were not yet) aware of the source of salvation, Luke and other NT authors followed a large-minded fairness which had already repeatedly surfaced in the OT.

The subsequent covenants with Abraham and Moses, so central to the special salvation history of the Jews, did not nullify or abrogate the universal covenant made through Noah, pictured after the great flood as the second founder of the human race (Gen. 9: 1–17). The blessings of this covenant extended to Noah's three sons, regarded as the ancestors of all the nations (Gen. 10: 1–32), to all living creatures, and even to the earth itself. That covenant covered the religious traditions developed beyond the special history of Judaism and Christianity.[5] We find that the cosmic covenant with Noah remained firmly in place in a late list of seven covenants that ended with King David (Sir. 44–7). Sirach had already blended the universal with the particular in its picture of Wisdom. A vivid, feminine personification of the divine activity, she enjoys a universal domain: 'I dwelt in the highest heavens, and my throne was in a pillar of cloud...Over waves of the sea, over all the earth, and over every people and nation I have held sway' (Sir. 24: 4, 6). This worldwide presence and influence goes, nevertheless, hand in hand with Wisdom's particular mission to Israel. She makes her home in the holy city of Jerusalem

Luke's writing, see J. A. Fitzmyer, *The Gospel according to Luke I–IX*, Anchor Bible 28 (Garden City, NY: Doubleday, 1981), 79–82.

[5] See G. Odasso, *Bibbia e religioni. Prospettive bibliche per la teologia delle religioni* (Rome: Urbaniana University Press, 1998).

and sends out an invitation for her great banquet: 'Come to me, you who desire me, and eat your fill of my fruits. For the memory of me is sweeter than honey, and the possession of me sweeter than the honeycomb. Those who eat of me will hunger for more, and those who drink of me will thirst for more' (Sir. 24: 8–11, 19–21). Here Sophia or Wisdom herself is the food and the drink, the source of nourishment and life. The NT will apply this language to Jesus (Matt. 11: 28), while John's Gospel will go beyond Sirach by portraying Jesus as permanently satisfying for everyone: 'Those who come to me will not hunger and those who believe in me will not thirst' (John 6: 35).

Before we leave the OT, we should not ignore the distinguished and varied list of 'outsiders', such as Melchisedek (Gen. 14: 18–20), the Queen of Sheba (who visits King Solomon in 1 Kgs. 10: 1–13), Ruth (the great-grandmother of David and ancestor of Christ, according to Matt. 1: 5–6 and Luke 3: 31–2), Job (probably an Edomite, whose story probes at length the mystery of one who is innocent and yet suffers terribly), and Balaam, a priest-diviner from Babylonia who delivered four oracles from God, with the final oracle being a prophecy of the coming Davidic dynasty (Num. 22: 1–24: 25). These figures helped lay the ground for two convictions held together by Luke: both a universal call to faith in Christ as Saviour (Acts 4: 12), and a recognition of how the Holy Spirit also operates before that call may be effectively received (Acts 10: 1–11: 18). The mysterious priest-king Melchisedek, described in Genesis 9 as a 'priest of the most high God', receives the homage of Abraham and offers him bread and wine. The king is addressed in Psalm 110: 4 as 'a priest forever according to the order of Melchisedek'. The NT uses both these passages to demonstrate how Christ's priesthood is superior to that of the levitical priesthood (Heb. 6: 20; 7: 1–25). From the time of Clement of Alexandria (d. around 200), the bread and wine offered by Melchisedek were seen as a type of the Eucharist, and in this connection he was introduced into the Roman Canon of the Mass (which seems to go back to the fourth century): 'Look with favour on these offerings and accept them as once you accepted the gifts of your servant Abel, the sacrifice of Abraham our father in faith, and the bread and wine offered by your priest Melchisedek.'

Jesus himself mentioned with approval the Queen of Sheba, who 'came from the ends of the earth to hear the wisdom of Solomon'

(Matt. 12: 42 par.). He also recalled the effect of Jonah's preaching to the people of Nineveh, who 'repented at the preaching of Jonah' (Matt. 12: 41 par.). The Book of Jonah had told of the wholesale conversion of the city, a conversion from 'evil ways' and not as such a conversion to the Jewish faith (Jonah 3: 1–10).

In his preaching Jesus largely confined himself to his own people. At times he made exclusive claims about the vital importance of following him and confessing him before the world: 'everyone who acknowledges me before others, the Son of Man also will acknowledge before the angels of God. But whoever denies me before others will be denied before the angels of God' (Luke 12: 8–9 par.). At the same time, a certain universalism marked the ministry of Jesus. He proclaimed a God who cares for all men and women (e.g. Matt. 5: 43–8 par.). He cured people who came from non-Jewish areas (Mark 3: 7–8). He found more faith in a Roman centurion than in anyone else in Israel (Matt. 8: 10 par.). He declared that the final kingdom of God will include non-Jews (Matt. 8: 11 par.). The gathering of the nations began already in the ministry of Jesus. He recognized the great faith of a Canaanite woman and her claim that a Gentile might share in Jewish privileges (Matt. 15: 21–8). He praised the faith of a Samaritan cured of leprosy (Luke 17: 18–19). Jesus preached a divine kingdom inseparably connected with his own person (e.g. Matt. 12: 28 par.). Yet this kingdom of God was universal and not limited by frontiers of race and religion.

But how did NT Christians hold what they did about the crucified and risen Christ as universal redeemer? Why did they believe him to be the universal mediator of salvation?

(2) THE GROUNDS FOR THE UNIVERSAL CLAIM

On any showing, claims about Jesus as the mediator of salvation for all people emerged from faith in him as risen from the dead. His resurrection was understood to have created a new possibility by inaugurating the general resurrection to come at the end of history (Rom. 8: 29; 1 Cor. 15: 20–8). The passage from 1 Corinthians to which reference has just been made could hardly be clearer about the universal impact of the risen Christ and his saving work; repeatedly it speaks of what he will effect for 'all', for 'all things', and for 'everyone'. The resurrection set up a situation that affected the whole human race. In his universal lordship Christ is present 'always'—right to the close of time (Matt. 28: 20). At the end he will be the saving goal for all men and women: as the universal judge (e.g. Matt. 25: 31–46) and the 'light' of the heavenly Jerusalem (Rev. 21: 23). Their ultimate destiny leads all human beings towards Christ. They are called to be raised like him, know him, and through him share in the divine life forever. In his glorified humanity he will remain the means by which the blessed know the Trinity and enjoy the fullness of salvation.[6] There can be no bypassing Christ when we come to the goal of salvation and revelation. He will be there for everyone as Saviour and Revealer.

The teleological conviction that 'the end commands everything', when applied to what the general resurrection anticipated by the glorious vindication of Jesus, goes hand in hand with the strong sense which the NT shows of Christ's universal salvific role here and now. To profess faith in his redemptive function for everyone at the end necessarily entails faith in his acting redemptively for all people even now. Not only in the world to come but also in this present world, Christ mediates salvation universally. The NT and early Christians clearly held that it will be true and is already true that 'outside Christ there is no salvation', to which they implicitly add: 'there is no outside Christ'. We are all part of his saving story. At least *five further considerations* underpin and illuminate the logic of the NT faith in the universal saving function of the risen Christ.

First, in a central exposition of redemption, Paul celebrates the Holy Spirit who delivers 'from the law of sin and death' and communicates life here and hereafter (Rom. 8: 1–27). The Apostle invokes the Spirit sixteen times in this passage. 'The Spirit of Christ' (Rom. 8: 9) is there for all, Jews and Gentiles alike (Gal. 3: 2–6: 8), to lead them to 'eternal life' (Gal. 6: 8). One cannot 'have' the Spirit without being 'in Christ' a son or daughter of God (Gal. 4: 4–7).

---

[6] See G. O'Collins, *Incarnation* (London: Continuum, 2002), 36–42; K. Rahner, 'The Eternal Significance of the Humanity of Jesus for our Relationship with God', *Theological Investigations* iii (London: Darton, Longman & Todd, 1974), 35–46.

More clearly than Paul, Luke (e.g. Acts 2: 33) and John (e.g. John 7: 37–9; 19: 30, 34; 20: 22) present the Spirit as given by the crucified and risen Christ (and his Father). As the Cornelius episode classically illustrates in Acts 10, the Spirit of Christ operates beyond the confines of baptized believers to bring others to Christ. The universal relevance and impact of the Spirit enacts the universal relevance of Christ's redemptive work. Active everywhere, the Holy Spirit relates the whole history of humanity to Christ and vice versa. To share in the Spirit is to share in the new sonship and daughtership effected by Christ.[7]

Some theologians have also developed what amounts to the same argument, but have done so through the themes of grace, divine self-communication, or justification. They argue, for instance, that since God's grace is offered to all and since all grace comes from and leads to Christ, through the universal offer of grace Christ is redemptively present to all. The argument is almost tautological. Since Christ is the prototype of our grace and since grace means a new likeness to Christ that turns human beings into God's sons and daughters in the Son, grace necessarily entails the presence of Christ. Thus the universality of grace bespeaks the universal role of Christ as Saviour here and now. Once we agree that there is no grace apart from the grace of Christ, even as there is no Holy Spirit apart from the Spirit of Christ, we must draw the universal conclusion. No one can experience the offer of salvation without experiencing, however obscurely, the presence of Christ as Redeemer. Any and every acceptance of saving grace and the Holy Spirit, whenever and wherever it takes place, is an acceptance of Christ. There is no zone 'outside Christ', since there is no zone 'outside' grace and the Holy Spirit. All experience of salvation is Christological. This kind of argument encouraged Karl Rahner to call Christ 'absolute Saviour'.[8]

---

[7] See K. Rahner, *Foundations of Christian Faith* (London: Darton, Longman & Todd, 1978), 316–18. It is the Holy Spirit who activates the capacity of human beings to pray and believe. Just as human beings can pray in less 'authentic' ways (e.g. Luke 18: 9–14), so too faith can express itself in less 'authentic' ways. Nevertheless, it is always the Spirit who activates in human beings the two strictly connected graced realities of prayer and faith.

[8] Ibid., 193–5, 204–6, 279–80, 318–21.

The use here of 'absolute' illustrates the need for a high level of clarity in this and other theological contexts. 'Absolute' can convey the unique universal role of Christ in human salvation. As Saviour of all men and women of all times and places, he is the only one of his class, and brings definitive salvation to the human race and to human persons in their totality (as material and spiritual beings). But 'absolute' has also been often used in the sense of 'totally necessary', 'utterly unconditioned', 'uncaused', and 'unlimited'. Only God is just that. One cannot describe that way the created humanity the Son of God assumed at the incarnation and his specific human, redemptive actions. Moreover, the incarnation itself was a free act of God's love and not unconditionally necessary. Apropos of the universality of grace and the universal presence of the often 'hidden' or 'anonymous' Christ, Rahner at one point spoke of 'anonymous Christianity'; he did not use the term in the masterpiece of his mature years, *Foundations of Christian Faith*. Apart from being offensive to followers of other religions (who can turn around and speak of Christians as 'anonymous Hindus' or 'anonymous Buddhists'), 'anonymous Christianity' can too easily distract from the heart of the matter: the grace that comes from and leads to Christ himself.

Second, what has been said above and, even more, in Chapter 5 about the earthly ministry of Jesus has shown how he linked his own person with the presence and coming of God's kingdom. There was a universal dimension to this preaching. His main and immediate audience was found in 'the lost sheep of the house of Israel', but he also looked beyond them to all those who would come 'from east and west' into God's kingdom (Matt. 8: 11; 15: 24). The first Christians knew how his resurrection from the dead authenticated his claims, and, in particular, the claim to being in person the agent of the divine kingdom that is and will be all-inclusive, or—in other words—to being the agent of universal salvation.

Third, the incarnation also bears on this point. Through his incarnation, Christ moved into historical solidarity with all human beings, as well as with the whole created world. He entered history and became, in a sense, every man and every woman. Hereafter to receive divine grace through other men and women and through the world would be to receive that grace through the incarnate Christ. The story of the last judgement in Matthew 25 singles out strangers, hungry and thirsty people, the naked, the sick, and prisoners to support the point: not only in meeting and caring for those who suffer but also in being graced by them, we meet and are graced by Christ. By his incarnation 'the Son of God has in a certain way united himself with every human being', said the Second Vatican Council (*Gaudium et Spes*, 22). Hence to experience and receive God's grace through other human beings is to experience and receive that grace through the incarnate Christ.

Fourth, unlike Genesis, the Psalms, Deutero-Isaiah, and other OT books, the NT does not have a great deal to say about creation. But in what is said (as we saw in Chapter 2 above), Christ, identified as the Son or the Word, takes over the role attributed by Jewish theology to the divine word and wisdom. He is acknowledged to be the agent of creation: 'all things were created through him and for him. He is before all things, and in him all things hold together' (Col. 1: 16–17; see John 1: 1–4, 10; Heb. 1: 3; 1 Cor. 8: 6). Despite their different nuances, these texts agree that through Christ all things were created. They confess him as the universal and exclusive agent of creation. This belief underpins a conclusion about Christ's universal role for salvation. Wherever the created world and its inner and outer history mediate God's grace, those who receive this saving grace are in fact receiving it through Christ. As divine agent of creation, Christ also brings the grace of God through the external world and the inner experience of human beings. Christ's agency, through his sharing in the divine nature and its operations, is as broad and as old as creation itself.

The sense of Christ as the creative Word, who is present from the beginning, sustains all things, and permeates all things, became a frequent theme for the Greek fathers from Justin in the second century to Athanasius in the fourth century and beyond. They followed and expanded the NT teaching by appreciating the revealing and redeeming presence of the Word or 'Logos spermatikos' ('the seed-sowing Word') in the whole cosmos and all history. In their version of things, the salvation offered to those living before Christ came through the Word of God who was to become flesh in the fullness of time. As agent of creation, the Word was and is always present, to sow seeds of truth in the minds of every human being. Thus those who lived before the incarnation were nourished by the divine truth and set on the way of salvation by the Word of God. The same holds true of those who have not yet received the message of the incarnation, death, and resurrection of Christ. Christ is hidden, yet uniquely active among the peoples of the world.

Fifth, talk of the divine Word brings us to what forms the ultimate ground for maintaining Christ's universal role as the Life of salvation (and the Light of revelation). As divine, Christ is universally present, actively influencing the mediation of redemption to all. Those who accept his divinity have no choice but to acknowledge also his universal role for salvation. Those who deny or doubt his divinity will not be able to justify his definitive, unparalleled, and universal function as Redeemer. For them, he can only be one in a multiplicity of saviour figures, differing perhaps from the others in degree but certainly not in kind. At best he could then be only a revealer and saviour (both lower case) for those who know his message.

(3) THE SALVATION OF THE NON-EVANGELIZED

What then of the religions of the world, the impact of their founders, and, even more broadly, of the situation of those many millions of people who did not or have not yet heard and accepted the message of salvation through Christ?[9] We can extend the language of Luke about 'the unknown God' (Acts 17: 23) to speak of the unknown Christ who has been and is effective everywhere, for everyone, and in all history—albeit often hiddenly. He has mediated and continues to mediate the fullness of revelation and salvation through particular historical events. Yet he is more than a simple reality of the temporal and spatial order. He is effectively present in all creation and history, and yet not in a way that depersonalizes him and reduces him to being a mere 'Christ idea' or universal principle. Salvation and

---

[9] See G. D'Costa, 'Other Faiths and Christianity', in A. E. McGrath (ed.), *The Blackwell Encyclopedia of Modern Christian Thought* (Oxford: Blackwell, 1993), 411–19; J. Dupuis, *Christianity and the Religions* (Maryknoll, NY: Orbis Books, 2001); various essays in D. Kendall and G. O'Collins (eds.), *In Many and Diverse Ways*; F. Whaling, 'Religion, Theories of', *Blackwell Encyclopedia of Modern Christian Thought*, 411–19.

revelation come personally—through the divine person who became incarnate as Jesus of Nazareth.

The universal presence of Christ has been thematized in three ways, which have their deep OT roots (see Chapter 2 above). He is present through the Spirit, as Word, and as Wisdom. First, the function of the Holy Spirit as vital principle or 'soul' of the Church (see 1 Cor. 6: 19) in no way excludes the presence and activity of the Spirit beyond the Christian community. While being the primary agent in carrying out the mission of the Church, the Holy Spirit's influence extends everywhere. The mysterious working of the Holy Spirit offers everyone the possibility of sharing in the saving grace brought by Christ's dying and rising, as Vatican II observes (*Gaudium et Spes*, 22). Second, we sketched above some lines of thinking about Christ's role as the creative and redemptive Word before and beyond Christianity. Yet, third, we might gain more by clarifying that role through another image which Christians drew from their Jewish origins: the image of Lady Wisdom. At the end of three millennia of a strongly masculine consciousness reflected in the Bible, what might this feminine, nurturing image convey about Christ's salvific function for all people?

Chapter 2 recalled the NT identification of Christ with Lady Wisdom, a theme then developed in Eastern Christianity. This feminine image helps to suggest the universal role of Christ, who invites and draws all to share in the divine banquet—like Lady Wisdom in Proverbs and other OT sapiential books. The Christian community has long been identified as 'Holy Mother the Church'. Within this visible, feminine community Christ has been primarily identified by his masculine qualities, as the 'Spouse' of the Church (e.g. Eph. 5: 21–33). But the feminine image of Lady Wisdom catches his role beyond the visible community—in mysteriously and anonymously gathering and healing human beings around the world.

An obvious advantage about interpreting Christ's role of universal Saviour through the image of wisdom comes from the fact that the Jewish-Christian scriptures and religion do not have a monopoly on wisdom. In one way or another, at least some wise teachings and wise ways of life turn up in all cultures, societies, and religions. Being found everywhere, sapiential modes of thought make an obvious bridge between the adherents of Christianity and others. Christian faith can see in any and all genuine wisdom the saving and revealing presence of Christ: 'ubi sapientia, ibi Christus (where wisdom is, there is Christ)'. To recognize in Christ the full revelation of God and the Saviour of all is not, then, to deny to other faiths any true knowledge of God and mediation of salvation. The unique and normative role of Christ in the history of salvation extends to the numerous and varied ways he works as divine Wisdom in the lives of people who follow other religions, honour their founders, and receive salvation through their faith. In one way or another, all peoples experience divine Wisdom, expressing it through their own inherited cultures and religions.

A persistent challenge for any efforts to correlate Christ, members of the Church, and others comes from the conviction, even if it is not always fully articulated, that some unfair element lurks in the background. It is all too clear that life's lottery does not distribute evenly life's blessings. There can be no denying that public fact. But once we move our focus from the merely human scene to our relationship with God, is it fair that merely a minority of the world's population consciously know and accept Christ as their Saviour, while the majority experience only his anonymous presence? Is it tolerable to think of the incarnation as the full and explicit manifestation of divine Wisdom in person at a particular point in human history, while other times and places have to be content with partial and implicit manifestations of that Wisdom? In response we might call attention to the mysterious freedom of God's saving love (see Chapter 9 above). That love, which inspires one cosmic plan of creation and redemption, discloses its presence in an endless variety of choices, ways, degrees, and intensities. Love constitutes, as I have maintained, the heart of redemption. Active presence, which assumes endlessly different forms, is its mode.

A CODA

So many issues are at stake and so many themes are involved in this chapter that it could be filled out and become a book in its own right. Let me address in conclusion at least two questions: the relationship between salvation and revelation; and the kingdom and the Church.

SALVATION AND REVELATION

The dense opening chapter of *Dei Verbum*, the Second Vatican Council's Dogmatic Constitution on Divine Revelation promulgated in 1965, uses 'the economy of revelation' and 'the history of salvation' in the singular. There is *only one* economy of revelation/salvation, even if we can and should distinguish between its various periods and modalities.[10] Moreover, the terms used here, 'revelation' and 'salvation', are more or less interchangeable. As far as Vatican II was concerned, the history of revelation is the history of salvation and vice versa. The text of Chapter 1 of *Dei Verbum* shuttles back and forth between the two terms.[11] Article 4 announces that it is 'above all through his death and resurrection from the dead and finally with the sending of the Spirit of Truth', that Jesus Christ 'completes, perfects and confirms *revelation* with the divine testimony: namely, that God is with us to *liberate us from the darkness of sin and death and raise us for eternal life*' (italics mine). Here the revealing and saving activity of God belong inseparably together in constituting the one history of divine self-communication. This theme of God's personal 'self-communication' in history, which comprises a self-*manifestation* that is *salvific*, comes up when article 6 of *Dei Verbum* declares that 'God wanted with the divine revelation to communicate himself'.

[10] Thus Vatican II's Decree on the Church's Missionary Activity (*Ad Gentes*) spoke in the plural of 'the ways' by which God brings those who 'through no fault of their own do not know the gospel' to the '*faith*' (without which, as the Letter to the Hebrews teaches (11: 6), 'it is impossible to please God'). It is not a question here of *mere beliefs* that result primarily from some human search and that, not being faith, would not 'please God' (*Ad Gentes*, 7).

[11] 'The economy of *revelation* occurs through deeds and words, which are intrinsically bound up with each other. Thus the works performed by God in the history of *salvation* manifest and bear out the doctrine and realities signified by the words; the words, for their part, proclaim and illuminate the works and the mystery they contain. The most intimate truth, which this *revelation* provides not only about God but also about the *salvation* of the human person, shines forth in Christ, who is both the mediator and the fullness of all *revelation*' (*Dei Verbum*, 2; italics mine).

A mindset which appreciates the two distinguishable but insepar-able dimensions of the divine self-communication, revelation and salvation, finds its justification in the Johannine terminology of 'grace and truth' (John 1: 14) and is needed for any evaluation of the religious situation of those who are not Christians. To understand their situation one needs to *hold together* persistently the revelatory and salvific activity of God, or the illumination that liberates people from darkness and brings them into the divine communion of love. Otherwise one might repeat the unacceptable view espoused decades ago by Carl Braaten, who recognized in Christ a universal role for salvation but not for revelation. For such a view Christ is the Saviour of all but not the Revealer to all[12]—a view simply incompatible with the universal action of the Son highlighted by Irenaeus. The Son 'from the beginning *reveals* the Father to all' (*Adversus Haereses*, 4. 20). One cannot separate the communication of salvation from that of revelation, as if—for instance—the world religions might be for their members means towards salvation but not towards knowing something of the self-revelation of God.

In 1964 the Second Vatican Council espoused the appropriate double terminology when describing Christ's activity: 'The one mediator, Christ, established and ever sustains here on earth his holy Church...as a visible organization through which he commu-nicates *truth and grace* to all men' (*Lumen Gentium*, 8; italics mine). Some paragraphs later the same constitution applied a parallel dyad, not to what is communicated through the visible Church, but to what the Church finds among those who, without any fault of their own, 'have not yet arrived at an explicit knowledge of God, and who, not without grace, strive to live an upright life. Whatever that is *good and true* which is to be found in them is considered by the Church to be a preparation for the gospel and given by Him who *enlightens* all human beings that they may at length have *life*' (ibid., 16). The Johannine language of revelation and salvation (in that order: 'enlightens' and 'life' (John 1: 4, 9)) alternates with the recognition of elements of salvation and revelation (in that order 'whatever is good and true') to be found among upright non-believers.

<hr />

[12] C. E. Braaten, *History and Hermeneutics* (London: Lutterworth, 1966), 15.

Two documents from the fourth and final session of Vatican II (of 1965) included similar 'double' terminology. Implying that other religions, even often, can exhibit elements of truth and holiness, the Declaration on the Relation of the Church to Non-Christian Religions (*Nostra Aetate*) stated: 'The Catholic Church rejects nothing of what is *true and holy* in these religions. She has a high regard for the manner of life and conduct, the precepts and doctrines which, although differing in many ways from what she herself believes and teaches, nevertheless not rarely reflect a *ray of that Truth which enlightens all human beings*' (no. 2; italics mine). Once again, echoing John's Gospel, the Council here combined terms in the usual order of revelation and salvation ('true and holy'). When proclaiming *Ad Gentes* six weeks later, it followed the same order, while showing itself more critical in the way it thought about other religions: 'Missionary activity... delivers from evil influences every element of *truth and grace* which are *already* found among peoples through a hidden presence of God' (no. 9; italics mine). Despite 'evil influences', a hidden presence of God has introduced everywhere elements of 'truth and grace' even before missionaries come to proclaim the Christian gospel.

To remark on this double-sided terminology may seem to border on the banal. However, this persistent usage in the documents of Vatican II suggests two conclusions. First, we may not raise the issue of salvation without raising that of revelation, and vice versa. When interpreting anyone's situation before God, we need to recall the two inseparable dimensions of the one divine self-communication. Second, the conciliar terminology follows John's Gospel in bearing witness to the way in which Christ's mediatorship entails his being universal Revealer as well as universal Saviour. He cannot logically be accepted as Saviour of all without being accepted as Revealer for all. His revelatory and redemptive activity can and should be distinguished but never separated. How one interprets this activity in terms of those who have not been baptized and may never have even heard of Christ is another and difficult issue. But, for Christians, such interpretation should start from the firm principle that Christ is both the Light of the world and the Life of the world.

Some early Christians left striking testimony to Christ as the Light and Life of the world by combining on the tombs of their beloved dead the two Greek words *phôs* (life) and *zôê* (life). *Phôs* ran down the cross-shaped inscription and intersected in the letter 'omega' with *zôê* which ran across. The central position of 'omega' recalled that Christ, who is Life of the world and the Light of the world, is also the end of all things.[13]

KINGDOM AND CHURCH

Mainline Christians agree that the fullness of the means of salvation are to be found in the Church—in particular, through the proclamation of the Word and the basic sacraments of baptism and the Eucharist. What then is the role of the Church for the salvation of those who are not baptized and go to God after a life spent in practising their religious faith? Most Catholic theologians (and their friends) remain grateful that the Second Vatican Council never repeated the old slogan of 'outside the Church no salvation'—a slogan that many had explained (or should one say explained away?) by talking of people being saved through 'implicitly desiring' to belong to the Church or by an 'implicit baptism of desire'. The Council used rather the language of all people being 'ordered' or 'oriented' toward the Church (*Lumen Gentium*, 15–16).[14] What, if any, is the 'necessity' of the Church for the salvation of all human beings?

To answer this question one needs to explain first *what* is the Church and *where* the Church is to be found. Given my confessional allegiance, I point, first, to the Roman Catholic Church. But I also strongly endorse what the Second Vatican Council taught in its Decree on Ecumenism, *Unitatis Redintegratio* (1965): 'all who have been justified by faith in baptism are members of Christ's body and have a right to be called Christian, and so are correctly accepted as brothers [and sisters] by the children of the Catholic Church' (no. 3).

---

[13] See R. Bultmann, '*Zaô*', in G. Kittel *et al.* (eds.), *Theological Dictionary of the New Testament*, ii (Grand Rapids, Mich.: Eerdmans, 1964), 832–75, at 841 n. 66.
[14] On this see J. Dupuis, *Toward a Christian Theology of Religious Pluralism*, 347–56; id., *Christianity and the Religions*, 208–10.

To ensure that this teaching would not be misinterpreted as referring only to individual Christians and not to their membership in a community, the Decree on Ecumenism acknowledged that the churches and communities not in full communion with the Roman Catholic Church possess 'many of the elements and endowments which together go to build up and give life to the Church itself' (ibid.). There is obviously very much small print to add to these headlines. But this paragraph provides the main outline of my answer to what the Church is and where it is to be found. For the small print I recommend a book by Cardinal Edward Cassidy, who headed the Council for Promoting Christian Unity from 1989 to 2001.[15]

First, for Christians the reign of God is or should be the decisive point of reference. The Church exists for the kingdom and at its service, not vice versa. Second, it is significant for me as a Roman Catholic that official teaching has become more cautious and less precise about the Church's role in mediating grace to those who are not baptized Christians; the mystery in God's plan to save all must be respected.[16]

Third, the Church mediates grace to its members and does so principally, although not exclusively, through the proclamation of the Word and the sacraments, the centre of which is the Eucharist. It intercedes for 'the others'. The eucharistic prayers distinguish between the invocation of the Holy Spirit to maintain the holiness and unity of the faithful and the intercessions for 'others' (intercessions which do not take the form of an *epiklesis* of the Spirit). Here 'the law of praying' should encourage theologians not to blur the distinction between the Church's role for the salvation of her members and for the salvation of 'the others'.[17] At the same time, the power of prayer ('for others' or, for that matter, for anybody) should not be underplayed, as if prayer were a 'merely moral cause'. The power of intercessory prayer should not be written off in that way. All baptized Christians are called to intercede for the whole

---

[15] See E. I. Cassidy, *Ecumenism and Interreligious Dialogue* (Mahwah, NJ: Paulist Press, 2005).

[16] See John Paul II's 1979 encyclical *Redemptor Hominis*, 9–10.

[17] See J. Dupuis, *Christianity and the Religions*, 210–12.

world. Through their prayers the salvation of 'the others' can come. Christians have received the astonishing gift of faith in Jesus, a gift that creates an essential responsibility to be fulfilled towards 'others'—not only through action but also through persevering prayer.

12

Bodily Resurrection and the Transformation of the World

> Earth felt the wound, and Nature from her seat
> Sighing through all her Works gave signs of woe,
> That all was lost.
>
> John Milton, *Paradise Lost*, 9. 782–4.
>
> Life has to end...love doesn't.
>
> Mitch Albom, *The Five People You Meet in Heaven*, 185.

One can hardly imagine a sharper difference between the ending of Mel Gibson's *The Passion of Christ* (2004) and that chosen by Pier Paolo Pasolini for *The Gospel according to St Matthew* (1964). Gibson does not picture a glorious resurrection but merely a reanimated corpse. Jesus stands up alone and without others being involved. Pasolini's presentation of the resurrection bursts with a revolutionary newness for the whole world. At the empty tomb an angel announces Jesus' victory over death. While we hear a joyful 'Gloria' taken from the African 'Missa Luba', we see the eleven disciples and other followers of Jesus, full of fresh energy and running up a mountain towards the risen Christ. He sends them on a mission with the comforting promise: 'Go, make disciples of all nations...I will be with you all days, even to the end of time' (Matt. 28: 19–20). Pasolini's ending is in a class of its own for suggesting something of the redemptive impact of Christ's rising from the dead.[1]

---

[1] I refer those concerned with grounds for believing in the risen Jesus to my *Easter Faith* (London: Darton, Longman & Todd, 2003).

THE REDEMPTION OF JESUS

Experience of seminar discussions has shown me how some Roman Catholic students find it strange when their reading of Thomas Aquinas's *Summa Theologiae* brings them to the statement that Christ himself was redeemed: 'Christ by his passion merited salvation not only for himself, but also for all who are his members' (3a. 48. 1 resp.). They have been so nourished with the idea of Christ as Redeemer and the language of his 'rising from the dead' (through his divine power) that it seems strange to picture the crucified and buried Jesus as 'meriting salvation also for himself' and being the object of the redeeming power of God. Nevertheless, that is the way passages in Paul and other early expressions in the NT stated the resurrection: 'God (the Father) raised Jesus from the dead'. In a new event, distinct from and subsequent to the crucifixion, God saved Jesus by bringing him from the condition of death into that of new and everlasting life. The Letter to the Hebrews uses 'save (sôzein)' to say just that about the Father, the One who 'could save him [Jesus] from death' (Heb. 5: 7). In this context Hebrews refers to the agonizing prayer of Jesus in Gethsemane, a prayer which brought him to accept obediently the divine will and his imminent death. But through resurrection we would be 'saved' definitively 'from death'. Matthew's passion story employs an equivalent verb ('ruomai') when, without intending to do so, those who mock Jesus on the cross say the truth about what God the Father will do: 'Let God rescue him [Jesus] if he wants to' (Matt. 27: 43).

(1) Mark's Eight Final Verses

In thinking and speaking about the redemptive event of Christ's resurrection, we do well to follow the reverent discretion shown by the closing verses of Mark's Gospel (16: 1–8). Those spare eight verses prove rich for any who, by espousing 'apophatic' theology, recognize the inadequacy of all attempts to describe the mystery of God and divine actions. Three contrasts are built into Mark's closing story:

darkness/light, absence/presence, and silence/speech. They enhance the telling of the story.

First, Mark's text contrasts not only the darkness of the night (between the Saturday and the Sunday of the resurrection) but also the darkness which enveloped the whole land at the crucifixion (Mark 15: 33) with the light of the sun which has just risen when the three women visit the tomb (Mark 16: 2). The women go to the tomb as the light fills the sky and as something they never imagined is about to be revealed: God has decisively overcome darkness and death.

A preliminary hint of the redemptive deed about to be revealed comes when the women 'raise their eyes and see' that the enormous stone, which blocked the entrance to the tomb and their access to the body of Jesus that they intend to anoint, 'has been rolled away' (Mark 16: 4). From the 'theological', passive form of the verb the attentive reader knows that God, while not explicitly named, has been at work in bringing about what is humanly impossible—by opening a tomb and raising the dead to new life. The women receive the first hint of what God has already done in unexpectedly reversing the situation of death and vindicating the victimized Jesus. Without being properly aware of it, the women find themselves confronted with the first disclosure of God's redemptive action in the resurrection. But Mark will not say what is ineffable nor describe what is indescribable. He leaves in place the awesome quality of what has already happened. So many Christian artists have failed to maintain this discretion, and set themselves to depict directly the moment when Jesus comes forth from the tomb.

A *second* contrast emerges once the women enter the tomb itself. The absence of Jesus' body contrasts with his personal presence, mediated through the interpreting angel who appears as a well-dressed 'young man'. This absent/present contrast has a deeper, numinous quality to it. God is literally absent in Mark's eight verses, through never being mentioned explicitly. Yet the mysterious, powerful presence of God comes through two verbs. God has been at work, since the stone 'has been rolled away' and the crucified Jesus of Nazareth 'has been raised' (Mark 16: 6). The awesome, redemptive power of God pervades the story, even if (or especially because?) God is never explicitly named.

A *third* contrast pits the confident *words* of the heavenly figure ('He has been raised. He is not here. See the place where they laid him.') against the *silence* of the women when they flee from the tomb. Its triple shape adds force to the announcement of God's saving act. The angel proclaims, initially, the great deed that concerns everyone and will change the universe forever: 'He has been raised'. Then the angel turns to the particular setting in which he is addressing the women: 'He is not here'. Finally, he points to the specific spot in the tomb where the body of Jesus had been left: 'See the place where they laid him.' Both these words of the angel and then the silent flight of the women highlight the dramatic nature of God's saving deed which has now been revealed. The women 'fled from the tomb. For trembling and astonishment had seized them, and they said nothing to anyone, for they were afraid' (Mark 16: 8).

Some commentators have explained the silent flight of the women as their disobedient failure to carry out the command, 'tell his disciples and Peter that he is going before you into Galilee; there you will see him' (Mark 16: 7). First of all, the male disciples of Jesus have failed, and now the women also prove to be disobedient failures. They break down and disobey the commission they have received from the angel. So Mark's Gospel is alleged to close with total human collapse. This dismal explanation, however, (a) glosses over the difference between the 'track record' of the male disciples and that of women in Mark's narrative, and (b) does not reckon with a feature of this Gospel which we find right from Chapter 1. Beyond question, (a) the male disciples of Jesus start going downhill from Mark 6: 52, where the evangelist states that they do not understand the feeding of the five thousand and their hearts are 'hardened'. Their lack of faith leads Jesus to rebuke them for their failure to understand and believe (Mark 8: 14–21). A little later he reproaches Peter sharply for perpetuating Satan's temptations by refusing to accept the suffering destiny that awaits his Master (Mark 8: 31–3). Then James, John, and the other disciples prove just as thickheaded (Mark 9: 32; 10: 35–40). Judas betrays Jesus into the hands of his enemies. When their Master is arrested in the Garden of Gethsemane, all the male disciples desert him (Mark 14: 50). Peter creeps back into the courtyard of the high priest while Jesus is being interrogated. But under pressure he twice denies being a follower of Jesus and then swears that he does not even know Jesus

(Mark 14: 66–72). None of the male disciples show up at the crucifixion, and it is left to a devout outsider, Joseph of Arimathea, to give Jesus a dignified burial (Mark 15: 42–7). The progressive failure of Jesus' male disciples—and, in particular, of the Twelve—begins at Mark 6: 52 and reaches it lowest point in the passion story.

Meanwhile, women have entered Mark's narrative (Mark 14: 3–9; 15: 40–1, 47). They function faithfully as the men should have done but have failed to do. The women remain true to Jesus right through to the end, and are ready to play their role by completing the burial rites. The women have 'followed' Jesus and 'ministered' to him (Mark 15: 41). Does the frightened silence with which they react to the angel's message express a sudden collapse on their part—a failure for which Mark's story has not prepared us?

Those who interpret the ending of Mark's Gospel by claiming that the male and then the female disciples all fail do not reckon with a persistent feature of this Gospel. Over and over again people respond to what Jesus does in his role as Redeemer (and Revealer) with amazement, silence, fear, and even terror (e.g. Mark 1: 22, 27; 4: 40–1; 6: 50–1). His activity manifests the awesome mystery of our saving God come personally among us. This was and is the appropriate human response to the awesome power and presence of God, revealed in the teaching, miracles, death, and resurrection of Jesus. The silence of the three women at the end must be understood as provisional; they remained silent until they could pass on their message to the appropriate persons, Peter and the other disciples. But their flight, fear, and initial silence are proper reactions to the climax of divine redemption revealed in the crucified Jesus being raised from the dead. God has triumphed over evil, the divine kingdom is breaking into the world, and the victimized Jesus is known to have been delivered from death and vindicated as the Son of God (Mark 1: 1, 11; 9: 7; 15: 39).[2]

(2) The Language of Resurrection

Many years ago Rudolf Bultmann pointed out how the adjectival clause 'who raised him from the dead' turns up as a formula-like

---

[2] For further details, see ibid., 73–6, 114.

attribute of God in Paul's letters and elsewhere in the NT.[3] Thus the Apostle begins his Letter to the Galatians with an appeal to 'God the Father who raised him [Jesus] from the dead' (1: 1). He warns the Corinthians against fornication by recalling their bodily destiny: 'God raised the Lord and will also raise us up by his power' (1 Cor. 6: 14). In Christ's resurrection the action was that of God (the Father). The only exception to Paul's normal way of stating the resurrection occurs in 1 Thessalonians 4: 14: 'We believe that Jesus died and rose again (anestê)'. Yet even here the overall stress is still placed on God's action. The verse continues: 'through Jesus, God will bring with him those who have fallen asleep'. In any case Paul begins the letter by reminding the Thessalonians how they 'turned to God from idols, to serve a living and true God, and wait for his Son from heaven, whom he raised from the dead' (1: 9–10). In Pauline terms God may be said simply to have raised Jesus from the dead (Rom. 10: 9), or to have raised him 'by his glory' (Rom. 6: 4), through his 'Spirit' (Rom. 8: 11), or 'by his power' (1 Cor. 6: 14). Christ's risen existence Paul calls life 'out of the power of God' (2 Cor. 13: 4). This merges with the notion of this risen state being life 'for God' (Rom. 6: 10).

The Apostle takes the resurrection of Jesus (together with ours) as the specifically Christian way of presenting God. To be wrong about the resurrection is to 'misrepresent' God essentially, since Paul defines God as the God of resurrection (1 Cor. 15: 15). One could not imagine a worse error in religion. It would be bad enough for our faith to be 'futile' and for us to be still in our old state of sin (1 Cor. 15: 17). But to misrepresent God would be the most extreme religious mistake we could make. What Paul says negatively in 1 Corinthians 15: 15 can be aligned with what he often says positively about the God who has raised Jesus and will raise us with him. Whether positively or negatively, the Apostle declares the God worshipped by Christians to be the God of resurrection.

In parenthesis it is worth remarking that subsequent to Paul other NT authors attribute to Jesus an increasingly active role in the resurrection. Acts represents Jesus as the agent of his post-Easter appearances, although not yet the agent of his resurrection *tout*

---

[3] R. Bultmann, *Theology of the New Testament*, i (London: SCM Press, 1952), 81.

court: 'He presented himself after his passion' (1: 3). In the Marcan predictions of death and resurrection, the Son of Man 'will rise again (anastêsetai)' (9: 31; see 8: 31; 10: 34)—presumably by his own power, but this is not made quite clear. The developing role of Jesus climaxes in John's Gospel. First, Jesus is the agent who will raise others (5: 21–9; 6: 39–54). Second, he names himself as the agent of his own resurrection (2: 19; 10: 17–18). Finally, the resurrection itself is simply identified with him: 'I am the resurrection' (11: 25).

To return to Paul, let us examine briefly the two key verbs Paul uses for the resurrection of Jesus: 'egeirô' and 'anistêmi'. The transitive verb 'egeirô', when used literally, denotes waking up or rousing from sleep; in an extended sense it applies to waking the dead. Just as a person can be awakened from sleep and rise, so Jesus 'has been raised' (1 Cor. 15: 4).[4] To clarify the metaphorical sense in which Jesus was 'woken up', Paul and the traditional material he quotes sometimes add 'from the dead' (Rom. 10: 9; 1 Cor. 15: 20; Gal. 1: 1). Paul draws our attention to this extended use of the verb by also adopting a conventional description of the dead as 'those who have fallen asleep' (1 Cor. 15: 6; 1 Thess. 4: 13) and calling the resurrected Christ 'the first fruits of those have fallen asleep' (1 Cor. 15: 20). 'Anistêmi', used transitively or intransitively, denotes being put back on one's feet, standing up, and being made to stand up. In an extended sense, this verb can be applied to those who have been made to stand up again (from the dead), put back on their (living) feet, or have themselves stood up again on their feet after being laid low by death.

Apropos of what has been said in the last paragraph, let me remind readers that to speak of the *metaphorical* sense of two key verbs ('egeirô' and 'anistêmi') is simply to draw attention to their being used in an extended, not in a literal, sense. But they do point to reality, the new reality of Jesus woken from the sleep of death, put back on his feet, and living gloriously after death and burial. Reference to reality is in no way limited to the literal use of language. Language used in the brave new world of computers and internet constantly exemplifies the *metaphorical* use of words (e.g. the 'world

---

[4] See D. Kendall and G. O'Collins, 'Christ's Resurrection and the Aorist Passive of egeirô', *Gregorianum* 74 (1993), 725–35.

wide web', the 'mouse', and 'hardware' versus 'software'). These metaphors may be false in the literal sense: we do not imagine that we are connected with a global-sized carpet or tapestry or that a tiny animal is wired to a machine on our desk. Yes, they are metaphors, but it is at our peril if we forget that they truly put us in touch with reality. Moreover, things expressed metaphorically can normally be further described (in literal and/or metaphorical language) and historically verified. They do not necessarily elude description or lack 'objective' reality. In short, metaphorical use of language (about the resurrection of Jesus or anything else) has *as such* nothing to do with the status in reality of that to which the metaphors refer.[5] In the particular case of Jesus' resurrection, historical verification has its (limited) role to play, even if Easter faith goes beyond the evidence.[6]

There is much more to be said about the language used by the NT in presenting what happened to Jesus after his death and burial. We find the new situation being set out in such terms as Jesus being 'assumed into glory', 'entering into his glory', 'exalted', 'exalted to the right hand of God', 'glorified', 'going to God', and 'moving from this world to the Father'. Let me limit myself to one term: life. Without abandoning the language of resurrection (Luke 24: 7), Luke shows a particular liking for the language of victorious life. At the tomb of Jesus, the two interpreting angels who speak with one voice challenge the party of women: 'Why do you seek the living among the dead?' (Luke 24: 5). Then, at the heart of the Emmaus story, this challenge is recalled by the two disciples. They tell the mysterious stranger about a vision of angels who told the women: 'he is alive' (Luke 24: 23). This language of life in the Easter context is not a Lukan monopoly; other NT authors apply it to the risen Christ (e.g. Rom. 14: 9; Rev. 1: 18). Nevertheless, the explicit use of this language sets Luke's Easter chapter apart from the Easter chapters of the other evangelists.

Since Luke's primary audience was probably Gentile rather than Jewish, (1) this may have been one of his reasons for introducing

---

[5] Here I follow what J. M. Soskice, especially in *Metaphor and Religious Language* (Oxford: Clarendon Press, 1985) and W. P. Alston, especially in *Divine Nature and Human Language* (Ithaca: Cornell University Press, 1989), have written about the use of metaphor as building on literal utterances and meanings but going beyond them when referring to reality.

[6] See G. O'Collins, *Easter Faith*, 25–50.

alongside the language of resurrection that of life. The terminology of life, which was in any case biblical, could communicate better with non-Jewish readers. Luke may have had at least two other reasons for using the language of life. (2) It sets out the present situation of Jesus: he has been raised from the dead and therefore he is gloriously alive. 'Life' expresses the permanent condition into which the resurrection has brought Jesus. There is a hint of the need to say this, when the 1989 *Revised English Bible* maintained the earlier translation of the *New English Bible* by rendering 'egêgertai' (1 Cor. 15: 4) as 'he was raised to life'. Strictly speaking, this is an exegetical comment. In any case, it would also have respected the perfect tense of the verb better by translating it as 'he has been raised to life'. This would have conveyed the implication of the Greek original: what happened in the past continues to exercise its influence in the present. But my main point here is that the addition 'to life' follows what Luke intended by sometimes introducing the language of life. The evangelist felt the need to indicate the present and permanent situation of Jesus that has resulted from the event of the resurrection. (3) A third motive behind Luke's choice of 'life' could well have been the desire to suggest what Jesus wishes to share with us here and hereafter. He has been raised from the dead in order that we might live in God now and forever.[7]

In the thirteenth century Aquinas wrote of Christ, through his love and heroic obedience, 'meriting salvation for himself'. This chimes quite well with Hebrews 5: 7, while not being the normal language of other NT authors. Nevertheless, what they did write supports interpreting the redemptive impact of the resurrection as primarily concerned with the crucified and buried Jesus. At the same time, Paul and other NT writers were not content to represent the resurrection as merely a unique action by God (the Father) on behalf of the dead Jesus. From start to finish this resurrection deeply affects humankind and the whole world. In Paul's words, 'he [Christ] was handed over for our sins, and was raised for our justification' (Rom. 4: 25).

---

[7] Curiously such large commentaries as D. L. Bock, *Luke*, vol. ii: *9: 51–24: 53* (Grand Rapids, Mich.: Baker Books, 1996), J. A. Fitzmyer, *The Gospel According to Luke X–XXIV*, Anchor Bible 28a (Garden City, NY: Doubleday, 1985), and J. Nolland, *Luke 18: 35–24: 53*, Word Biblical Commentary 35c (Dallas: Word Books, 1993) have little to say about Luke's important Easter theme of life.

THE RESURRECTION OF HUMAN BEINGS

Comments on the appearances of the risen Christ and the associated outpouring of the Holy Spirit (see, above all, John 20: 23) could fill a whole book. Here at least this should be said. The men and women to whom he appeared, and who become the founding fathers and founding mothers of Christianity, were brought to understand that the risen Lord was bringing them into a new relationship with him and into a new fellowship in the Spirit, an unprecedented way of life that could never be broken by death. Hope for their own resurrection was integral to their experience of and reflections on what had redemptively happened to Jesus himself. Chapter 15 of 1 Corinthians witnesses eloquently to the centrality of this hope to share in Jesus' risen existence and so experience forever life not only after death but also life without death.

This coming life without death entails a full and final salvation that will complete our being made in the image and likeness of God (Gen. 1: 26–7). The original creation had meant just that. The new creation (2 Cor. 5: 17), initiated by all that Christ did and went through, centres on the resurrection or being remade in the image and likeness of the risen and glorified Christ. Creation itself is mysterious, and the new creation of resurrection even more mysterious. If Job could not plumb the mysteries of creation (Job 38–42), what chance do any of us have to grasp something of the new creation which is bodily resurrection? Nevertheless, any theological work of redemption would be patently incomplete without some serious reflection on the risen existence to come.[8]

(1) Art and Literature

Great paintings, both classic and modern, inevitably shape our images of the risen life to come. Stanley Spencer's *The Resurrection* (1924–6), now in the Tate Gallery (London), pictures the dead rising

[8] See R. Bieringer, V. Koperski, and B. Lataire (eds.), *Resurrection in the New Testament* (Leuven: Leuven University Press, 2002); B. P. Prusak, 'Bodily Resurrection in a Catholic Perspective', *Theological Studies* 61 (2000), 64–105.

in a country churchyard. They are emerging from their graves in a leisurely fashion, rather like people getting out of bed in the morning. There is a last judgement of sorts going on, but it is a very gentle, merciful one. Christ is represented as a motherly figure, who nurses two babies lovingly held in her arms. Many details of Spencer's work project this-worldly actions into the scene of general resurrection. A woman brushes the jacket of her husband, as she is reconciled to him; another woman, modelled on Spencer's first wife, smells a flower and then climbs over a stile towards the river Thames, where a pleasure-boat is waiting to take the resurrected dead to the higher and better form of life in heaven. The painting does provide hints of what resurrection will be like, especially through the maternal presence and love of Christ with whom human beings will be united in lasting and completely satisfying happiness when they are raised after death. Spencer does not aim at portraying the 'mechanism' and moment of resurrection. He sets out rather what happens in its immediate aftermath; it will result in the dead being peacefully reunited with one another in the communion of saints at the 'heavenly banquet' and experiencing a new life centred on the all-loving Christ. Spencer's painting yields a sense of people being available to each other, yielding their self to others, and then receiving it back from them. The whole impression is totally different from the ruthless self-assertion of isolated or self-separating individuals, which is euphemistically sometimes called autonomy or independence.

In *The Five People You Meet in Heaven*,[9] Mitch Albom may not introduce Christ as such, but he does suggest the mysterious depth of individual identity and the totality of our life brought beyond death into eternity. Death appears to rupture our particular network of relationships, that ensemble of events, effects, and individual relationships which over time constitute our self. Albom lets the reader sense the interconnectedness of all human lives, including those lived before us and after us. Each human existence is a unique cluster of relationships and bodily performances, which together make up one story. As Albom puts it, 'the secret of heaven' is that 'each affects the other and the other affects the next, and the world is

[9] (London: Little Brown, 2003).

full of stories, but the stories are all one'.[10] St Augustine of Hippo would agree, while expressing this interconnectedness in terms of the exalted Christ and his proper self-love. At the end, 'there will be one Christ loving himself (erit unus Christus amans seipsum)' (*In Epistulam Johannis*, 10. 3). In chapter 51 of her *Showings*, Julian of Norwich endorsed a similar belief: 'Jesus is in all who will be saved, and all who will be saved are in Jesus.'[11] The third Eucharistic Prayer hints at this belief in the prayer that 'we, who are nourished by his body and blood, may be filled with the Holy Spirit, and become one body, one spirit in Christ'.

One could suggest other and greater examples from literature, art, and music that might provide some hints and imaginative insights into resurrection. Those who treasure the work of Dante Alighieri (d. 1321) will glean much from his *Paradiso*, the third part of his *Divine Comedy* where thirty-three cantos take us through heaven until we arrive at the divine love that 'moves the sun and the other stars'. Painters and sculptors have provided almost innumerable scenes of humanity's resurrection (often coupled with the last judgement). Michelangelo's *Last Judgement* in the Sistine Chapel must be the most famous example of such works. Just a few yards away in the Vatican, the chapel of 'Redemptoris Mater' has been decorated by the modern mosaics of Marko Rupnik, who depicts a similar combination of resurrection and judgement but with a feeling of luminous joy. The baroque churches of Rome abound with frescos showing what results from the resurrection: the risen life of saints in heaven. But one needs to go to Ghent and Madrid for more brilliantly and mysteriously evocative examples. The *Adoration of the Lamb* (1432) by Hubert and Jan Van Eyck in Ghent shows a blossoming meadow in which carefully arranged groups of angels and saints adore Christ enthroned on an altar. The *Holy Trinity* (from the mid-sixteenth century), executed by Titian and now in the Prado, depicts risen humanity drawn tumultuously up toward the triune God. Settings of the Creed for the Latin Masses by Bach, Beethoven, Bruckner, Mozart, and other classical composers evoke the joyful mystery of Christ's resurrection ('et resurrexit tertia die'), as do

[10] *The Five People You Meet in Heaven*, 208.
[11] *Showings*, trans. E. College and J. Walsh (New York: Paulist Press, 1978), 276.

Mahler's Second ('Resurrection') Symphony and the works on the resurrection, risen bodies, and the resurrected environment by Olivier Messiaen (d. 1992).[12] Music, like literature and the visual arts, can lend credible insight into the glorified, bodily existence of the risen Jesus and risen humanity.

(2) The Sign of the Tomb

Before we grapple with the risen body and resurrected existence, we might usefully pause to think about the value of Jesus' empty tomb as a redemptive sign.[13] Here and there the NT notes how the Easter *appearances* also functioned as a sign of continuity between the earthly Jesus and the risen Christ (e.g. John 21: 7). His pre-resurrection followers were able to recognize him as the same person whom they had lived with and seen or known to have died on the cross. The NT, however, offers little on the sign-value of the empty tomb of Jesus. All the same, it seems reasonable to go beyond the fact of the empty tomb to what it might express and symbolize.

First of all, the emptiness of Jesus' grave reflects the holiness of that it once held, the corpse of the incarnate Son of God who lived totally for others and died to bring a new covenant of love for all people. This 'Holy One' could not 'see corruption' (Acts 2: 27). Second, tombs naturally express the finality and irrevocable loss of death. Jesus' open and empty grave readily suggests and symbolizes the fullness of new and everlasting life into which he has risen. Here emptiness paradoxically bespeaks fullness.

Third, the empty tomb expresses something vital about the nature of redemption: namely, that redemption is much more than a mere escape from our scene of suffering and death. Still less is it a kind of second creation 'from nothing (ex nihilo)'. Rather it means the transformation of this material, bodily world with its whole history of sin and suffering. The first Easter began the work of finally bringing our universe home to its ultimate destiny. God did not

---

[12] See J. Bowden, 'Resurrection in Music', in S. Barton and G. Stanton (eds.), *Resurrection* (London: SPCK, 1994), 188–97.

[13] On the historical reliability of the empty tomb, see e.g. G. O'Collins, *Easter Faith*, 43–9.

discard Jesus' earthly corpse but mysteriously raised and transfigured it, so as to reveal what lies ahead for human beings and their world. In short, that empty tomb in Jerusalem is God's radical sign that redemption is not an escape to a better world but a wonderful transformation of this world. Seen that way, the open and empty grave of Jesus is highly significant for anyone who wants to appreciate what redemption means.

(3) Christ's Case and Ours

But what is a risen, bodily existence like? What could be meant by the final goal of redemption, the resurrection of the body and life everlasting? First of all, an introductory 'confession' and a word of caution. I am well aware that (a) many people hold that death simply brings the extinction of our personal, human existence or at best a kind of recycling—namely, the re-absorption of our material/ spiritual being into some supra-personal material/spiritual reality. (b) Many others, however, maintain the survival of our souls, either as transferred to some enhanced state or else as reincarnated in a fresh body. Those who belong to this second group espouse a wide variety of beliefs about the soul's origin and destiny.[14]

Whether they belong to group (a) or (b), those who do not accept resurrection may well find the reflections that follow a sheer waste of time, as absurd as looking for something north of the North Pole. Yet reflect we must. It seems odd to believe in Jesus' resurrection and hope for our own, while steadily refusing to hazard any thoughts on what the resurrection of the whole person could be like. St Paul, to be sure, wrote of 'the things revealed to us through the Spirit' as 'what no eye has seen, nor ear heard, nor the human heart conceived, what God has prepared for those who love him' (1 Cor. 2: 9–10). But 'what God has prepared for those who love him' does belong among 'the things revealed to us through the Spirit', and the Apostle will press ahead in chapter 15 of the same letter to explore tentatively what risen existence could be like. What then can we say about the

---

[14] See the nine articles on 'Soul', in M. Eliade (ed.), *The Encyclopedia of Religion*, xiii (New York: Macmillan, 1987), 426–65; for beliefs about the soul's origins and destiny, see 'Breath and Breathing', in ibid., ii. 302–8, and 'Afterlife', in ibid., i. 107–27.

new, transformed life which will be 'me' risen from the dead and not my spiritual successor or some mere duplicate of me?

Then a word of caution. Whatever way we try to depict the resurrected and glorified human existence, we should always remember the difference between Christ's case and ours—something rejected by Arthur Peacocke among others. In the name of the fundamental solidarity which the incarnation involves, he argues that Jesus must share our lot with regard to bodily corruption in the grave. There is supposedly a perfect parallel, so that what happens to us corresponds precisely to what happened to Christ.[15] Yet an incarnation-centred theology need not and, indeed, should not lead to a rejection of the empty tomb. Peacocke formulates the doctrine this way: the Son of God became *man*. My own formulation would reverse the emphasis: *the Son of God* became man. Christ differs from all other human beings in that he is a divine person who assumed the human condition and had the unique role of being the Saviour of the world. While Peacocke feels that it is imperative that Christ should fully share our fate, I would argue that his primary role is that of saving us human beings and summoning us to what lies beyond our powers. The redemptive goal of the incarnation needs to be respected, and that justifies the scope of the empty tomb. By first confessing the incarnation and Christ's resurrection and then expressing hope for ours, the Creed does not take the two cases of resurrection to be simply the same. His corpse laid in the tomb near Golgotha entered directly into Christ's risen existence in a way which will not be true of ourselves.[16]

We are dealing here, of course, with mystery, the deliverance of Jesus from death and his final, glorious transformation. He does not return to his old life, but breaks through to a new kind of life. He becomes a new creation, not a patched-up version of the old one. Nevertheless, once we accept that his tomb was found to be empty and did not become so through some merely human intervention (removal or theft of the corpse), we must conclude to some special

---

[15] A. Peacocke, *Theology for a Scientific Age* (Minneapolis: Fortress Press, 1993), 279–88, 332.

[16] On the special continuity between the earthly body and the risen body in the case of Jesus, see G. O'Collins, *Jesus Risen* (Mahwah, NJ: Paulist Press, 1987), 224–6.

divine activity. Someone could argue, I suppose, that God simply annihilated the corpse of Jesus and fitted out his soul (in which his 'real' identity is lodged) with a brand-new, 'pneumatic' body or with a copy of the body laid in the tomb. Taken simply as such, a divinely caused disappearance of the corpse does not necessarily say anything about the nature of the material continuity between that corpse and the resurrected Jesus. Nevertheless, the Gospels indicate some kind of direct continuity between the corpse laid to rest by Joseph of Arimathea and Jesus' risen existence, a continuity which made it possible for the disciples to recognize the glorified Jesus whom they met as the same person who died on the cross. This more direct continuity sets his resurrection apart from ours.

Reasons are available to render such special continuity plausible. The corpse buried by Joseph of Arimathea differed in two ways from all other corpses anyone has ever or will ever place in a tomb. This corpse had been the body of the incarnate Son of God who had suffered on the cross to bring all men and women deliverance from evil. The *divine identity* and *universal redemptive role* of Christ put his resurrection in another class. In being raised from the dead, only he assumed his rightful divine identity (e.g. Acts 2: 32–6; Rom. 1: 4) and became the effective Saviour of the world (e.g. Acts 4: 12; 1 Cor. 15: 45). On both counts some peculiarly close continuity between the corpse laid in the tomb and Christ's risen, bodily existence can seem believable.

A partial reading of Paul could obscure the real differences between Christ's resurrection and ours. The talk about Christ being raised as 'the first fruits of those who have fallen asleep' (1 Cor. 15: 20) and the Apostle's attempts to say something about 'the resurrection of the dead' in general (1 Cor. 15: 42–51) do not necessarily bring out how different Christ's case is. Yet Paul indicates that difference. It is true only of Christ that his resurrection brought 'justification' to all human beings (Rom. 4: 25). He alone will effect the resurrection of the dead: 'as in Adam all die, so also in Christ shall all be made alive' (1 Cor. 15: 22). Paul does not say of any other risen person that 'he must reign until he has put all his enemies under his feet' (1 Cor. 15: 25). In short, Paul does not present Christ's resurrection as a precise prototype of ours.

His personal identity and redemptive function make it plausible that Christ's dead body should be 'incorporated' immediately into his risen existence, and hence that he would enjoy 'more' bodily continuity than we will. Furthermore, in his case a clear sign of continuity between his earthly and risen existence (the empty tomb) is incomparably more important that it is in the case of any mere human being.

In what follows, however, I do not wish to stress the differences between Jesus and ourselves, but rather to reflect on the earthly body and its possible relationship with the risen body. Some insights into the possible meaning and nature of a personal, risen existence automatically bolster the position of those who look to share in Christ's resurrection and deny that we 'go the way of the grasshopper'.[17] I have just written of 'some insights' into risen existence. No one can describe exactly and fully the life and activity of risen persons. To be able to do that, we would need to have already experienced resurrection for ourselves. The limits in our experience condition the way we may conceptualize and describe resurrection. Perhaps it would be wiser to say very little and speak only of a new life for the whole person who will be transformed and live 'beyond' the limitations and evils that affect our present existence. In these terms, resurrection will be the ultimate freedom from domination (brought by Christ the Liberator) and the totally satisfying participation or 'koinônia' of the Holy Spirit. To the extent that the final reality of resurrection is more than a spatio-temporal reality, language fails. Hence I do not pretend to say anything about *how* the resurrection takes place. I confine myself to reflecting on what its result, the risen bodily existence of a human being, could be like.

(4) Matter and Spirit

Nowadays it is common to stress the spiritual and bodily unity of the human person. All the same, a certain 'dualism' remains between matter and spirit. But it should be added at once that dualistic

---

[17] Echoing André Malraux, Ernest Becker wrote of the years of suffering and effort it takes to make an individual, and 'then he is good only for dying... He has to go the way of the grasshopper, even though it takes longer' (*The Denial of Death* (New York: The Free Press, 1973, 269)). If there is no resurrection, everything about human life seems a matter of indifference, like the life and death of an individual grasshopper.

thinking about our present existence does not necessarily steer us to a Platonic conclusion in which 'we' (as soul or spirit) are 'in' a body or 'have' a body. To speak of our present matter and spirit need not suppose that they are utterly, totally disparate realities which, like oil and water, will not mix. All matter has something spiritual about it. A pure materiality that would be utterly 'unspiritual' seems impossible. One is dealing here partly with a question of definition. Matter could be flatly defined in opposition to spirit and, if so defined, would not have something spiritual about it. Nevertheless, all *human* matter has something spiritual about it. Moreover, all the atomic material in our universe is at least potentially human matter.

The spiritualizing and personalizing of matter take place incessantly through eating and drinking. By being taken into a human body, matter becomes vitally associated with the functions of a spiritual being. The world of art exemplifies a similar phenomenon. Paintings, pieces of sculpture, and stained-glass windows are material objects. But by being organized and spiritualized in the hands of makers, these works of art can embody a rich cargo of personal meaning. Christian believers acknowledge a similar process in the life of the sacraments, above all in the case of the Eucharist. There a piece of bread and a cup of wine are spiritualized and personalized through the power of the Holy Spirit to become the risen Christ's most intensely real presence. The use of material objects (e.g. water and oil) in all the sacraments visibly associates the bodies of the worshippers with the material universe. But the rite aims to link them symbolically with highly personal realities: the body of the Church and the body of Christ himself. Obviously matter can be understood and interpreted in many ways. Nuclear physicists know it as mainly empty space, the field of several basic forces. Electrons and other particles appear as either mass or energy. Nevertheless, eating, drinking, painting, celebrating the sacraments, and other human activities disclose another face of matter: its possibility of being partly spiritualized and personalized.

The resurrection of the dead will mean the full and final personalizing and spiritualizing of matter, not its abolition. Through the Holy Spirit the human spirit will dominate matter, in the sense that the body will clearly express and serve the glorified spirit of human beings. Accepting this demands a leap of imagination. Four functions of our earthly body and four contrasts between the earthly and risen body can carry us forward in making that leap.

(5) Four Functions

As human beings we are bodily, or—if you like—we are bodies. What can we appreciate about the nature of the present human body that could point ahead to our bodily destiny in the resurrection? First of all, our bodies obviously insert us into the material world. We become a tiny part of the cosmos and the gigantic cosmos part of us. Once upon a time people naively assumed a far-reaching autonomy and stability for the human body. Scientists had not yet discovered that our life is a dynamic process of constant circulation between our bodies and our material environment. To adapt John Donne's words, no body is an island. Our bodies make us share in and incessantly relate to the universe.

An essential part of this insertion into the universe is our relationship to God. To be sure, for various reasons and to various degrees many people fail to live out this relationship. Nevertheless, as human bodily persons we participate in the universe, and that entails being related to God as the ultimate origin, ever-present partner, and final goal of our existence. We cannot participate in the material universe, without participating in God, the inmost ground of all being, the One on whom the created world remains constantly and radically dependent.

Second, our bodiliness creates the possibility of being *communicators*. Through our bodies we act, express ourselves, relate, and communicate with others. Without our bodies, there would be no language, no art, no literature, no religion, no industry, no politics, no social and economic relations, and none of that married love in which verbal and non-verbal communication reaches a supremely intense level. In short, without bodies we could not have and make any human history. Through our bodies we build up a whole web of relationships with other human beings, with the material universe, and with God. Our bodies enable us to communicate, play the human game, and compose our story.

Although our bodies enable us to communicate, at the same time they set limits to our communication. Being subject to the constraints of space and time, our bodies set us apart and restrict our chances of relating and communicating. People talk, hug, kiss, telephone, write letters, and in other ways try to make up by quantitative repetition for what they lack qualitatively. Through sickness, old age, imprisonment, and other causes, our bodies can bring us radical solitude and terrifying loneliness. That bodily loneliness and breakdown in communication find their ultimate expression when the tomb contains a newly-buried corpse or a crematorium the fresh ashes of someone.

Our material bodies do not merely separate and alienate us from one another, from the world, and from God. Through weariness, physical weakness, sickness, and sleep, they alienate us from ourselves. Our embodied condition can make us feel not fully free to be ourselves and to be with others.

Third, here and now our bodies ensure our *continuity* and our being recognized as the same person. To be and to be recognized as the same person, we must remain the 'same' body. Despite our constant and massive bodily changes, personal identity and continuity are somehow bound up with bodily identity and continuity. We are/have the same body, and therefore remain the same person. Bodily continuity points to personal identity. Some deny the link between bodily continuity and continuity of personal identity, understanding the latter in terms of continuity of memories and character. Unquestionably memories have a role in maintaining our *sense* of personal identity. The memory of what I have personally experienced constitutes the 'evidence' within me of my persisting identity. Yet one's enduring personhood cannot simply depend upon one's memory. Otherwise loss of memory would entail loss of personal identity. The case of amnesia rebuts attempts to promote memory as the (sole?) means for constituting and preserving personal continuity or the one unique life story which is 'me'.

To press this case, one might imagine the case of a murderer who not only repented and underwent a radical change of character but also suffered a total loss of memory about his crime. Let us suppose that many years later he was arrested by the police. His physical appearance had changed over the course of time. But fingerprints and DNA tests positively identify him as the person who had committed the murder. We can bracket off what a court of law might do in such a case. At all events one thing is clear: bodily identity and continuity would be decisive in establishing the continuity of the murderer's personal identity.

Fourth, at all stages of our human life we experience our bodiliness as the 'place' and means of grace, happiness, sin, and misery. The sacraments act as a massive reminder of this. Our personal communion in the life of God through Christ and the Holy Spirit begins and then grows through our heads being sprinkled with water, our forehead being smeared with oil, our mouths opening to receive the eucharistic elements, and so forth. For ancient and modern hedonism, the body has taken on an exaggerated importance, as if the pursuit of happiness could and should be defined in terms of physical pleasure alone. Nevertheless, this sad exaggeration should not be allowed to cover up the fact that all human happiness has something bodily about it. It is the same with sin and misery. It is hard to imagine either unhappiness or sinful human acts which could remain completely 'unbodily'. Through his brilliant miming of the deadly sins, Marcel Marceau used to bring out wonderfully how all seven of them, including pride and envy, have something bodily about them. In short, our body enters essentially into what we experience of grace, happiness, sin, and misery.

(6) Four Contrasts

The four 'functions' of our human bodies which I have just outlined can help us refine what we might say about the risen life. First, resurrection brings matter to a most intense *participation* in the universe and in the life of God. By being raised from the dead, human beings as embodied spirits will not only belong in a new way to the universe but will also in a new way share in the divine life. As both *material* and spiritual beings they will receive their ultimate divinization so as to 'live to God' (Rom. 6: 10). In his bodiliness the risen Jesus himself takes part in a most intense way in the life of the universe, and is a 'piece' of this material world which has already been inserted into the life of God—to be fully and finally with God.

Second, resurrection will maximize our capacity to relate and *communicate*. Let me select the supreme example. As raised from the dead through the power of the Spirit, Jesus now relates to the Father, human beings, and the whole cosmos in a manner that has shed the constraints of his historical existence. Wherever, for example, two or three gather in his name, they find the risen Lord in their midst (Matt. 18: 20). Nothing expresses better the new communicative power of Jesus than the Eucharist, his worldwide presence and offer to communicate a life that will never end.

To hope for resurrection means hoping that we will be set free to go far beyond the limitations and triviality of so much of what passes for communication in this world. We will be liberated to be truly ourselves and to be with others in a new, loving way.

Third, perhaps the greatest difficulty in grasping something about the nature of risen existence gathers around the issue of *continuity*. As we saw, personal identity remains somehow bound up with bodily continuity. Irenaeus emphatically applied this principle to the personal identity that will be preserved in resurrection. He asked: 'With what body will the dead rise? Certainly with the same body in which they died, otherwise those who rise would not be the same persons who previously died' (*Adversus Haereses*, 5. 13. 1). But in what sense will we rise with the *same* body? What counts here as bodily sameness or identity? Even in this life the enormous and constant interchange of matter with our environment can make us wonder how far it is correct to speak of someone being or having the 'same' body at six, sixteen, and sixty. If it is difficult to say how we keep the 'same' body within our human history, we need to be even more hesitant about 'explaining' bodily continuity between this existence and our risen life.

One answer could be found here by noting the connection between saying 'I am my body' and 'I am my history'. Through our bodiliness we create and develop a whole web of relationships with other people, with the world, and with God. Our history comes from our body being 'in relationship'. As bodies we have our history—from conception to death. As human beings, we enjoy a bodily or embodied history. Through resurrection our particular embodied history will be raised from death. That human, bodily history that makes up the story of each person will be brought to new life. In a mysterious, transformed fashion their risen existence will express what they as embodied persons were and became in their earthly life. Put that way, the view of Irenaeus can make good sense:

'With what bodily history will the dead rise? Certainly with the same bodily history at the end of which they died; otherwise those who rise would not be same persons who previously died.'

I realize that to some this suggestion of mine can seem like pure poetry—in the pejorative sense of 'pure poetry'. Nevertheless, if I ask what has made me what I am, it has surely been my particular embodied history and not, for instance, merely the millions of molecules which in a passing parade have at different moments constituted my particular physical existence. Furthermore, my whole bodily history is much more 'me' than the physical body which breathes its last, say at eighty years of age. In short, I propose resurrection as God bringing to a new personal life the total embodied history of dead individuals and so ensuring their genuine personal continuity. This approach makes very good sense of what happened to Jesus himself. As Henry Scott Holland (1847–1918) put it, 'when he [Jesus] rose, his life rose with him'.[18] In his risen state Jesus possesses fully his whole human story. His glorification has made his entire life and history irrevocably present.

My proposal about our continuity being preserved by our embodied history being resurrected must face the question: How can our history in time be resurrected in an existence which is not temporal? Any full response would need to establish two conclusions. First, time and eternity are not exclusively different. Just as some kind of eternal life can already be present in temporality, so there could be some kind of temporality in eternal life. Second, time is more than a pure and mere succession of events (as someone in the tradition of David Hume (1711–76) would lead us to believe), but has also something cumulative about it. Every moment is a coming together of many things which are all somehow preserved. Likewise, or rather even more so, resurrected life could be a coming together of a whole, accumulated past which remains present to us. In resurrection our time is summed up and completed.

My proposal about our embodied history being resurrected finds support from Caroline Walker Bynum's *The Resurrection of the Body in Western Christianity, 200–1336*.[19] She illustrates extensively the

---

[18] Quoted by D. M. MacKinnon, *Borderlands of Theology* (London: Lutterworth Press, 1968), 115.
[19] (New York: Columbia University Press, 1995).

persistent conviction of Christians that resurrection will preserve for all eternity their gender, family experiences, and other personal characteristics. They rejected Gnostic-style talk about Jesus living 'male' but rising 'human'[20] or, more generally, about themselves living 'male' or 'female' but rising 'human' with some kind of unisex, spiritual body. Such views detach the risen Jesus from the particular characteristics and circumstances (especially the sexual, racial, religious, and geographical ones) that shaped his history as a first-century Jewish male who lived in Palestine. Since his particular history is thus not supposed to rise with him, what he was, did, and suffered during his earthly life no longer matters—at least *sub specie aeternitatis*. There are those who continue to maintain that we will rise neither male nor female but simply as human. If this were so, our personal history shaped not only by our language, culture, and other factors but also by our sex would be radically flouted. We will rise with our integral history. Our sex forms an essential part of that history. If we were to rise as neither male nor female but as undifferentiated human beings, we would not be the same persons who had previously lived.

Fourth, here and now bodiliness enters essentially into our life of sin, grace, and happiness. Our bodies are the *place* where we experience them. In our future existence, our risen bodies will be the 'place' where we will experience full freedom and happiness. The truth of a beatific vision for our minds can obscure the essential bodiliness of risen life and even wrongly suggest that we will become pure spirits to contemplate the infinite beauty of God. Yet the vision of God face to face will not be at odds with the redemption and transformation of our bodily, social selves. Rather, both here and hereafter we receive God's loving presence through our bodily humanity. To apply and extend one of Tertullian's classic sayings, 'caro cardo salutis (the flesh is the hinge of salvation)' (*De Resurrectione Carnis*, 8. 2), our bodiliness is the hinge or pivot of our grace now and of our glory to come.

This section has lingered over four points (participation, communication, continuity, and the place of salvation) which may

---

[20] For a latter-day version of this Gnostic view, see V. R. Mollenkott, *The Divine Feminine: The Biblical Imagery of God as Female* (New York: Continuum, 1983), 70–1.

help us to leap imaginatively from our present to our future bodiliness. Seen in those terms, our present body points to and symbolizes, albeit inadequately, our final redemption in our risen body.

(7) Physical Fantasies

Over the centuries people have often taken final resurrection from the dead to involve a mere resuscitation of a corpse or at best an improved earthly body which enables risen persons to resume eating, sexual activities, and other previous activities. This false interpretation turned up in a debate with Jesus initiated by some Sadducees (Mark 12: 18–27). A few years ago a crudely materialistic view of resurrection lay behind an appalling episode witnessed by a friend of mine. To stop them rising from the dead, the bodies of some government troops were dismembered by those who had ambushed and killed them.

It is a mistake to think of present human bodiliness in merely material terms and ignore or play down its spiritual and personal aspects. It is even more mistaken to take the risen body primarily in physical terms. This happens with all those recurring speculations about our physical appearance in the life to come: 'Will I look the same as I did at thirty?' In this life a person's external characteristics can suffer massive changes over the years, and he or she remains the same person. My maintaining my identical selfhood in a risen state does not depend on my enjoying an appearance totally similar to that of some supposedly optimum phase of my earthly life. Rather my remaining in resurrection the particular person I have been depends on my particular embodied history being raised from death to new life.

THE TRANSFORMATION OF THE UNIVERSE

Modern astronomy has tended to demote humankind from its traditionally exalted place in the universe to what can appear to be a relatively unexceptional and very insignificant role in the cosmic process. The sheer size of the universe seems to render humanity and its destiny unimportant. Astronomy has shown that our universe is too big for thinking. There are around 100,000 million galaxies in the universe, each containing about 100,000 million stars. In this gigantic setting human beings look so small. Yet all created things, including humanity, are interconnected and even interdependent. In that web of cosmic relationships there remains something uniquely valuable about human beings and their behavioural capacities as contrasted with the rest of nature. This makes it appropriate for God the Son to take on the human condition, and it encourages us to take up again the scriptural link between our race and the rest of the created world in the whole story of redemption.

A passage from Milton's *Paradise Lost* (9. 782–4), quoted at the start of this chapter, expresses the wound that nature suffered when Eve succumbed to the wiles of the serpent, ate the forbidden fruit, and initiated the story of sin. No doubt Milton wanted to recall the Jewish conviction that through human sin the earth itself was cursed and corrupted (Gen. 3: 17–19; 6: 11–13).[21] Nevertheless, the psalms invite animals, plants, and other created things to join human beings in praising God (e.g. Ps. 148: 3–10). The song of the three young men, which Greek versions of the Book of Daniel contain (after 3: 23 or after 3: 24), develops this theme at greater length. The 'Prayer of Azariah' calls on rivers, seas, the earth, mountains, cattle, fish, and all created things to unite in a cosmic praise of God. Such hymns raise the question: If all created reality somehow joins now in the praise of God, will it also do so in a transformed life to come?

Such language from the psalms and Daniel resonates with cultures which, like those of the Australian aboriginal peoples, maintain a strong spiritual link between humanity and nature. This sense comes more easily to 'modern' people who think of the whole universe as almost one living organism rather than a vast machine. Interestingly *The Lord of the Rings* closely associates nature with the salvation of

---

[21] If he had written in the twenty-first century, Milton would have referred to the wounds inflicted on the earth by human beings ruthlessly depleting natural resources, polluting rivers, seas, and the air, and even threatening the ozone layer that protects our existence. Milton would have been horrified at human beings ravaging the global ecological system.

human beings; trees, for instance, join the battle against the forces of evil.

In telling the story of Jesus' passion, Matthew goes beyond what Mark says about 'darkness over the whole land' (Mark 15: 33) to speak of the earth shaking and rocks being split when Jesus died (Matt. 27: 51).[22] Various fathers of the Church like St Jerome took up this theme of creation showing through the darkened sun and trembling earth how it was affected by the redemptive death of Christ.[23] William Langland (d. around 1400) exploited the fuller imagery from Matthew when depicting the aftermath of the death of Jesus: 'Daylight shrank in terror; the sun was darkened./ Walls stirred from their bases and split asunder./ A shudder ran through the whole wide world' (*Piers Plowman*, 6. 18). Artists have conveyed a similar sense of the cosmic impact of the crucifixion and resurrection. In his *Christ of Saint John of the Cross* (1951), Salvador Dalí represents the monumental figure of the crucified Christ suspended in space, with the earth beneath him. Grünewald (Mathis Gothardt Neithardt, d. 1528) expresses the resurrection's effect on creation by depicting the radiantly transformed Christ rising in a blaze of light against a dark, midnight sky.

Faced with a world damaged by sin, some OT prophets dreamed of a future, messianic harmony between human beings and the whole of nature, a time when 'the wolf shall live with the lamb, and the leopard shall lie down with the kid, and the calf and the lion and the fatling together, and a little child shall lead them' (Isa. 11: 6; see Ezek. 47: 1–12). This poetic vision has encouraged many Christians to take seriously again the biblical sense that final redemption embraces the transformation of the world, and not an apocalyptic destruction of the material universe. Ecologists have fastened, in particular, on Paul's vision of the whole creation groaning in travail, waiting for its liberation from futility, and hoping to be 'set free from its bondage to decay' and so share in 'the glorious freedom of the children of God' (Rom. 8: 19–22). Here I agree with those commentators who interpret the Apostle's reference to 'creation' as going

---

[22] See R. E. Brown, *The Death of the Messiah*, ii (New York: Doubleday, 1994), 1118–23.

[23] See J. A. W. Bennett, *Poetry of the Passion* (Oxford: Clarendon Press, 1982), 14.

for their continuing existence and operation. The resurrection of Jesus—not to mention other such matters as the role of God in Israel's history, the event of the incarnation, miracles, the writing of inspired scriptures, and special graces that touch individual human lives—involves some special divine action that goes beyond the normal order of the world. To produce different effects like the resurrection of Jesus, God acts in ways that are qualitatively distinct and different from the 'ordinary' divine work in creating and sustaining the world.[25] At the end God will be free to change the laws of nature, so as to transform the material world.

In the resurrection of Jesus and what will follow (the resurrection of human beings and the final transformation of the universe), God's love is effectively shown and present. The power of love always creates the conditions for a human life to grow and fully unfold. Easter faith maintains the recreative love of God at work in an extraordinarily different kind of divine activity: the resurrection of the dead Jesus. Only the free, loving involvement of God illuminates and makes possible that particular, yet universally significant, event.

Finishing this chapter fifty years after his death in 1955, I am reminded of what a priest-palaeontologist, Pierre Teilhard de Chardin, wrote about humankind as the universe come to self-consciousness and the role of the resurrection in the progressive spiritualization of matter. Teilhard lined up against those who support any dualism either here and now or hereafter. 'Matter', he maintained, 'is the matrix of Spirit. Spirit is the higher state of Matter.'[26] He could sing a 'Hymn to Matter',[27] when he contemplated the story of the unfolding cosmos, the Christ story as the cosmos moves in a process of becoming towards the Omega Point—through cosmogenesis, biogenesis, noogenesis, and Christogenesis. Teilhard called the resurrection 'Christ's effective assumption of his function as the universal centre'.[28] So far from the resurrection leaving behind

[25] On the divine activity involved in the resurrection, see G. O'Collins, *Christology* (Oxford: Oxford University Press, rev. edn., 2004), 106–12.

[26] *Science and Christ* (New York: Harper & Row, 1968), 27, 35.

[27] Ibid., 75–6.

[28] Ibid., 63–4. 'Cosmogenesis', 'biogenesis', 'noogenesis', and 'Christogenesis' refer, respectively, to the creation of matter, the emergence of life, the emergence of mind, and the coming of Christ (his incarnation leading to his resurrection and its results).

Christ's crucified body, it made that material body the proper and perfect vehicle of the Spirit, and mediated God's creative power in bringing the world towards the final unification of matter and spirit.

Teilhard called love 'the most universal, the most tremendous, and the most mysterious of the cosmic forces'.[29] With Christ's resurrection from the dead, the energy of love was released in a qualitatively new way to organize the noosphere and move it towards the Omega Point. After 1930 Teilhard worked out a view of love as *the* most enormous and universal force in a world which is dynamically converging towards Christ, the unifying point of everything. He saw the resurrection as a cosmic event in which Christ overcame matter's resistance to spiritual ascent, effectively assumed his functions as centre and focus of the created universe, and guaranteed the upward and forward development of the whole universe. As 'the Personal Heart of the Cosmos', the risen Christ inspires and releases the basic energy of love that progressively carries both humanity and the material universe towards its future goal.[30]

[29] *Human Energy* (London: Collins, 1969), 32.

[30] See C. F. Mooney, *Teilhard de Chardin and the Mystery of Christ* (London: Collins, 1966), 120, 135; R. Faricy, *All Things in Christ: Teilhard de Chardin's Spirituality* (London: Collins, 1981), 13–31.

Epilogue

As much as ever, the whole world faces turbulent and dangerous times. As we move further into the third millennium, Christians remain bound by their faith to proclaim Christ the Reconciler and to do all they can to reconcile alienated groups and nations. Any witness to Christ the world's Redeemer requires steady commitment to the service of justice and peace. This book has aimed at helping that commitment by clarifying what it means to call Christ 'our Redeemer'.

A final rereading of this book suggests a closing emphasis on the personal causality of love. What is the causality of divine and human love? How does it have its effects? Common human experience testifies to the way intimate relationships embody a causality of their own and transform one or both of the parties involved. If hate destroys, love gives life. The redemption effected by Christ has revealed and communicated the divine love to humanity. The tri-personal God has created the conditions in which our response can be made. One should speak then about the 'empowering', creative quality of the divine love which draws men and women to respond freely in love. They are enabled to love by being loved. Human love has the power to generate love; ever so much more has the divine love the power to generate love. For generation after generation of Christians, the story of the two disciples at Emmaus recognizing the risen Jesus in 'the breaking of the bread' has suggested the loving union of the Eucharist, when God's redeeming love for us is vividly actualized. Through communion we become in love what we receive from the divine Lover.

Human sin sharpens our focus on the divine love. God responds to the desperately bad situation created by our sins by personally entering into that situation at the incarnation, being united with sinful humanity, and serving them with self-sacrificing love. The death that Christ died on the cross at the hands of sinners was the consequence and climax of the life which he led on behalf of others. On the cross the love of the Trinity became visible. In his most intense identification with the human condition, the totally innocent Christ suffered with and for human beings and bore in his body the consequences of their sin.

Provided we reckon seriously with the tragedy that sin involves, we may a little more easily appreciate the 'cost' of rectifying that awfully bad situation and 'cleansing' a terribly contaminated world: the horrendous death of Christ by crucifixion (see Chapter 8 above). What may not fit so readily into human ways of thinking about redemption is the thought of Christ as *the* innocent adult. The novels of Graham Greene and such films as *One Flew over the Cuckoo's Nest* offer us figures who are in some sense genuinely redemptive but in no sense innocent. We are perhaps a little more used to the innocent redemptive figures of children, like Tiny Tim in *A Christmas Carol* by Charles Dickens. Adults, we feel, are flawed characters. Hence the utterly holy and loving adulthood of Christ our Redeemer cuts right across normal human perceptions. Yet the innocent Jesus is the only one in a position to forgive and expiate with gratuitous love, since he is both completely free of guilt and truly divine. In this way we can appreciate the unique significance of the unmerited suffering of the innocent Son of God.

In Western iconography 'the throne of grace (Gnadenstuhl)' is undoubtedly the most important representation of the Trinity. Turning up for centuries in a painted or carved form, it shows the Father holding the cross with the Son dead on it (or the Father simply holding the dead body of the Son), with the Holy Spirit as a dove hovering above, between, or below them. One cross links the three figures. Frequently, as in the version by El Greco exhibited in the Prado, the luminous quality of the dead body of the Son already hints at the coming resurrection. The composition's name is theologically significant and correct: not 'the judgement seat', still less 'the punishment seat', but the seat or throne of grace and love.

The sending of the Holy Spirit from the throne of grace was and is *the* great act of love on the part of the Father and the Son at the crucifixion and resurrection. One ever-popular hymn at Pentecost prays to the Spirit: 'Come down, O Love divine'. Yet the hymn thinks, apparently exclusively, of the impact of the Holy Spirit on the individual believer. It continues: 'seek thou this soul of mine, / and visit it with thine own ardour glowing; / O Comforter, draw near, / within my heart appear, / and kindle it, thy holy / flame bestowing.' Primarily, however, the Spirit acts in the whole body of believers and then on individuals. The invisible Spirit works to make the visible Church *the* place which manifests the divine love, the community which on behalf of all humanity (and the whole cosmos) voices praise and thanksgiving to the Trinity, and which reaches out in loving prayer to all humankind.

The picture of 'the throne of grace' embodies a final reply to the three questions with which this book began. First, the picture challenges its viewers to acknowledge the love of the divine persons at work here and now for our salvation. Second, the crucified body of Jesus reminds us that, so far from being self-sufficient and virtuous, our existence is characterized by a sinfulness and evil that calls out for divine forgiveness and healing. Third, the throne of grace conveys, gently but powerfully, what should be our dominant image of God as the loving Father who, holding like a mother the dead body of Jesus in his arms, loves us and wishes to share with us the fullness of life, both here and hereafter.

Select Bibliography

Anselm of Canterbury, St, *Why God Became a Man* (*Cur Deus Homo*), ed. and trans. Jasper Hopkins and H. Richardson (Toronto/New York: Edwin Mellen Press, 1976).

Beattie, T., *Woman*, New Century Theology (London: Continuum, 2002).

Bennett, J. A. W., *The Poetry of the Passion* (Oxford: Clarendon Press, 1982).

Bigaouette, F., *Le cri de déréliction de Jésus en croix: Densité existentielle et salvifique* (Paris: Cerf, 2004).

Bradley, I., *The Power of Sacrifice* (London: Darton, Longman & Todd, 1995).

Brown, R. E., *The Death of the Messiah*, 2 vols. (New York: Doubleday, 1994).

Daly, G., *Creation and Redemption* (Dublin: Gill & Macmillan, 1988).

Daly, R. J., *The Origins of the Christian Doctrine of Sacrifice* (Philadelphia: Fortress, 1978).

Davis, S. T., Kendall, D., and O'Collins, G. (eds.), *The Incarnation* (Oxford: Oxford University Press, 2002).

—— *The Redemption* (Oxford: Oxford University Press, 2004).

Dillistone, F. W., *The Christian Understanding of the Atonement* (London: Nisbet, 1968).

Dunn, J. D. G., *The Theology of Paul the Apostle* (Grand Rapids, Mich.: Eerdmans, 1998).

Dupuis, J., *Toward a Christian Theology of Religious Pluralism* (Maryknoll, NY: Orbis Books, 1997).

—— *Christianity and the Religions: From Confrontation to Dialogue* (Maryknoll, NY: Orbis Books, 2002).

Fiddes, P., *Past Event and Present Salvation: The Christian Idea of Atonement* (London: Darton, Longman & Todd, 1989).

Ford, D. F., *Self and Sacrifice: Being Transformed* (Cambridge: Cambridge University Press, 1999).

Gunton, C. E., *The Actuality of the Atonement* (Edinburgh: T. & T. Clark, 1988).

Hastings, A., Mason, A., and Pyper, H. (eds.), 'Atonement', 'Love, 'Redemption', 'Sacrifice', 'Salvation', 'Sin', 'Suffering', and further relevant entries, in *The Oxford Companion to Christian Thought* (Oxford: Oxford University Press, 2000).

Hengel, M., *The Cross of the Son of God* (London: SCM Press, 1986).

Hultgren, A. J., *Christ and His Benefits: Christology and Redemption in the New Testament* (Philadelphia: Fortress, 1987).

Jones, L. G., *Embodying Forgiveness: A Theological Analysis* (Grand Rapids, Mich.: Eerdmans, 1995).

Jossua, J. P., *Le salut, incarnation ou mystère pascal* (Paris: Cerf, 1968).

Kendall, D., and O'Collins, G. (eds.), *In Many and Diverse Ways* (Maryknoll, NY: Orbis Books, 2003).

Lyonnet, S., *Sin, Redemption, and Sacrifice* (Rome: Biblical Institute, 1970).

McGrath, A. E., 'Soteriology', in A. E. McGrath (ed.), *The Blackwell Encyclopedia of Modern Christian Thought* (Oxford: Blackwell, 1993), 616–26.

McIntyre, J., *The Shape of Soteriology* (Edinburgh: T. & T. Clark, 1992).

Moses, J., *The Sacrifice of God: A Holistic View of Atonement* (Norwich: Canterbury Press, 1992).

O'Collins, G., *Christology: A Biblical, Historical and Systematic Study of Jesus* (Oxford: Oxford University Press, rev. edn, 2004).

—— 'Salvation', in the *Anchor Bible Dictionary*, v (New York: Doubleday, 1992), 907–14.

O'Collins, G., and Kendall, D., *Focus on Jesus* (Leominster: Gracewing, 1996).

Padgett, A. G., 'The Body in Resurrection: Science and Scripture on the "Spiritual Body" (1 Cor 15:35–58)', *Word and World* 22 (2002), 155–63.

Peters, T., Russell, R. J., and Welker, M. (eds.), *Resurrection: Theological and Scientific Assessments* (Grand Rapids, Mich.: Eerdmans, 2002).

Placher, W. G., 'Christ Takes Our Place: Rethinking Atonement', *Interpretation* 53 (1999), 5–20.

Powers, D. G., *Salvation through Participation* (Leuven: Peeters, 2001).

Rahner, K. *Foundations of Christian Faith* (New York: Seabury, 1978).

Schwager, R., *Jesus in the Drama of Salvation: Toward a Biblical Doctrine of Redemption* (New York: Crossroad, 1999).

Sesboüé, B., *Hors de l'Eglise pas de salut. Histoire d'une formule et problèmes d'interprétation* (Paris: Desclée, 2004).

—— *Jésus-Christ l'unique médiateur. Essai sur la rédemption et le salut*, 2 vols. (Paris: Desclée, 1988–91).

Sherman, R., *King, Priest, and Prophet: A Trinitarian Theology of Atonement* (New York/London: T. & T. Clark International, 2004).

Sherry, P., *Images of Redemption* (London: T. & T. Clark, 2003).

Sobrino, J., *Christ the Liberator: A View from the Victims* (Maryknoll, NY: Orbis Books, 2001).

Sullivan, F. A., *Salvation Outside the Church?* (New York: Paulist Press, 1992).

Swinburne, R., *Responsibility and Atonement* (Oxford: Clarendon Press, 1989).

Sykes, S. W., *The Story of Atonement* (London: Darton, Longman & Todd, 1997).

—— (ed.), *Sacrifice and Redemption* (Cambridge: Cambridge University Press, 1991).

Van der Watt, J. G. (ed.), *Salvation in the New Testament* (Leiden: Brill, 2005).

White, V., *Atonement and the Incarnation: An Essay in Universalism and Particularity* (Cambridge: Cambridge University Press, 1975).

Young, F., *Sacrifice and the Death of Christ* (London: SPCK, 1975).

beyond human beings to the whole of nature. A similarly broad meaning turns up when a NT hymn celebrates the 'reconciliation', through the death of Christ, of 'all things, whether on earth or in heaven' (Col. 1: 19–20). This redemptive reconciliation will bring into conformity with the divine plan not only human beings but also their cosmic environment, which will be completed, spiritualized, and transformed.

The Book of Revelation, through a wealth of exotic imagery, invites its readers to contemplate the victory of the suffering and risen Christ, a victory which embraces the created world, as well as the whole of human history. It sums up the goal of redemption as 'the new heaven and the new earth' (Rev. 21: 1; see 2 Pet. 3: 13). The Book of Revelation fills paradise with leafy trees and rich fruits on either side of the river of life (Rev. 22: 1–2). Christian iconography took up this theme: for instance, in the wonderful mosaics in Ravenna that picture animals in verdant landscapes, peacocks (representing immortality), stags (representing souls), and doves drinking from the fountain of life. We saw above how the brothers Van Eyck follow this theme of the heavenly park in their *Adoration of the Lamb*. Heaven as a luxuriant garden recurs in many Christian paintings, mosaics, and tapestries.

Thinking nowadays about such a transformation of the material universe inevitably involves a dialogue with modern science.[24] Fortunately, astonishing advances have generally rendered obsolete determinist views of the world as a rigidly closed system of causes and effects. A growing sense of wonder at the material universe, its immense size, and its mysterious forces have often produced a new willingness to admit the exercise of the special divine causality required by the resurrection of the dead. God has created and respects the natural order of the world and its functioning. Yet the course of events is not utterly fixed and rigidly uniform. For good reasons and in the appropriate circumstances (e.g. the death of Christ), God can suspend the operation of some laws. These laws need not have existed nor did they have to be precisely the way they are; created by God, they depend from moment to moment on God

---

[24] See T. Peters, R. J. Russell, and M. Welker (eds.), *Resurrection: Theological and Scientific Assessments* (Grand Rapids, Mich.: Eerdmans, 2002).

Index of Names